HC

Susan Ekins was born just outside London and,
after a cheerful post-war London childhood, and
five years at school at the Grey Coat Hospital, she
began her studies to become a librarian. But music
called, and she then trained as a classical mezzo-
soprano, performing for music societies, orchestras
and light opera companies in England and Europe,
under the name of Susan Lofthouse, for over 45
years. She is also not only deeply involved in local
issues in Battersea's Safer Neighbourhood Panel
included, but was also involved in the campaign to
save Battersea Park from electric motor racing. For
her, community is deeply important. Other interests
include history, theatre and Italian. She is married
to an environmental economist and their son is a
classical pianist.

HOOD
WINK!

A 'true' medieval whodunnit

SUSAN EKINS

THE REAL PRESS
www.therealpress.co.uk

Published in 2024 by the Real Press.
www.therealpress.co.uk
© Susan Ekins.

ISBN (print) 9781917443050
ISBN (ebooks) 9781917443067

Acknowledgements

To my dear family - all of them, but especially Paul, JP, Lyn, Robert, Gabi, A. and Jean, and Lucie who all showed interest. And to all my friends, especially to Gian, and to Rahul, whose computer enabled me to write, research and edit this tale problem-free. To JP who helped with the final edit and to the patience of David Boyle, who helped this book see the light of day.

Contents

I

He pushed open the door from the kitchen to the yard, wrapped himself in his cloak, and crept towards the street, first seizing a piece of bread from yesterday's baking. The morning was cold, and still dark, puddles lying on the path, and water dripping from the eaves.

He thought he could get there and back before work began at the tannery. He had told his mother he was going fishing. He was still unsure about whether to approach the other one. The thing was still in his satchel. He asked himself why his visit yesterday had got nowhere? It had been frightening, in a way, although the other one's eyes had smiled at him.

The watchman leaning at the gates, half asleep, his hat tipped over his eyes, barely opened them to spot the skinny boy now running towards the heath. Wasn't that young William, the tanner's apprentice? He wondered if his family knew where he was at that hour in the morning. Rabbiting? Fishing? He wouldn't be the first one out this morning; Sister Legarda, for example, clutching her basket for any herbs which did not grow in the hospital garden, and mushrooms, too.

The priory bell rang in the far distance, giving the Brothers barely half an hour to wash and prepare for Prime. What a life. But he couldn't really say anything against them. Hadn't the Brother Infirmarian saved the life of his youngest, suffering with a summer fever? He closed his eyes again, so did not see Messire Hugh pass on his bay mare, his lips tight and his face grey in the dawn.

By now more people were passing through the gates – some arriving with goods for the market, others going the other way to the fields. Then Peter de Champs appeared to take over the shift. Not before time. Breakfast called. His belly was complaining. And a few hours' sleep. Then he might just take an hour or so by the river and see what he could catch. And the vegetable patch needed some work, too. He slapped Peter on the shoulder, then made for his house in Bread Street, by now smelling of hot bread and buns. That was a good thing about living next to the baker's – fresh bread always available.

At home, Wlward was grumbling. Where was that boy? Always slipping off somewhere – never to be found. Bed empty – although made, he had to give him that. His daughter calmed him down. "Just fishing. You know what he is. And you wouldn't object to a nice fat trout, after forty days of nothing but herring."

"Chance would be a fine thing, Elviva. If that's really what he's doing. If he doesn't get a move on, he'll be late for work. His father had to pull quite a few strings to get him that apprenticeship, and Daniel's not a bad master. And people tip well. He says the Jews are particularly generous. Well, time I was off. I don't want to miss the service. By the way, what was that you were telling me about the cook?"

"Nothing much. I'm not even sure I believe it."

"What?"

"Some man claiming to be the archdeacon's cook, called here yesterday afternoon and spoke to Leviva. He said he could get William a job in the kitchens. Offered her thirty shillings if I were to let him go – which I couldn't, of course. Why didn't he approach you, I wonder? Or me?"

"Quite right. The boy's indentured. And the man must have known, or why offer her money? Did William say whether he'd been approached?"

"He said not. And he's generally a truthful lad. But he did ask his aunt what the man looked like, and when she told him, he didn't seem that worried, rather more puzzled. The man was well dressed apparently – some sort of high class servant, if not a noble – rode a fine black horse. And a large gold ring. Far too fine to be a cook."

"See if you can get anything else out of him. When's he back?"

"Not until Good Friday evening – heavy workload, he says. He'll sleep over with the other lads."

Wlward strode out through the yard, pulling up his hood against the rain, lifting the skirts of his cassock, his dog snuffling after him through the puddles. The carts were out in force, splashing anyone who got in the way. He wondered what William did with himself when he wasn't working? He wasn't sure he quite believed his daughter's story about the fishing.

But as Daniel hadn't said anything was wrong, he'd best leave the boy to himself. He'd have it out of him on Sunday when they broke the Fast. The boy was due for a new jacket, in any case, and he would certainly have that; he'd been wearing his father's old cut-down for far too long. It was a shame Wenstan had died; the boy really needed a father; he himself was getting too old.

Master Daniel Le Peche stood looking down the path from his front door, wondering where William had got to. The other lads were already here, each with a bed roll ready to stop over these next two nights. The orders for fur and leather were rolling in; no sign yet of the Spring.

Suddenly the lad skittered into view, slipping on the damp, muddy cobbles. What was wrong with the boy? He looked as pale as skimmed milk. Mind you, he was never that healthy-looking – rather the look of a half-starved novice – although his dead father had been tall and strong, and his mother was a good cook. But the boy was strong enough – just look at the way he hoisted those bales of skins for Master Eleazar. No milksop there.

"Sorry I'm late, Master Le Peche."

"What happened? Over-sleep?"

"No, Master, forgot the time."

"That's no excuse, boy, there's no mistaking the bells. There's work to do here, if you want time off for the Easter feast. I don't want to have to call on your grandfather." Not that he would, but it didn't harm to keep the lads in check.

"Off you go. Jehan will give you your instructions."

William considered he had got off lightly this time, with just a gentle warning. Why had he ever thought they would be cowed by what he knew? What he had seen? And, thinking about it, the same man must have been the so-called cook who called on his aunt. He had not made the connection when his mother told him.

He shuddered, though taking comfort from the

fact that he was now away from home and surrounded by bigger lads, not to mention the dogs.

But he had seen something that day, something that he knew was wrong, he knew it was. Maybe he shouldn't have asked for something in return for his silence. Or maybe he should tell someone anyway. But who? A priest? He couldn't really tell his grandfather or his uncle.

The day soon passed. He always liked visiting Master Eleazar. There was always a penny or two dropped his way, sometimes even a cake from the Gentile maidservant, "To sweeten the way home."

Over the next three days he was sent on so many errands he hadn't much time to think. Not even time to stop and watch the preparations for the Easter celebrations. On Thursday, around Angelus, passing by the cathedral, he thought he saw the man again, but on his own this time. No sign of the other.

II

At dusk, on Friday – no holiday for him - last delivery done, he cut through the woods, hoping to get home in time for supper, and maybe look in on the nesting owl on the way. His mother would be glad to see him after three days, although he kept a wary eye out for the black dog, which the other boys said haunted the woods.

"It'll rip your throat out, soon as look at you", sniggered spotty, sweaty Ethelbert. He was the worst of the lot – grubby stories behind the privies, and it was surprising how many people he knew who had been massacred by black dogs, poisoned by witches, stabbed by roaming Moors. He half didn't believe him, but then, how much did one really know?

There was a rustle in the bushes, the chucking of a blackbird. He half froze from fear. He ran stumbling towards the town, tripping, clutching his stick, his hand searching for his penknife.

Gasping, he stopped to check, then found he had lost his way.

He turned, then something smashed on his head, and he fell into nothing.

That night his mother, busy stirring something on the fire, wondered where William had got to. Not like him to miss a meal. There was a new jacket waiting for him, too, and the little ones would be glad to have him back. His grandfather was already washing in the yard.

She waited a long time. Maybe Master Daniel had kept him over with a later delivery. Wlward told her not to worry, but how could she not?

In the end, with curfew fast approaching, she told Wlward she was going to see Master Le Peche. His reaction was only to be expected.

"I'm not having you going through the town this late. I'll go. They'll not rob a priest. It's probably nothing." And he seized his cloak and strode out into the lane. Ten minutes later he was knocking on Master Daniel's door.

Daniel Le Peche was not best pleased to be roused from his supper and the warm fire. It had been a long week.

But he understood the man's concerns.

"No, I've not seen the lad after I sent him with a delivery to Master Eleazar. Around mid-day. I said he could go home afterwards, as I had nothing else for him. And he's not home yet, you say? Give it another few hours, and we'll set up a search. Try not to worry."

But they did not even have to set up a search. At dawn, Sister Legarda, out looking for mushrooms, stumbled over something. She gave a cry and stooped down to look.

It was the body of a boy, scarcely more than a child, wet with the overnight rain, blood on his jacket. She crossed herself and lifted him. But there was no sign of life. She wondered what to do. She was still dithering when a forester came by.

"Let's see what we have here, Sister." And he too knelt to look at the boy.

"By Our Lady, it's a murder. Has to be. Look at those injuries. And he seems to have been dead for quite a while. Who would do that to a child? Have you a name for him?"

The nun shook her head.

He covered the lad with his cloak and, asking the nun to keep watch, rode towards the town. The nun knelt and said the Ave Maria, stroking his head as she did so, taking little note of the blood on her hands.

By now a group of men had arrived in the woods, led to the place by the forester, whom they knew as Henry de Sprowston. It took a while for the body to be recognised; some wanted to bury him where he lay, but others said he should have a Christian burial, once they had found out who he was. Then the watchman, just off duty, and roused by the commotion, recognised him, and someone sent for his grandfather and uncle. Both priests. They would know the correct procedure.

The crowd was joined by others, all with their own ideas about who had murdered the boy. They clustered round Wlward and Godwin Sturt, the boy's uncle, who had arrived in haste, and were now kneeling by the body, deep in prayer.

"We must take him to the Priory," said Godwin. "Lift him gently. Here, wrap him in my cloak. There must be an inquest, although I fear this Holiest of Feasts will delay it awhile. Has anyone gone for the Constable?"

They had. Several of them. He should soon be on his way.

Henry said, "At least there'll be no Murdrum. We'll be spared that. The boy's Saxon, not Norman."

"Ay," said a voice from the crowd, "But who murdered him, eh?"

Henry replied: "That's for the crowner to decide. At least give the boy the dignity of making no wild assumptions, Aelward Ded. Come, let's go."

"Not yet," said a voice. It was the Constable, leaning down from his horse to gaze at the body. "Who found him?"

"I did, or rather, it was the Sister." said Henry. "Henry de Sprowston, Constable, forester to the Priory. Just out checking there was no unlicensed woodcutting."

"I thought I knew your face. Anybody else?"

Sister Legarda came forward.

"I did, Sir. Sister Legarda, I was picking mushrooms for St Mary Magdalene's Hospice. I fell over the poor lad. Then Master Henry arrived. I... I... I said a Hail Mary for the boy, but I fear he will have died unshriven." And she started to weep.

"Sister, you did a good thing. Sir John will soon be on his way. Lucky that he was in the castle today and had not yet left on his circuit. Is anyone else here a witness to this? No? Then let us take the boy to the Priory for the time being where he can lie in peace. I suggest the rest of you go home. If you are needed, you will be called."

"And pointless calling Hue and Cry. I think he's probably been lying out here all night, poor lad."

And the sad little group turned and slowly started walking the long damp path towards the Priory.

III

The bell at the gate rang dolefully, summoning the Porter. When he saw what the men were carrying, he crossed himself, and led them inside, calling one of the Brothers to fetch Brother Anselm, the Infirmarian.

A resting place was laid for the boy at the end of the infirmary, outside the pharmacy, and a Brother brought warm water to wash the body, but not before the Infirmarian, under the watchful eye of the Sheriff, who had by now joined them, made a lengthy examination. He drew a wide curtain to give privacy from the eyes of the two Brothers in bed with the usual winter chest infections.

"See, here, masters. The boy has been struck on the head by a heavy, metal item – it has a spiked head. You can see where it has ripped the flesh and drawn much blood. In fact, there are several wounds – almost as if the assailant was overcome with uncontrollable rage." He crossed himself. "Now, what sort of weapon would that have been?"

The Sheriff looked closer. "Nothing that I quite recognise. A mace, possibly. But with added spikes? I wasn't involved in the last crusade –not even born. In any case, it was mainly a French affair. But I've heard of weapons like this. And I dare say there are plenty of items like this stored in castles and manors throughout the land. But to bring it out to kill a young boy? Certainly risky. And vicious."

"How long would you say he has been dead, Brother Anselm?"

The Infirmarian wrinkled his brow. "Difficult to be exact, but at least fourteen to sixteen hours. There is rigour. And his clothes are damp – it rained in the night. The fact that he was out in the cold and damp will delay any passing of the rigour, which in any case would not be for at least another twelve hours or more. Let's say four o'clock yesterday. We shall know more when we know when he was last seen."

Wlward spoke, his voice gritty with emotion. "We haven't seen him since Tuesday, when he went to Master Le Peche, the Tanner. Master Le Peche said he sent him out on deliveries to the Jewry at noon yesterday. Maybe we should ask Master Eleazar what time he saw the boy last."

"Then we'll do that at the inquest," said Sir John. "Brother, can you draw up a report? We'll need it for the hearing. It looks as if we have a manhunt on our hands. Nasty business. I'll let you all know more when the inquest is arranged." And he strode hurriedly from the room, surreptitiously wiping his eye with his cuff. Then, recollecting himself, he returned. "Master Wlward - if the boy's mother needs assistance, I know you will both of you be her support, but the boy will no longer bring in an income. Let me know."

Wlward and Godwin stood staring down at the child. Brother Anselm took the bowl of water and the soft cloths. He sprinkled herbs into the water. "Come," he said. "Help me prepare the lad for his last rest. He should have family about him at a time like this. And prayers."

They gently removed the old blue jacket. He'll never wear that fine new coat, thought Wlward. Something fell on the floor. He picked it up. It was a ring. A gold posy ring. So small it could have fitted no-one but a lady.

Godwin held out his hand and looked inside. It said: *Mon desir me vaille.* So, a love token, he thought. What was the boy doing with this?

He spoke out loud: "He is no thief, I'll swear." Anselm looked up.

Wlward was looking around. "It's nothing,

Brother. Did they bring in his scrip?"

Godwin pointed. "It's over there in the corner. But it was empty. Not even his penknife. Maybe someone already found the body, emptied the satchel, and left. Without reporting the death."

Wlward said, "That in itself is a crime. Much more likely that the murderer rifled his bag. But why take the knife? Why not just take the whole bag? How desperate were they, Godwin?"

"I think that must be for Sir John and the crowner. In the meantime, I think Brother Anselm needs our help. Then we must go home to support Elviva. A sorry business, Wlward, a sorry business."

Brother Anselm tried to comfort them. "We shall say prayers for the boy's soul. And he will not be left alone, I promise you, we shall keep watch until a day is decided for his burial. And even after. Come, help me move him to the little chapel."

IV

Easter morning came soon enough, and the faithful came to celebrate the Risen Christ. But it was not the usual rejoicing. Many wrestled with their consciences in an effort not to rail against a providence that allowed the murder of a young boy. In vain did Bishop Eborard, standing at the altar, insist that the lad was an innocent now in God's hands. The evil was with the man who had done this deed. They knew that the boy had died unshriven. Who would wish to die such a death? Doom paintings abounded on church walls. Doubtless more would appear in their new cathedral. They knew what awaited unrepentant souls.

They filed out afterwards – artisans, farmers, labourers – all in their best garments, gazing at the splendour of the nobility, gathering ready for the breaking of the fast in their manors and big houses. Sir John in a splendid russet cloak, his lady in green. Lord Revil in black, his young bride in tawny, her blond hair in ringlets on her shoulders, the silver veil fluttering in the breeze.

Sir John beckoned to Lord Revil, who spoke in his wife's ear.

"I must talk to Sir John. I think it is about the inquest on that unfortunate lad. Come, my lady, there is no cause for tears, you did not even know the boy."

"Sir, he came on several occasions to the house with those furs that you gave me for Christmas. I remember him. He used to wear an old blue jacket. And he whistled."

"Then remember him as he was. What's done is done. We'll find the murderer, whoever he was. And he shall hang for it. Here is Hugh. He will escort you home. Let me help you onto your pony."

He stopped suddenly. He looked at her hand. He snatched it towards him. "Your ring. Our ring. Where is it?" She gasped in pain.

"Oh, leave it. I must not keep Sir John waiting. We shall talk later." And he left her, not noticing her ashen face. Hugh barely looked at her, but handed the bridle to the waiting page, and mounted his own fine bay horse. They moved on.

It was a while before Revil left Sir John. The inquest was called for the next morning, Monday, in the cathedral Chapter House.

There were many witnesses to interview. Father Anselm, Henry the Forester, Sister Legarda, Eleazar the Jew, friends of William, his grandfather, his uncle, Daniel Le Peche, the Constable. All must be in order. The public would want to attend, of course. They always did. Just a matter of keeping any troublemakers in order. There was always one.

By now most of the congregation had left for their homes, to break the fast in their own way. The monks returned to their refectory.

Others still stood around, probably discussing the murder.

In the manor, Lady Alys sat in the solar room, still shaking. What excuse could she make about the ring? Where was it now? Someone had it, but who? Revil was not an easy man. Possessive. At times cruel. She looked at the red mark where he had gripped her wrist. She wished he were dead. Then regretted it. That was not a Christian thought. Her fate was to bear her lot; there could be no comfort now after the boy's murder.

There was a knock on the door. It was Brangwen. "My Lady, my lord is returned, and wishes your presence."

Surely he would not raise the subject of the ring at table. She rose and slowly went down the stairs into the hall, where the others were already gathered, some holding cups of wine and warming themselves in front the fire. There was the smell of roast lamb, roast goose. She felt slightly sick. Almost she would welcome the dried fish of the Lenten fast.

Her husband turned towards her. She could see from his face that he had not forgotten the missing ring. He took her hand again, and spoke to the woman on his left, tall, with red hair confined under a white veil.

"See here, Margaret, my wife cares so little for me that she has "mislaid" (he sneered) the posy ring I gave her on our betrothal."

"I am sorry, my lord, but I do not know where it is. I wear it every day, and I never take it off." She coloured at the necessary lie. "I cannot remember it slipping off."

"A lesser man would beat you for that, madam."

Margaret looked shocked. "Brother, do not make such a threat, even in jest. It is a simple enough matter to lose a ring. When the weather is cold, the finger shrinks, and the ring slips. I have known it myself. Indeed, I lost the finger ring that Luke gave me, and it was never found. But he certainly did not beat me. Just bought me another ring from Master Orfe."

"Then more fool him. Does money grow on trees?" and his thin lips twisted into a sneer. "But that's the last gewgaw I give you, my lady."

He strode away to the other side of the hall,

leaving his sister and wife together. Margaret took Alys's arm and pulled her into a corner. "I am sorry about my brother, Alys. He was always difficult, even as a child. I could have shown you bruises. I wish I could do more. Maybe you could spend some time with us in Sprowston. If he will allow." She gave a wry smile. "Maybe when you have children?"

Alys tried to stop her tears. "What sort of a father will he be, Margaret? I know I am disloyal, but I am frightened for the future."

Margaret tried to comfort her, but they were being watched. Luke was talking to Hugh and one never quite knew what Hugh was thinking. Did he even like women? He certainly had no time for Alys. Barely even looked at her. But then, Revil would have had something to say if he did.

A servant entered to announce dinner, and all the guests took their seats, the pages going round with the bowls of scented water and soft napkins. The first course was brought on, and the feast began. A minstrel struck up some gentle melodies.

At the head of the table Revil ignored his wife, and talked with Hugh about the farm, the promises for the harvest, and the rents. Alys picked at her food and was swift to leave the table at the end of the meal, pleading a headache. This time it was not a lie. Margaret went after her.

She looked down at the girl lying on the bed.

"Alys, what is wrong?" She placed her hand on the girl's forehead. It was hot, though her cheeks were pale.

"It's nothing, Margaret. Just a headache. I often get them."

"Nonsense, there's more to it than that. It started with the missing ring, didn't it? What's going on?" She went to the door and called down to the maid, sitting with the pages in the Hall. Brangwen ran swiftly up the stairs.

"Brangwen, go to the kitchens and ask cook to make a tisane of camomile."

"Alys, as soon as you feel a little better, I am taking you back with me to Sprowston. Has your physician seen you?"

"No. I hate him. Him and his bleeding, his cupping, his strengthening brews."

"You mean this has been going on for a while? What does Revil say?"

"He just wants sons. The witch's brews are to make sure I do. They are disgusting. I won't see him. I won't."

"Then we shall call in Brother Anselm. I and the children have sometimes consulted him. He is gentle. And I have never yet had a medicine that I could not stomach. I will ask Luke to have a word with him at the inquest tomorrow."

They sat in silence for a while, until the maid entered with the draught. When Alys had drunk it,

Margaret told the maid to put a few things in a bag, while she went to speak to Revil. His face was sour when he heard her request.

"I've married a milksop, a weakling, an idiot. It won't do, Margaret. I want sons. God knows what Alys will produce. Why did I marry her in the first place?"

"You married her because you wanted her manor and her money."

"While you married that ninny of a Luke - a third son. An excellent choice."

Margaret smiled as she thought of her husband. "He is kind, gentle, and does not use his fists. Yes, I saw the bruises. It seems I did indeed make an excellent choice. And we have two sons."

She regretted this when she saw his face whiten in rage.

"You must do what you wish. At least I shall not have to see her whey face every day. In any case, tomorrow I shall be wanted at the inquest. Alys mewling about a dead boy she barely knew is the last thing I want. I will ask Hugh to accompany you."

"No need. Luke is all we need. But we shall take Brangwen. She can mount behind Luke. Revil, let us not be enemies. I will look after Alys, and maybe a change of air from Catton will strengthen her. I hope the inquest runs smoothly."

24

And she turned and climbed the stairs to the solar room.

V

The inquest did not start on time. To begin with, there were so many people, the townsfolk had to be asked to stay outside. One or two of them nominated themselves unofficial newsmongers and stationed themselves at the open door. One of them was Aelward Ded.

"Trust him, dirty scobberlotcher. Must have been sleeping out all night to get here this early," said a disgruntled Edwin Chepe.

There was the sound of horses. The Bishop had arrived, followed by a small delegation of monks, among them Brother Anselm. Sir John, Revil, Hugh and Luke were already seated at a long table. On the surrounding stone seats sat Henry de Sprowston, Sister Legarda, Daniel Le Peche, the Bailiff, Godwin and Wlward. On wooden benches sat several young lads, shuffling their feet. The Bishop sat on his throne. At a writing desk sat a clerk.

Next arrived Eleazar the Jew, his son, and the

Gentile maidservant. Someone found him a stool.

Sir John stood. "I now declare this enquiry into the death of William, son of Wenstan, deceased, open. I charge you all that you will tell only the truth."

"Who found the body?"

Sister Legarda rose to her feet. "I did, my lord. It was very early on Saturday morning. I was collecting samples for the pharmacy of St. Mary Magdalene, something I do on most mornings. I tripped over his body."

"What happened then?"

"Sir, I did not know what to do, but then a forester came past."

"Is that man in the room?"

"Yes, sir," and she pointed to Henry.

Henry was matter of fact. "The boy was obviously dead. I left him in the care of the Sister and rode towards the town to fetch help. Later the Constable arrived, and yourself, of course. We also summoned the boy's grandfather and uncle, since someone later recognised the lad."

"And what happened then?"

"We took him into the Priory, into the care of Brother Anselm, the Infirmarian."

"Brother Anselm? May we have your report?"

Brother Anselm rose to his feet. He told how he had examined the body. He and the boy's grandfather and uncle had then washed the body.

"Brother Anselm, what were your conclusions?"

"That he had been killed by a heavy blow to the head by a sharp item – possibly a mace but spiked. There were no other marks or injuries."

"Ah," said John "Yes, that was my conclusion, too. Go on. When do you think the lad died?"

"Difficult to say exactly, Sir, but not later than four in the afternoon of the day before. Rigour was not fully established, and he had last been seen by his Master at mid-day on Good Friday, when he was sent out with some deliveries. Oh, and one other thing. It seems that, although they found his satchel, it was empty. Not even a penknife. Now, who would rob a child? The boy would hardly have had anything of value on him."

"Do you have all that, Master Clerk? Good, then may I call Master Le Peche, the boy's Master."

Daniel Le Peche was also brief. "I was called to the scene where I confirmed that the boy was indeed my apprentice, William. The last time I had seen him was when he was sent out with deliveries on Friday. I assumed he had then gone home. I had told the lads that work was over until today."

"And the deliveries were where?"

"Master Eleazar, in Jewry, my Lord."

"Thank you, Master Le Peche, you may go." Daniel sat with his apprentices.

"Master Eleazar."

28

The tall, stooping, bearded man rose to his feet. "Your servant, My Lord."

"Master Eleazar, would you tell the hearing, please, about William's last visit."

"Yes, my Lord. The boy often visits us with deliveries. He is polite and efficient, and I believe my servants like him. A trustworthy boy, I would say." He smiled. "He arrived shortly after noon, and when I had checked the bundles, I gave him a penny or two, and sent him to the kitchen for something to eat. I did not see him again. Maybe Ardith can tell you more. Our housemaid, sir."

Ardith rose. She was a rosy, cheerful girl, aged around 14. "What would you know, sir?"

John was gentle with her. "Ardith, what is your position at Master Eleazar's?"

"I am his housemaid, sir. And I do the things which he and his household are not permitted to do on their Sabbath. I cook, I light the candles, make up the fires. I am a Christian, Sir, so you see to me it is not forbidden."

"And when did you last see William?"

"Just after mid-day on Good Friday, sir. He came with a delivery."

"What happened then? Did he go straight home?"

"Not immediately, sir. I usually give him a cake or two to sweeten the journey home, but this time Master Eleazar suggested he might like some-

29

thing rather more substantial. So, I gave him some vegetable broth, and some bread and cheese."

"Ardith, do you remember how he cut his bread and cheese? Did he use his own knife?"

"With his penknife, sir. Like always. Then, when he was ready to go – he said his family would be worried, and he wanted to see something in the woods first – I gave him a couple of cakes. Like always."

"Ardith, you were fond of William, weren't you? Can you tell us something about him."

He addressed the room. "I make no apologies. Here we are, talking about a young boy, cruelly murdered with no idea of what he was really like."

Ardith said, "Yes, sir, I was fond of him. But nothing in it, sir. It was just that he reminded me of my older brother, John, who died young - of the summer pestilence. He was a good lad, just as my Master says, polite, hardworking. And interesting to talk to. He knew a lot about the nger
s. He often walked through the woods for that reason. And always whistling - like a blackbird, he was.' Sister Legarda wiped away a tear,

Sir John cleared his throat. He, too, seemed moved.

"Just one thing, sir. I think William may have

gone to the woods to look at an owl's nest. He said a tawny owl was nesting in an oak."

"Thank you, Ardith. That is very useful. You may sit down now."

"Lastly, to his grandfather and uncle, I offer my condolences. And to his mother, too. I see she is not here. Be assured that if help is needed, you may call on me."

Godwin said, "No, Sir John, she is so distraught, she is in the care of her sister, my wife. It is not that long since she lost her husband."

The Bishop rose. "My sons, I will have special prayers said in the cathedral, and all other churches, for William's soul, for I truly do not believe that William will not find a place in heaven."

"Let the little children come to me, and do not hinder them, for the kingdom of God belongs to such as these."

"Saturday was the feast day of the Blessed Virgin. Pray to Her."

"And pray that the evil doer be brought to justice. Pray continue, my lord."

Sir John bowed.

"We declare that William, son of the late Wenstan, was unlawfully killed by person or persons unknown at some time around dusk on 24th day of March in the year of our Lord 1144, in his 13th year."

"No payment of Murdrum will be required."

"It has been arranged that he will be buried in the Brothers' graveyard tomorrow."

A voice shouted from the back. "Person or persons unknown? When the murderer is right here among us?"

Sir John's face darkened.

"Who is that? Who dares interrupt this solemn inquest. Bring him here."

One of the two men-at-arms seized the man by his arm and dragged him before Sir John.

"Who are you? Your name, man."

"Aelward Ded, Sir. Citizen of Norwich. An honest man, sir. Nothing ever against me."

"Master Ded, you appear to know more than the witnesses. Why did you not speak up before? Why did you not come forward? What is your evidence?"

Aelward Ded seemed to lose some of his bravado. "Well, sir, it's like this. Everyone knows."

"Everyone does not know. Know what?"

"The Jews, sir. It was Saturday when they found him, murdered on Good Friday. You said so. Obvious, sir. They murdered him. Just like they murdered Our Lord. That's where you should be looking. In his house" – and he pointed towards Eleazar, who rose, appalled.

Sir John's anger was barely concealed. "How

32

dare you slander an honoured citizen of Norwich with these lies. You know the penalty for that? Do you wish to lose your tongue? The Jewish Community is under our protection. Sergeant, throw this man in the lockup for a day or so. Then I shall decide on his punishment."

The muttering that had arisen outside when the townsfolk heard Ded's outburst suddenly died down, as he was dragged outside by the guard.

Sir John continued. "Perhaps I had better ask if any of you have anything else to add?"

A hand went up from the benches.

Sir John sighed. "Yes, boy, what do you have to say?"

An unappetising, spotty youth, he thought.

"Ethelbert, sir. I was his best friend."

"No, you weren't," added the other two boys in unison "No, you weren't. He hated you."

"Go on."

"He was killed by the Black Dog, sir."

"The Black Dog. Really."

"Yes, sir. William was scared of him, sir. It lives in the woods."

"Then why did he visit the woods to look at the birds?"

"Like I said, sir, it was the dog what killed him."

"No doubt with a spiked mace." Master Le Peche looked furious.

"It was his fangs, sir. His gory fangs."

"If I hear any more nonsense like this, you will be sent to join Master Ded. It is only my respect for your long-suffering Master that keeps you from a whipping." The other boys smirked.

"As I said: Murdered by person or persons unknown."

"The Hearing is closed. All rise."

As Ded was shoved towards the Town Gaol, nobody noticed the monk that came out after him. Indeed, his brethren in the priory barely knew him either. He was a visitor. From Monmouth.

The townsfolk moved on. One way or another it had been quite exciting. Who would have thought Ded would end up in the lockup. Edwin Chepe did. "Had it coming to him," he said. "Like a gossipy old woman – and twice as dangerous."

Others were not so sure. Others thought the Jews might well have had something to do with it. Others thought that sort of talk was the crackling of thorns. Not all Jews were bad. Look at Joseph of Arimathea, said Abel Boucher. And the disciples, added another. Ah, but they became Christian, didn't they? All right then, how about all the others. Thousands of them. What about the five thousand? And anyway, it was the Romans who did the crucifying.

It was a conversation that would be visited often over the next few months.

The monk from Monmouth mingled with them,

listening, his pale eyes gleaming. He was on fire. There would be more. And he turned and took the path back to the Priory.

VI

Alys sat on a cushioned chair by the fire, her knees covered by a rug, her feet on a stool. Her embroidery was on a small table at her side. Margaret's two boys were playing with bricks and a Noah's ark. Wanda the hound was worrying a bone. Already Alys looker calmer, although her dreams had been painful.

At that moment Luke came in, followed by Brother Anselm, who was carrying his satchel of medicines.

"I'll pass the Brother over to you, my love," he said to Margaret, and took himself off, followed by Wanda and the boys.

Margaret took the monk's hands. "Thank you so much for coming. We really need your help and advice."

Anselm looked at Alys. The young woman was pale, dark shadows under tired eyes. He sat down and took her hand. It was cold. The pulse was fast.

Far too fast. And what was this bruise?

"My Lady Margaret, may I ask why you are o worried?"

Margaret tried to put it as simply as she could. "She has something on her mind, something is worrying her. I am frightened for her, Brother. That is why I thought she might be better off with us for a while."

"But is not the lady married? Did I not see her husband at the inquest this morning? Does he not have his own physician?"

"Yes, Brother. But he is not... sympathetic. And the medicines and treatments are doing no good. Alys dreads the cupping and bleeding. She sleeps badly. She has nightmares. I think this business with the boy, William, has also had an effect."

He nodded.

"Is this true? Did you know the boy?"

Alys nodded. "Slightly. He came to the house once or twice. But he was so young, so young, Brother. How could anyone kill a young child? How can people be so cruel? He comes into my dreams sometimes."

Anselm said. "I am going to ask you some questions which you may think are nothing to do with your sickness. But be patient. The mind and the body and the soul are all linked. After all, were they not created by God? Joseph knew the importance of dreams, which often send us important messages."

"Tell me, when did you last go to Mass?"

"I... I... I cannot remember."

"Did you not go on Saturday?"

"I felt too ill. And then, there was the news of the boy."

"Tell me, Alys. What are these marks on your arm?" He had rolled up her sleeves. Margaret gasped. Even she had not seen these. Some were fading, some were recent.

"Does your husband..." he hesitated... "Does your husband chastise you?" She nodded.

"Often?"

"Yes."

"Does he have a reason?"

"I think he believes I am weak. And that I cannot give him sons."

"Is that the reason for the visits from his physician?"

"Yes. I'm sorry."

"Do not be. There are gentler forms of medicine, and I shall prescribe some, if you will let me. I shall also prescribe rest, fresh air, plenty of fruit and vegetables. And a visit to your priest. Sometimes we need to empty our consciences."

"One more question. Is there a chance you could be with child?"

She nodded.

"Then your husband should be pleased. Does he

know?"

She shook her head.

"Why have you not told him?"

"Because he will be pressing on me all the time to produce a boy. And what if I cannot?"

"That is for God to decide, not your husband who is, if I may say so, but a mere mortal. And I mean no disloyalty."

"And what if the child, if it is a boy, is violent like its father?"

"Child, you will have the upbringing of his early years. We do not inherit violence; we learn it."

He turned to Margaret.

"Let us get her back to health and then we can think about informing his lordship. And it may stop any more of these – well, let's just call them blackberries. You and I will know what is meant. If you will allow me into your still-room I will make up a draft for today, but I will also leave you infusions of valerian for sleep – not to be taken for more than three weeks; some honey; some arnica and calendula balm for the blackberries, and a strengthening tonic. Nay, Lady Alys, it is quite pleasant to take."

"And I promise you – no cupping, no bleeding. And when next I come, I hope to hear that you have kept that appointment."

Margaret kissed Alys on the cheek, then led Brother Anselm down the stairs and out to the still room.

"I will ask Luke to take you back to the Priory. We really are most grateful."

"How did you become so involved? If I may be bold enough to ask?"

"It all started with a ring. Such a little thing. Alys lost the posy ring that Revil gave her, and it blew up into something quite unpleasant."

Anselm started. A ring? Now, what was it he had seen? Heard? No, he must be mistaken.

"Then I hope it is found. For her sake, and for the sake of your brother's soul."

"Thank you, Brother. Will you be at the funeral tomorrow?"

"All the community will be present. He will have our prayers. As do you." And he then turned away and busied himself with his herbs.

And she left him and returned to Alys.

"Margaret, I want to go to the boy's funeral."

Margaret said. "That would not be wise, Alys. You are unwell."

"But you don't understand. I wish to pray for his soul."

"That can be done anytime here, or in any chapel. The Lord knows we have plenty of them in Norwich and round about."

"But I want to be there. I want to say goodbye. Maybe drop some flowers on his grave."

"Alys, this is morbid. It will do no good. Ah, and

now you are crying again. Think of the child. Look – why don't I ask Luke if you could just watch the cortège? That is, if you are strong enough?"

Alys seemed content. She took up her embroidery.

A little while later there was a knock on the door. It was Anselm.

"Here we are, my ladies. Valerian – no more than 3 weeks, mind, to be taken before sleep. I have labelled it. And honey. The balm was already made up. And here is a strengthener – twice a day, as instructed. With the honey, if you wish. Or you may have the honey on bread or on its own. It is from our own bees."

"And now I must leave. Master Luke has arranged transport for me" – he smiled – "as passenger on his squire's fine horse. I am well served. Do not hesitate to send for me if needed."

And five minutes later they heard the horse's hoofs clattering on the flags as he returned to the priory.

VII

The morning was grey, with the promise of rain. Prayers had been said in the Priory and in other churches in town. The Bishop himself would attend, and a burial plot had already been found for the child.

The townsfolk were out in force.

The small coffin was born by Wlward and Godwin, Godwin's son Alexander and Master Le Peche. Behind came the Bishop, the monks, Sir John, the Master and Wardens of the Tanners' Company, which, like other societies, was a religious fraternity, and other notables – among them Revil. At the back a small group of nuns from the convent. Some townsfolk tacked on behind.

It was a simple ceremony. The usual prayers for the dead, and the Bishop repeated what he had said at the inquest.

"I truly do not believe that William will not find

a place in heaven."

"Let the little children come to me, and do not hinder them, for the kingdom of God belongs to such as these."

As the coffin was lowered into the grave, a woman rushed forward, weeping uncontrollably. It was William's mother. Two women in the crowd stepped forward to comfort her. They were Godwin's wife and a neighbour.

Alys had to resist the urge to rush forward. But, restrained by Margaret, she had no choice but to stay where she was. Then Hugh arrived and helped her onto her pony.

As they passed through the cathedral gateway, they noticed the groups of townsfolk huddled in doorways, talking. There was a monk, raising his voice in an excited manner, surrounded by a small crowd. The whole atmosphere felt like the minutes before a storm. Alys saw William's mother being led back to her house by the women. She felt cold; she pulled her cloak closer.

Tuesday arrived, with everyone back at work, although the chatter continued. Anselm, busy in his still-room, was surprised to receive a visit from the strange monk. And yet, in an odd way, he wasn't surprised.

"Yes, Brother? What can I do for you? Some ailment?" Loose tongue, if that is an ailment, he thought, then told himself that he was being uncharitable. But the monk's behaviour yesterday had not gone unnoticed.

The visitor was still in his thirties, whey-faced, with wispy red hair, and pale, almost colourless, eyes that had the touch of the fanatic. His hands were soft – a cleric then. No work in the fields for him. He smiled, and Anselm was reminded of a pike. Was it the teeth? There was rather a large specimen where the river flowed past the Dyers Yard.

"Brother, I would have a word with you."

"Oh?"

"Were you not the Brother who laid out the body of young William?"

You know quite well I was, said Anselm to himself. But he kept his lips tight, waiting for more.

"Tell me, did you notice anything strange about him?"

"Such as?"

"Any particular odour?"

Anselm was blunt. "Apart from the herbs in the water, no. And, in any case, the infirmary always smells of herbs. I burn them to keep away unpleasant miasmas."

"You are sure?"

Anselm tried to remain calm. What was all this?

"Quite sure. Brother, let me be frank. I am very busy, yet you come in here without even introducing yourself, and question me about odours."

"Ah, I see you have not heard. My name is Thomas. I am here from my community on an important mission to deliver documents to the Prior and to the Bishop." Anselm noted the way he slithered over the words 'important mission.'

"Then, Thomas, either you had better explain what this is all about, or you must leave. I have two sick Brothers who need my attention."

Thomas smiled. "I can say nothing yet, but, having received special favours, I believe that soon I shall have things to reveal that will surprise the world."

Anselm sighed inwardly. A religious fanatic. You only had to look at the eyes.

"Then I would suggest, Brother Thomas, that you should go to Father Prior and tell him what you have told me, which, at the moment, is nothing. I am sure he will be able to advise you," and he returned to pounding up the paste for the camomile balm.

"May God forgive you your hard words, Brother," said Thomas, as he slid out of the door. "I shall pray for you."

It was later that night, in the warming room, that the news started circulating. Someone had seen flickering lights round the boy's grave.

Who had? Nobody knew. But the word had got

round. Was it a special spiritual visitation? A sign of grace?

Anselm thought to himself that he might just have a suspicion or two. Should he try and put a stop to it before it went too far? He decided that in the morning he would ask for an audience with the Prior. Maybe he could suggest a calming draught for Brother Thomas. Something particularly unpleasant. What would Prior William have to say on the subject, he wondered? There was that case two years ago of Brother Antoninus who was suddenly convinced he could fly. It was a mercy they had managed to stop him before he jumped from the tower of St Leonard's. Was this another such case? Staying up for nights on end in prayer and excessive fasting? Against the explicit rule of St Benedict, as he recalled.

"Let each one deny himself some food, drink, sleep, needless talking and idle jesting, and look forward to holy Easter with joy and spiritual longing."

And as for sleep – eight hours was what the Saint required.

On second thoughts, thinking about it, Prior William himself was not above thoughts of the miraculous. Maybe he would sleep on it.

Having warmed up, he returned to his work. But the Brothers continued to chatter. How long before this hit the outside world, he wondered?

On second thoughts, his patients were doing well enough with his apprentice, Brother Martin. He might just collect a warm cloak and spend a few hours in the graveyard.

Wrapped in his hooded mantle, and armed with a stout stick, he tucked himself behind a yew to keep watch. It was chilly and damp, and any person wishing to play games must be very hardy indeed. Or very, very foolish. He hoped whoever was planning on another light display would not be too long about it. This affair needed to be put to rest before the hysteria grew.

The night drew on. Somewhere a fox chittered, and the owls were out and about. Nesting time. What was it Ardith had said? William was keeping an eye on a tawny owl in the woods.

Suddenly, in the distance he saw a tiny light. He drew back out of sight. The light came closer. And closer. Brother Thomas? No, Brother Martin, coming out to call him back to the infirmary. Brother Anastasius had taken a turn for the worse. Well, that was that for the moment. But he might take another turn tomorrow night. Things were becoming interesting. Prior William could wait.

VIII

Alys stood gazing out of the window at the yard below. Her brother-in-law was talking to his steward – probably about the lambing. She wondered how long she could hide away here, protected by Margaret and Luke. After a few days, she had begun to feel a little stronger. The sleeping potions did work, she had to admit that, but they did not stop the frightful dreams. She asked herself when they would stop. Maybe she should go to see a priest. But what could she say that would take away this awful burden? Would the confessor tell her to return to her husband? To obey him in all things? To accept her lot? How unfair life was.

The door burst open. It was Henry and Edward, her nephews, clamouring to be taken to see the lambs again. For such tiny creatures, they seemed to have taken to being her guardian angels. Henry, the younger, placed sticky fingers on her skirts. Edward placed a hand on Wanda's neck. The dog licked his hand. The boys had obviously been eating some kind of sweet cake.

"Alys, Alys. The kitchen cat has had kittens. Four them, A whole four. Wouldn't you like one to take back home? It could look after you – when it is grown up, I mean. Cook says its mother is a really good ratter."

Good heavens, she thought, how are they so wise at their age? How do they know how I feel? She smiled.

"Well, what a good idea. What colour are they?"

"Two black and white, and two tabbies. We could go and name them. Now."

She did not reply that in all likelihood two them would be drowned. Revil had done it himself on occasion. She shuddered. Much better to go along with their childish enthusiasms.

"Then let's go. Maybe I could choose two?" She wondered what Revil would have to say to that. "And then we could perhaps visit the lambs again."

The boys took her hands and barged through the door, almost knocking over their mother.

"Boys, boys, mind how you go. Your aunt has been a little unwell. Where are you all off to?"

"To see the lambs. And the new kittens, Mama. Alys says she will take two of them."

Margaret raised her eyebrows at Alys, who for

the first time in days, smiled back.

She was glad that the boys seemed to have taken to Alys. Maybe it would change her mind about the forthcoming birth. She still seemed to have the idea that her child would take after Revil in harshness. Now, if she could only come to see that children were born gentle. They did not lie, they were not cruel. As Brother Anselm said, these vices were learned from others.

And like Alys, she wondered what Revil would have to say about the two kittens.

There was another tap on the door. She was surprised to see her brother, Hugh.

"This is a surprise, Hugh. You've been rather a hermit these past two weeks."

"I came over to look at the new lambs. Luke tells me there have been several sets of twins."

"Yes. The children have worn their legs to the bone in their constant visits."

"Ah, I had hoped to see them." He reached into his satchel. "I thought they might like some additions to the ark." And he pulled out two wooden lambs.

"They've actually gone to see the lambs, and help Alys choose a couple of kittens to take back with her."

"Oh, is she here? I wondered why I hadn't seen her."

"Didn't Revil tell you? She was unwell at the

Easter weekend, so we brought her back here. He may be our brother, Hugh, but Revil is not a very sympathetic husband."

He looked embarrassed. "I hope she recovers soon, then. Did Revil not call in the physician?"

"His leeches and potions only made things worse. Brother Anselm has been helping her."

"And has he been successful?"

"She is a little better. But she has these terrible dreams. There is something troubling her, although I doubt you would know what it was."

"No." He fiddled with the lambs. "Well, I had best go and find Luke."

"Will you stay to supper?"

"No, probably not."

"Cook's making a tart made from last year's apples. And clotted cream."

He smiled slightly. "Well, all right then. And I can see the boys before they go to bed."

He kissed her on the cheek, and almost rushed out of the room.

"Well," she thought, "not much interest in Alys. Not like him. He was usually very thoughtful. Perhaps Revil was catching."

She took up Edward's hose and started darning. How on earth did he manage to get such enormous holes in the heels.

Later, at supper, there was more talk about William, although it dwindled to nothing because the boys were there. When Brangwen had whisked them up to bed, it began again, although Margaret made meaningful faces at Luke, with sideways glances at Alys.

However, it was not anything particularly concerning. People were saying that Godwin Sturt, William's uncle, had gone to the Synod and repeated the slander against Eleazar and his community. It was not well received, and Luke seemed a little puzzled.

"I got the impression on Monday that he was a very gentle man and was rather overcome by the whole thing. Isn't the boy's grandfather known for interpreting dreams? Not the sort of family that would succumb to that sort of hysteria. However, as I was not there, understandably, it may have been someone else. It may be all hearsay. And later, at the burial, William's mother was hysterical. But there was no mention of the Jews. This is maybe someone making mischief. And someone did raise the subject at the inquest, now I come to think of it. Someone called Ded."

Hugh agreed. "Yes, the Sheriff had him thrown into the lock-up and threatened him with the penalty for slander. I don't know what happened next, but it is likely that the man is now released."

"Then let us leave it until we know more," said Margaret. Alys cast her a grateful look. "Those lambs you brought over for the boys. They are delightful. Where did you find them?"

"There was a stall at the Tuesday market. I have more animals tucked away for their birthdays and for Christmas."

"You are a kind brother, Hugh. You will make a wonderful father." He looked startled. "When the time comes, I mean."

There was a drop in the conversation. Then Luke and Hugh started on a discussion about spring crops, and Alys said she would go up to bed. "I'm fine, Margaret," she said. "Just a little tired. Those boys of yours quite wore me out. If I am not careful, I shall be taking all four kittens back with me."

"And have you got names for them, yet?"

"I think the boys have already done that for me. Although not quite what I would have chosen."

"Oh?"

"Fox and Wolf. For such tiny creatures, too. But who knows. I am told their mother is a ferocious ratter." And she bid goodnight and went upstairs.

Conversation finished, Luke and Margaret went to the yard to bid Hugh farewell.

Afterwards, Margaret was a little thoughtful. Hugh seemed very distant with Alys. That was unlike him. Maybe it was just a case of not making Revil jealous and encouraging more violence. She remembered that weekend before

53

Easter when Revil had come to visit and was furious about a lost brooch. She smiled wryly. Alys was not the only one who lost things. She would remind him of that the next time.

And Alys, too, had barely looked at Hugh the whole evening.

She sighed, and followed Alys upstairs, thinking to remind her to take the sleeping draught.

The rumours of accusations against the Jews were also being discussed in the Sturt household.

Godwin was adamant, that he had made no such accusations in the Synod. And neither had William's grandfather. He had merely attended, along with Wlward as injured parties, and to thank Bishop Eborard for his promise of support.

Wlward patted his daughter's hand. "This is pure spite, my dear. And we must take steps to stop it, even if I have to go to the Sheriff." The candles and the fire cast a flickering light on his worried face, and on that of his daughter, still swollen with frequent weeping.

"Tongues are even saying that a light was seen near William's grave on the night of the burial. Yet none of the Brothers that I have asked have seen anything," said Godwin. "Elviva, I urge you to believe none of it. This all started with Aelward Ded at the inquest. The Sheriff was quite right to lock him up for a day or so. That man has always had a poisonous tongue. As Saint James says,

"Consider what a great forest is set on fire by a small spark."

"But Brother, they say that I also went about the town accusing them. And when I deny it, people say, ah, but we have heard it, so it must be true. And Leviva has heard them, too." Leviva nodded.

Wlward stood up. "Then I shall certainly go to the Sheriff. And the Bishop. Maybe the Prior, too, if these events are supposed to have happened in the monks' cemetery. Godwin, will you come with me to the castle tomorrow? As soon as possible would be best. These rumours need to be stamped on. And quickly. Now, let us to bed." And he signed a blessing over the little group.

IX

The next morning was grey with a promise of rain. Wlward and Godwin, watched by a worried Elviva, snatched a hasty breakfast, then set off for the castle. The stallholders were already setting up in the Market, and within twenty minutes or so the men had reached the castle mound where they stopped to discuss the best approach.

"Godwin, did you notice the Sheriff's response when those accusations were made?

"I did, indeed. He has always been a just man, who bears his responsibilities with honour. I truly believe he will listen to our concerns, especially after his offer of help."

"Then let us go up."

It was an imposing building. To build the original, over a hundred houses had been destroyed. Following a rebellion, the ditch had been deepened, and the height of the motte raised. Then they built the keep. Very little of the original wooden structure remained.

"And they built over our cemetery," said Godwin. "Indeed, to look at the countryside, is to really understand the impact of these Normans after the invasion. A sad thing, indeed."

They approached the gate and were hailed by the guard on duty, who directed them towards the external staircase and the forebuilding. Here another guard sent ahead to tell Sir John, and they slowly climbed the steps.

Sir John was seated at a long table in the hall. In front of him were pipe rolls and sheets of parchment. He was deep in discussion with a clerk. He looked up and smiled.

"Wlward, Godwin. You are most welcome. How can I help you? Please, sit. May I offer you some spiced wine? It is a cold day."

"Thank you, sir, but no. Sir, at young William's inquest you were kind enough to offer support, and we saw the way you dealt with the slanderous accusations against Eleazar. We are sad to say that these are again being voiced. And what is worse, rumours are circulating that Godwin himself raised them, as did also William's mother. A double slander, sir, a double slander."

John's face darkened. "I will not have it; I will not have it. The Jewish community are under our protection. And so are you. Have you been to see anyone else?"

"We did consider speaking to the Bishop, as it is to do with the religious community."

"It is a delicate point, but I believe that the Ecclesiastical Court has no jurisdiction over the Jews. Whilst we can certainly do something about the slander; Master Ded is only now out of prison."

"Without wishing to stir up the problem," said Godwin "I believe some of this stems from Master Ded."

"Then Master Ded needs our attention. Have no fear, I will deal with this. If necessary, I will take the Jews in here, for safety, should it get to that point. It would be most helpful if we could find the murderer, but there is no evidence of anything. It may just have been a passing footpad."

"Please, do not hesitate to call on me. This is a sorry business. I know we are the conquerors, so to speak, but it is my strong belief that communities should live in harmony. Honest men need protection."

He rose and showed them to the door. As they went down, they heard him speaking to a guard. They thought they heard the name 'Ded.'

As they hurried towards the cathedral for the morning service, a monk passed them, probably with the same purpose. Godwin called out, "Good morrow, Brother," and the monk turned.

He looked strangely familiar. Pasty, round face; pale eyes. Godwin muttered to Wlward, "Isn't that the Brother that was standing in the corner near the Chapter House the day of the inquest?"

Wlward was not quite sure. "If it is, then he's maybe the one that I kept seeing talking to people in the streets. A face I don't know. He isn't part of the community; maybe a visitor? I will call in on Brother Anselm. I have an excellent excuse. My joints are aching with all this damp weather. And he produces a very effective balm. It beats anything produced by Elviva. Anselm will know, if anyone does."

And after the service they did indeed call on Anselm, who was only too happy to speak.

He took Wlward over to the fire, and started moving his arm and leg joints, checking for where the pain was worst. "Well, Wlward, for someone of your age, you are not doing so badly. I shall prescribe the usual – plenty of movement, don't stand around too long, and some embrocation. I have added something to the usual recipe. Let me know how you get on with it."

He gave him a very straight look. "And dare I say that this is not the only reason for your visit this morning?"

"You may indeed, Brother. Tell us, have you a new Brother recently joined the community?"

Anselm gave a broad smile. "Now, why should

you ask that?"

"Nothing in particular; just out of interest, shall we say?"

"I have known you too long to think that is only just out of interest. Well, I shall put you out of your misery. But you must not share what I am about to tell you, since I think my reaction to this particular Brother on the one occasion I came into contact with him was hardly Christian. And I am still trying to make myself feel ashamed."

"As far as I can gather, Brother Thomas is from Monmouth although I do not think his current community is there. He arrived here with some documents for Prior William and the Bishop and seems to have taken upon himself the duty of inquisitor over the death of your grandson. If I tell you what he was asking, it must go no further."

Wlward raised his eyebrows.

"He asked me if I had noticed any sweet odours around the body."

"What!?"

"Exactly. This man is up to no good. There are strange rumours. Oh, not just in the Priory but in the town, among certain credulous people. Even some of my patients have heard them. It would not surprise me if he were at the bottom of them. And I am not talking about blaming the Jews for the murder. Oh, yes, I have heard that, too."

He looked at the faces of the others. "Someone has been talking about strange lights in the graveyard."

"Dear God. We heard that, too."

"Exactly. I did a bit of watching myself, and I can state in all honesty that there were no lights. Unless they arrived after I had left. Put plainly, I have seen people like him before. Fanatics. And fantasists. And dangerous. They prey on the minds of the gullible."

"Thank you for your time, Brother," said Godwin.

"Not at all. Between ourselves, I believe this situation needs dealing with. May I perhaps call on you one evening? You are in Colegate? Perhaps I could bring some herbs and ointments for Elviva. I know she is adept in these matters, but I can also understand that her mind has been elsewhere. Maybe some late apples, too?"

Godwin took his hand. He liked this Brother, with a warm heart and a sensible head on him, in spite of his young years. "You will be truly welcome, Brother. We must work together on this."

As he and Wlward walked towards the gate, they were aware of a shadow behind them. But when they turned back, whoever it was had gone.

Anselm busied himself over his various brews and what the priests had said. He wondered whether he should revisit his first idea of going to Prior William. Certainly, some of the younger monks were starting to gossip among themselves. The atmosphere was starting to become febrile. Unless something was done, it would only get worse.

He would sleep on it.

X

Anselm and the priests had done well to be concerned. They would have been even more so, had they followed the dark-robed figure that slipped through the priory gate after Terce the next morning. He had missed breakfast. Did not Benedict himself say that our life should be a continuous Lent, he thought, smugly. He strode out towards the castle and Eleazar's house, a fine, stone building, part of a block of dwellings.

He hammered on the gate, setting up barking from a large mastiff. A tall dark young man came to the gate. "Yes?"

"I wish to speak with the maid."

"Which maid? We have three."

"The one who knew the boy, William."

"Ah, that would be young Ardith. Wait there." And the man went back into the undercroft.

A few minutes later a worried-looking Ardith came to the gate. "Yes, sir?"

"I want a word with you, girl. You knew the boy, William?"

"If you mean, I met him when he visited here on his master's errands, then I did." She wasn't going to be browbeaten by this shiny-faced Brother with the sly smile. Too many teeth. Gave her the shivers. And what business was it of his whom she knew or didn't know.

"Girl, I think you know more than you say."

"My name is Ardith, Brother, and I gave my evidence to Sir John. Didn't I see you there, hiding in the corner? Then you will know what I said then."

"Insolent girl, I am here on God's business."

She smiled to herself. She had obviously hit his pride. "And I have work to do, so if you don't mind."

"I believe you are deceiving us. You know more than you have told. Ardith, is it? I want you to say what you really saw that day."

"I saw only what I told the Sheriff."

His pale face flushed, and he raised his voice. "Tell me what you really saw, you lying slut, or it will be the worse for you. Working for these Jews has twisted your tongue into the evil of deception." Spittle shot from his pale mouth as he spoke.

He tried to force his way through the gate, and the dog started up again. The young man

64

returned. It seemed he had been listening.

"Ardith, go back inside. I will deal with this. Sir, I would ask you to leave. This is a breach of the peace, and you have no business here. I would not like to have to set the dogs on you."

Ardith went inside, but stayed by the half-open door, listening.

The monk decided that bullying would not work, and, in any case, the man was tall and strong, so he lowered his voice. And there was the matter of the dogs.

"Of course, I regret causing any trouble, but I believe there is more to this story than has been told."

"And what leads you to that conclusion?" The young man's voice was smooth and courteous, but his eyes flashed.

"I have been visited by heaven with a mission to find the truth."

The young man stared at him. He was joined by a tall, bearded older man. "What is the trouble, Jacob?"

Jacob lowered his voice. "Father, this man believes he has a mission from heaven to find out the truth about the boy, William. He was bullying Ardith."

"Then he can stop there."

"Sir, you have disturbed our morning's work, and threatened my maidservant. If you have anything else to say, please go to the Sheriff, under whose protection we live. We are finished here," and he returned to the house, followed by his son.

Thomas stood motionless, biting his lips, muttering. He would say a prayer for these heathens, these God murderers. He knew their ways. Always sneaking around. Always peeping through keyholes. The girl must certainly have seen something. Then he would go to the Prior.

As he hurried down towards the Priory, he was passed by someone coming the other way, who turned to watch him for a minute or so, before continuing to Master Eleazar's house.

He knocked at the gate, and again Jacob arrived. Master Le Peche thought the young man's anger must be directed at him and wondered why. "I am sorry, Master Le Peche. Please excuse my manners. We have just had a rather unpleasant visitor. Pray, come in. I will ask Reuben to look after the pony. Will you need help with the skins?"

"No, I thank you, Master Jacob. They are easily managed. But your father will need to check them."

A shutter opened above, and Master Eleazar looked out.

"Pray, wait, Master Le Peche, I shall be down shortly. Jacob, bring him inside to the office."

The skins were checked, and spiced wine brought. Then Master Eleazar opened a chest and counted out payment. "I would that you take this now. A simple receipt will suffice. You must be short-staffed now that William is no longer with us. We miss the youngster."

"Indeed, that is most thoughtful of you. I will need to train a new apprentice. But I took this opportunity, as I also wished to warn you about something."

"Oh?"

"There are some nasty rumours circulating as to who murdered William. I am afraid..."

"Do not be, Master Le Peche. This will be nothing new. We Jews are always suspected. We had some of it, indirectly, just now. Come, sit by the fire."

Daniel gazed around the room, appreciated the hangings, the branched candlestick, the well-polished settle and sideboard.

"Ah, the monk? I thought I recognised him. From what I have gathered from William's grandfather and uncle, it is possible he is involved in this rumour-flap."

"However, it is worse than that. Even William's mother and uncle are said to be spreading these rumours. Yet they are completely innocent. I should add that yesterday Godwin and Wlward called on Sir John. At the time they did not mention the monk. It was the Infirmarian at the Priory who added his suspicions. May I ask what the monk was doing here?"

"He insulted our maidservant, and accused her of lying, of knowing more than she told at the inquest. And, for what it is worth, he told my son he had a mission from Heaven to find William's murderer."

Master Peche looked shocked. "Then it is as well William's family have spoken to the Sheriff. You may count on my support. Please do not hesitate."

"I thank you, Master Le Peche. Let us hope it will not come to that."

XI

Anselm did indeed sleep on it. For three days. Then, after Terce, and a good breakfast – unlike Thomas, he believed bodies needed feeding as much as the soul – he asked for an audience with Prior William. His visit to William's family could wait until he knew more.

Prior William de Turbeville was what one could almost describe as an ambitious, professional Religious, thought Anselm. He had been educated in the priory at Norwich, then took orders, first as a teacher, then as Precentor, and was now Prior. Where would he go next? It was not hard to hazard a guess. Bishop Eborard was not that strong and, of course, there was always the question of certain accusations of simony, although discounted.

He knocked on the door. A monk opened it. "Yes?"

"I am seeking audience with Prior William,

Brother."

"Wait," and the monk disappeared back inside. Two minutes later Thomas appeared, and smirking triumphantly, went down the stairs towards the cloister.

The monk reappeared and ushered Anselm into the room. There was a large fire burning, noted Anselm, conscious of the cold dorter where he had spent last night. And was that a carpet on the floor?

"Well, my son," said William. He was a tall man, although, sitting down, this was not immediately obvious. His hair had no grey, yet he was almost fifty. He would look well in Bishop's robes, thought Anselm. He also thought it was odd that his eyes resembled those of Thomas. Pale, emotionless.

"Father Prior," said Anselm. "I will get straight to the point since I see you are busy. I am concerned about the spiritual welfare of some of the Brothers, particularly the younger ones."

William's eyes glinted. "Brother Anselm, your duties are to care for the bodies of the community. Their spiritual welfare you can safely leave to me."

"Father, some of the Brothers spend their time gossiping about the murder of young William. They speak of lights in the cemetery. They are now starting to blame the Jews."

"Is that all?"

"Father, there are no lights. And Sir John has declared the Jews guiltless. And Brother Thomas – of Monmouth, is it? – pays me almost hourly visits with questions on the state of the boy's body, odours of sanctity. I can get no work done. He is spreading these rumours. It is against the Rule, Father."

"You are an adept in the Rule, Brother Anselm?"

"Father, did not Saint Benedict himself say: 'In all places gossip.' Brother, has it not occurred to you that Brother Thomas may be speaking the truth? However, if as you say, he has committed any sin, it is for him to come to me. It is not for you to appoint yourself his unofficial confessor."

"I find in Brother Thomas one who seems to have spiritual communion with our Lord. Indeed, he had shared with me some of his visions. He will shortly be returning to his own community, but I should tell you that I am asking his Superior to allow him to return and remain permanently with us in the community in Norwich, where he can perhaps continue with his meditations on the blessed William."

Anselm felt his throat dry up. So, this was the reason for that smug look. And what was meant by 'Blessed William'? Where did that come from?

"If that is all, Brother, then you may leave.

71

There is to be no more of this nonsense. And I would suggest you spend some time in prayer, examining your conscience. Envy is a deadly sin, Brother."

He slipped into the cathedral to spend time in prayer and meditation. Maybe the Prior was right. Was he jealous of Thomas? He almost laughed out loud but then besought himself to avoid the sin of pride. Did he truly understand the souls of others? How could he be sure that this was indeed something from a deranged mind, rather than a genuine vision? He asked for help that he might see more clearly.

He returned to the infirmary, only to find two of the younger novices seated on the bench, looking pale and worried. "Not more of them," he thought.

Indeed, yes. Poisonous dreams. Restless sleep. Fear of murder.

"Brothers, why would anyone seek to kill you? Keep the way straight before you, and may God forbid, should this ever happen, you would die in good odour." He nearly kicked himself and wished he had not used that phrase, remembering that Thomas had been widely spreading his lies about the odour of sanctity, in spite of Anselm's denials that first day.

"Come, let me take a look at you." He checked their pulses, their skin, their tongues, their eyes. "Now, tell me honestly, have you been unofficially fasting? You know the rules."

Benet blushed. "Yes, Brother. Brother Thomas said it would help us to achieve the visions with which he has been blessed."

So, now Thomas is a doctor of souls, he thought.

"And instead, Benet, you have been visited with nightmares. Should this not tell you something?"

Cuthbert added "But maybe this tells us that we have not fasted hard enough."

"Children, for that is what you are, whatever Brother Thomas suggests, you owe your duty to Father Prior and to the Community. You must fast only when required to. The Summer heat will soon be upon us, and I do not want you down with the Summer Pestilence. So, I shall give you both a strengthener, and my instructions are no more fasting. Come back in two days, and I hope to hear no more talk of fasting and visions," and he took down from a top shelf two waxed flasks of a rather unpleasant tonic. "No honey for these young nincompoops," he thought. "Let that be their penance."

He smiled to himself as he continued with his work and tried to remember himself at that age. But at the same time, the worries continued. Please God, Thomas would soon be gone, although the thought that he would return was no true comfort. Plenty of time to brew up more feverish fantasies ready for his return.

He needed fresh air. He thought he would visit the Lady Alys, before she returned home. He believed she was still with her sister-in-law's family. And there would be no harm in sounding out how far all these rumours were spreading. He hoped to see an improvement, not more bad dreams. He took a rush basket and added some dried herbs and more of the tonic, and leaving Brother Martin in charge, strode out towards the gate.

XII

Anselm was welcomed by Alys herself who was playing some kind of mumming game with the children. At least, he supposed that's what it was, as the elder boy had a scarf wound round his head like a turban, and the little one was banging a drum. Wanda was skittering about the room like a demon, trying to avoid the Turk's wooden sword.

"Boys, boys. Take care. Don't hurt Wanda." Alys was laughing.

"It's not Wanda, it's the dragon, and we are saving you from his teeth."

Ah, then quite obviously it wasn't an infidel, but someone else. Maybe the Archangel Michael himself. Patron Saint of Normandy, if he recalled rightly. Though he was not sure there were any young ladies involved in his story.

"You are looking much better, my Lady, there is more colour in your cheeks," he said. "Are your dreams improved?"

"They still come, but hardly at all now. And I am no longer afraid of them. Although..."

"Yes?"

"Brother, there are strange rumours that have reached us here – mainly brought by the servants. There is a monk..."

"Yes? Have no fear, my Lady, you may speak freely."

"Two days ago, my Brangwen heard him in the market, shouting at a crowd of people. Something about saints and Jews. When she came back here, she was very shaken. Would you like to speak to her?"

"Yes, I rather think I would. There is too much of this sort of talk, and I wanted to ensure you were not affected."

"Boys, would you go and ask Brangwen to come up, please? And when you have done that, go down to Cook and say I said that you may have an apple each."

Alys sat and Anselm did the same, admiring the fine embroidery lying on the stool. "That is to be a purse for Margaret's birthday. She has been so kind, Brother, you have no idea. But I have to do it when she is not here, as it is to be a surprise."

There was a tap on the door, and Brangwen came in. She looked worried. Anselm thought that he was seeing rather a lot of worry these days.

It was like a disease.

"Brangwen, could you tell Brother Anselm what it was you saw and heard in the marketplace?"

"Brother, it is difficult to explain, but it almost seemed as if the monk was trying to get people to attack the Jews. At least, he didn't actually say that, but it was the dreadful names he called them, and saying that they had killed the boy, William. At one point, it seemed the monk looked straight at me. It was as if he might even accuse me."

"And what happened then?"

"There was a bit of an uproar, and then the Constable appeared and told them to go home. He said they risked being thrown into prison, like Aelward Ded. Who is Aelward Ded?"

"Another scandal monger, I am afraid. I believe he spent a couple of days in the castle lock-up."

"Then I am glad. It wasn't right, what he was saying."

"And after that?"

"I came straight home. But the monk hung around for a bit until the Constable sent him back to the priory. But he didn't go that direction, though. I saw."

"Brangwen, that has been very useful. In this world, unfortunately, we have too many liars and troublemakers. I am just sorry that you should have seen this Brother in such a light. Now, go back to your work – I think the boys may need a substitute maiden. Try not to worry. In any case, the Brother is going back to his own community soon. And I hope that may be the end of it."

But he knew that Brother Thomas would be coming back for good. And that did not bear looking at.

The rest of the time passed in gentle conversation until it was the hour for his return. Alys was to return to Catton on the next Monday, as it seemed Revil wanted her back, when she would give him the news of the forthcoming child.

He emptied his basket, then strode out through the early dusk towards the cathedral. He wondered what the date was for Thomas's departure. He laid a bet he would not go without some sort of revelation or show.

He had not long to wait. He was met at the door to the pharmacy by Brother Martin. At least it wasn't another troubled novice.

"All well, Brother? No emergencies, I hope?"

"Brother Edmund is much improved, and Silas coughs much less. Oh, and there is news."

"Good news, I hope?"

Martin's face shone – almost with glee, thought Anselm. Surely not.

"Brother Thomas is returning to his community. On Friday."

Anselm wasn't sure whether to tell him that,

unfortunately, Thomas would return at Christmas, if not earlier. But why spoil the lad's enjoyment.

"Then let us hope he has spent his time with us well." Indeed, he had, he thought, indeed he had. Rather too well.

The next few days were calmer. Whether it was because of the Constable's intervention, or because of the weather. Late April showers they were not. The heavens opened, and the rivers rose. Perhaps, thought Anselm, now was the time to call on William's family. But maybe he would wait until the rains stopped and Brother Thomas had left. Then would be the time to judge whether the mutterings had truly stopped. At the moment, with everyone inside, there was far too much opportunity for gossip.

Finally, Friday arrived. The day was dry, and after a short service, the community gathered in the frater house, where Prior William bid farewell to Thomas, and accompanied him outside, followed by the others.

Thomas looked rather ungainly on the mule, but his smile remained unpleasantly seraphic. No doubt he was imagining palms before his feet, thought Anselm, who had been gifted with yet another of his visits that morning.

After a short prayer, Thomas went on his way towards the city gates, to join the small convoy travelling north-west. and the others returned to their duties. If Prior William was right, then they would be seeing Thomas again before Christmas. That is, if Thomas's own Prior could bear to release him. Anselm had his own rather unworthy thoughts on that issue.

He thought he would not approach the Bishop unless the rumours started up again. But he might just keep his promise and call in on William's family. And Alys was returning home after the weekend. She would need his prayers.

It proved more difficult to slip away than he had thought. The Novice Master popped his head round the door and asked for a moment of his time. He was worried about some of the novices who were rather unsettled. Anselm led him to the fire and poured him out some spiced cordial. Making sure they were not overheard, he shared his thoughts with Brother Dunstan, holding nothing back.

"I hope I am not being disloyal to Father Prior, Brother, but there seems little support there."

"So, you, too, went for advice?"

"I imagine you fared the same as I did," said Anselm, with a wry smile. "I did not know. We might have gone together."

"I suspect we might have been accused of some kind of plot," said Dunstan. "But that is not to say that we may not share our thoughts on the matter.

You and I can fend for ourselves, but these youngsters are young and impressionable. And it is not only rumours of lights and odours; once or twice I thought I overheard some unpleasant accusations against the Jews. Really it should be for Prior William to deal with this, but I am under the impression that he rather approves."

"So, what do you think Thomas is aiming for?"

"Between you and me, it would not surprise me if he were trying to turn William into some kind of saint. Yes, I know, it's against common sense and usual practice, but there is this sense of a fantasist. I have felt it strongly. And I daresay Prior William would not object to bringing some fame to the cathedral."

"Then let us keep our council. If we raise the issue at this point, we shall get nowhere. Let us see what happens now that he has left. And I shall have a quiet word with William's family. I gather they have already spoken to the Sheriff." And they changed the subject.

That evening, leaving the infirmary in the hands of Brother Martin, Anselm took a basket with apples, cordials and remedies, and set off to see William's family. He wondered whether Thomas would really wait until Christmas before returning? Was Dunstan right? Did Prior William really desire a saint for the cathedral?

Seated at the long oak table with Godwin and

Wlward, he shared with them what Dunstan had suggested. The other men were appalled. "William was a normal boy, not particularly pious – unlike his brother Robert. He was murdered by some passing thief. That should not make him a saint," said Godwin. "And what will happen when his mother hears? It may well tip her on the side of these rumour-mongers."

Wlward added, "And if this Brother is really inventing stories to further his sanctification, how can that be based on a lie? It is blasphemy, nothing more nor less than blasphemy. Maybe we should go to the Bishop?"

"He may be more sympathetic than Prior William," said Anselm, sharing with them what the Prior had said. "But he is frail, and from what I have heard, may soon be resigning."

"Then why do we not all go?" said Godwin. "He cannot refuse to see us. Bring Brother Dunstan, too."

Anselm nodded. "I will speak to Brother Dunstan. Let us agree to go in deputation to the Palace on Monday. Shall we say in the after-noon?"

And so it was agreed.

But something happened first.

XIII

On Monday morning, Alys took courage and took Revil's arm as he passed through the hall.

"What is it, can't it wait?"

She almost changed her mind, but it had to be done, "Husband, I need to talk to you. Please. It is important."

"Unless it is to tell me that you have found the ring, then you may hold your tongue. I have not forgotten."

"No, it is something more important."

"And now you tell me that you give little value to the loss of my ring?"

He stared at her, and she half thought that he was going to strike her. But something must have made him stop. "Well, come on then, woman, what is it?"

"I am expecting a child."

There was a silence and then, to her utter amazement, he took her in his arms. He was smiling. When did she last see him smile?

"At last. At last. A son."

"Husband, it is by no means certain."

"Of course it is a son. We have taken all the measures. At last. At last."

"Well," thought Alys, "it is only six months since we wed. Hardly a sudden miracle." She was surprised to find herself suddenly very angry. Not a word as to how she felt. She supposed he thought a smile was sufficient. But she hoped he would forget the ring for the time being. Her head had started aching. She went into the garden. He would not follow her there. He disliked flowers.

She sat down on a stone bench and looked into the little pond. Her reflection rippled, pale as a water sprite. Suddenly, another face appeared. It was Brother Anselm.

"I see you are taking some fresh air. How does it feel to be back at Catton?"

"Rather strange, if I tell the truth. Everything seems to be without life. I miss the liveliness of Sprowston."

"But you have your brother-in-law. And soon the kittens will arrive."

"Yes, I suppose so. And I do not see much of Hugh these days."

"And have you told your husband the news?"

"Yes, a short while ago. He was strangely

cheerful. He smiled."

"And that is so unusual?"

She did not answer.

He sat down beside her and pulled out something from his satchel. It was a tiny wooden cross.

"This you may hang over the cradle. Something to protect the child from nightmares," and he smiled. "This was mine as a child. For some reason I kept it with me."

"And did it work?"

"I cannot say. I was never one for bad dreams. Of course, my childhood was relatively peaceful. How is Brangwen, by the way?"

"She is still a little shaken. But she says the disturbances have quietened down in the past week."

She gazed into the pond. "Sometimes I think it must be very pleasant to be a fish and hide among the reeds in the cool water."

"Until a large pike comes along, or a fisherman catches you for supper." He wondered why he had thought of a pike. Thomas must be miles away by now.

There was the sound of a horse clattering into the yard, and Hugh calling for Revil. Revil came through the garden.

"What is it?"

"There has been a disturbance in Jewry. A spot

of stone throwing, and a few arrests, including Master Ded and Master Le Peche's apprentice. Master Le Peche has been sent for. Master Eleazar is not pressing charges – probably because he does not wish to raise any more anti-Jewish feeling. But Sir John is calling a council to discuss the situation. He is anxious that this should not get out of hand."

He noticed Anselm. "Brother, can I offer you pillion transport?"

"That would be most helpful. I myself am going to see the Bishop, together with William's family and the Master of Novices. We are of the same thought – this has gone far enough." And saying goodbye to Alys, and giving her the basket of remedies and herbs, he followed the brothers to the stables and was soon back at the Priory, where the other three joined him at the appointed time.

Before they went in, it was agreed that Wlward would start the conversation, although Wlward reminded them that Bishop Eborard had been one of those at the Second Council in 1129 discussing enforced celibacy on the clergy. "But since I have been widowed these past ten years, it is likely he will have nothing to say to me. Shall we go in?"

A monk met them in the hall. He went to find the Bishop's Chaplain, and they were soon in

Bishop Eborard's parlour. Again, Anselm noticed the carpet, the fire, although in this case probably needed. The Bishop must have been in his early sixties and looked frail. As they knelt to kiss his ring, Anselm noticed the swollen gouty joints.

"My sons, please, sit. How may I help you?"

Wlward spoke gently, almost as if he feared to blow away this man, old before his years.

"Your Grace, it is about my grandson, William who was cruelly murdered on Good Friday. As my friends here will testify, someone is spreading what we can only describe as lies."

"In what way?" The Bishop leaned forward.

"Has he not heard?" thought Anselm.

Wlward continued. "Rumours have blamed the Jewish community for his death. Even this morning there was an attack on the house of one of its most respected citizens. May I ask Brother Anselm to say more?"

"Yes, indeed. Brother Anselm, you are the Infirmarian, I believe. I have benefited from your medicines in the past. Pray, go on."

Anselm told him about the monk, the endless visits, the supposed lights, the non-existent odours. "Brother Dunstan, the Master of Novices can add more, your Grace."

And Brother Dunstan mentioned the young novices who were suffering from the effects of the hysteria.

The Bishop looked concerned.

"My sons, has it not occurred to you that these rumours, as you call them, may be true?"

"If I may be so bold, your Grace, I had the washing of the young lad's body. I had the watching of him whilst he lay in our infirmary until the burial. There was no odour. I have on occasion kept watch in the cemetery. Late at night. There were no lights. This was a passing murder for gain. Nothing more than that."

"This I know, since I was at the inquest. Yet has it not occurred to you that just because you have not been visited by these occurrences, it does not mean they are not true. Not everyone is so blessed."

Godwin intervened. "Sir John is concerned that this will get out of hand. As we have said, there was a small disturbance this morning. The house of Master Eleazar was stoned. Sir John has called a council."

The Bishop changed tack. It was obviously getting too much for him, thought Anselm.

"I am sure you quite rightly first went to Prior William with these concerns. What did he have to say? He has certainly not been to see me."

Not when he has the chance of his own tame saint, thought Anselm, uncharitably. But, give it time. He will, he will.

"To be honest, your Grace," said Dunstan, "he

sides with Brother Thomas."

"Then, my sons, since you owe obedience to Prior William, you must accept what he says."

Dunstan opened his mouth, but Eborard held up his hand.

"If the novices are proving difficult, then it is your duty, as Novice Master, to deal with it. I am sure both you and Brother Anselm can provide for the health of their bodies and minds. You are not strict enough with them, you are not strict enough."

"And the Jews, Your Grace?" added Godwin.

"Since they are not under my jurisdiction, not being Christian, they are not my responsibility. Leave that to Sir John." And he rang a small bell, a monk entered, and the petitioners were ushered out.

They stood by the gate and looked at each other. It was all very unsatisfactory. In the distance they noticed occasional men-at-arms standing at street corners. Sir John was taking no chances.

"Let us sleep on it," said Wlward. "If, as you say, Brother Thomas is not returning for several months, all being well, things by rights ought to calm down."

"It will depend on what today's Council decides," said Anselm. "Let us all remain vigilant, and I would suggest we report back to Sir John, if necessary. If today's troublemakers really have been arrested, then they are out of our way for the time being. I do not think Master Ded will get off so lightly the second time around."

Sir John also made the same point at the Council meeting. He told those attending that Ded was now in prison for a considerable amount of time. He had not yet decided how long that would be; it would depend on whether things quietened down. A guard had been placed on Master Eleazar's house, although Eleazar had not deemed it necessary.

John addressed the town worthies: "Masters, you have seen that Master Le Peche will deal with young Ethelbert. Master Daniel, I leave it to you how you deal with him. Let others of you who have apprentices, servants or artisans in your employ, I ask you to give them all due warning. I could, of course, send the crier round to make these announcements as to how we shall deal with public disturbances, but for the time being, your personal cooperation will probably be enough."

"Let us reconvene in two weeks' time. And let us hope I do not have to recall you earlier than that. I shall keep the guards on the streets for the next four days only. If necessary, I shall visit the Prior. But since no religious has been involved in the disturbance, I shall hold my hand for the moment."

"Now, go in peace. But please, share a cup of wine with me before you leave."

He drew Daniel Le Peche to one side. "Thank you, Master Daniel. Your swift response was much noticed. If there is anything, anything at all, please contact me directly. No need to wait for any further meetings. These youngsters – they are so impressionable. Those who take advantage of them should be shut away, and the key thrown into the Wensum." And he smiled.

And the next few weeks passed in calm and quiet.

XIV

It was Margaret's birthday, and the Sprowston family were celebrating. Alys's embroidered case was passed round and much admired, as were the little green earrings from Luke. The boys produced a special performance of St Michael and the Devil, and Alys felt she had not been so happy for a long time. She looked down at the two kittens who were soon to be accompanying her back home.

Revil, too, lately returned from London, seemed more cheerful, and took every opportunity to show what he had bought his wife. Almost as if rubbing in the loss of the first ring, thought Margaret.

It was a gold posy ring – with an intricate design of lilies and the words *ung temps viandra*. Was he perhaps alluding to the forthcoming birth, wondered Margaret. But it was good to see him looking more relaxed. She watched Hugh chasing the boys around, pretending to be a devil, and wondered whether Revil would ever unwind enough to do the same?

"That's a fine piece of work, brother," said Luke. "Local workmanship, or did you commission it in London's Chepeside?"

"Local, of course. Master Orfe. Where I commissioned the first ring. We should support our local tradesmen."

"That's right," thought Margaret, "Never let it go." Mischievously she added, "I see you have replaced that cloak brooch you lost before Easter. A handsome piece. Did Master Orfe also make that?"

She was surprised when his lips tightened, and he said, "What brooch are you talking about, Margaret? I never lost anything." She was about to argue, but saw his face, and let it go. It really wasn't worth the trouble.

"Shall we go into the garden? The first roses are out. And the servants have brought out the wine. Then we can come back in for the feast."

She knew the men would just talk business and discuss Revil's visit to the court. But she wanted to get Alys on her own and ask her how things were. She also wondered why it was that Alys and Hugh never seemed to talk to each other any more. Yet they had always been on very friendly terms.

They strolled through the gate, and Margaret noticed that Alys barely showed the expected child. Was it a girl, she wondered? She hoped not. Wanting an heir and more was natural for a man, but given what Alys had undergone, it would be good if she was spared some of that pressure for a while.

The smell of the white roses was intoxicating, and they spent some time with their noses buried among the blossom. Then Margaret led Alys to the wooden bench and spread down a mantle for her comfort. They were soon deep in conversation.

It seemed that Revil had been kinder, ever since he had learned of the child. She thought of the difference between the two brothers – and wondered why Alys had never been betrothed to Hugh. They would have been more suited. But then, he was the younger brother.

"Is there anything amiss between you and Hugh, Alys, only I notice you never seem to speak these days."

"No, we just seem to have drifted apart. Then there was the business with William."

Margaret decided, from the rather evasive look on Alys's face, that it would be best to leave it for the time being. Maybe she could talk to Hugh. Alys needed a friend in that great house.

They both fell into a gentle half-sleep amongst

all the blossom, lulled by the sound of the bees and the birds. Wanda pattered out to join them. Margaret could hear the sound of the boys in the distance. Just a few more minutes before they went into the hall.

Later, Hugh was no more forthcoming than Alys. "It just happens, Margaret," he said. "We grow up, we have responsibilities." She did not quite believe him.

"Hugh, that I understand. Yet with the child on its way, she will need a friend; Revil is seldom at home, and when he is, he takes no notice of her."

She felt, rather than saw, the start he gave. She looked up. He was pale.

"You did not know?"

"No. When is it due?"

"Sometime in mid-November, I think. I shall try to be there. If not, she must come to Sprowston. She is a delicate flower, Hugh. She needs our support. Maybe this is the time to heal rifts."

He nodded. then went over to speak to Revil and Luke, and they were soon deep in conversation.

Haymaking passed at Midsummer, with its great fires on Saint John's Eve to keep away the Devil. Not forgetting the shearing. To the great joy of Henry and Edward.

And slowly the summer strolled by.

There were no more disturbances, and everyone

thought that would be the end of it. Apart from Brother Anselm and Dunstan, who could still sense remnants of hysteria among the novices. "It looks like a waiting game," thought Anselm, and decided to brew some strong cleansing draughts to begin the winter. Dunstan thought he might start some kind of outdoor exercise for the youngsters. Footraces? Some kind of ball game? Maybe bouts of La Soule? Anything to tire them out.

"Not too rough, Brother," said Anselm. "I don't wish to be patching up broken heads, as I was after the Midsummer revels. Better broken nights than broken crowns."

Soon after came August and a good harvest gathered in. Praise God there had been no heavy rains. After weeks of back-breaking toil, the Harvest Home celebrations were a welcome respite. The churches were decorated with lammas loaves and fruit; and Alys and Margaret spent their hours sewing for the new child. Before long it would be the sowing and apple gathering. The nights would draw in. And before Christmas arrived, a new member of the family.

In the meanwhile, Revil and Hugh spent some time away at the King's court in discussions, since de Mandeville's rebellion was now over, and a pact had been signed with Ranulf of Chester, resulting in the handing over of a number of castles. However, the troubles in the west continued, and by sending men in support of Stephen, please God the east of the country would be protected, and the disturbances brought to an end.

Looking at the lush grasses and the trees, so fruit-laden, inhaling the green scents, soaking up the colour, gazing at the wildflowers, looking down into the gently flowing water of the river, it was very easy to forget about the serpent in Eden.

It might have been peaceful in Norwich, but things did not remain so for long.

XV

In October, the word soon got round, and the town folk once more turned out in force. They did like a great show, and it seemed, from the whisperings from the Priory, that they were to get one. Anselm, in his still room, speeded up his production of purges and tonics. After Prior William's announcement that day, he had had a feeling they would be needed.

It had started with William calling the community together after prayers, to make his announcement.

"My sons, I am glad to announce to you a happy event. Our dear Brother Thomas, who was with us at Easter, is returning from his order to join us permanently." And he brandished a letter.

"From what I saw in his time here, I truly believe he is sent from our Saviour to lead us to a more perfect life. He will be acting as my assistant in a very important project. I cannot tell you more at this point, but you will also take part in this tremendous journey. And as our Founder said:

'If he would find fault with anything, or expose it, reasonably, and with the humility of charity, the Abbot shall discuss it prudently lest perchance God has sent him for this very thing.'"

There was a flutter of sound. Anselm groaned. He caught the eye of Dunstan, who grimaced, then crossed himself as if to beg penance for an unworthy thought.

"Now, go in peace. We shall greet Brother Thomas on his arrival, and I have ordered that we shall have meat for supper tomorrow, in celebration."

Anselm glanced around. It seemed that it was mainly the younger brethren who were excited at the prospect of Thomas's return. Brother Terence's face was red with what he could only describe as anger. And as for Brother Peter...

Over supper he glanced around the table, and caught the eye of Terence, who nodded. Anselm jerked his head slightly in the direction of the infirmary and raised his eyebrows in a question. Terence nodded again. Maybe, if Thomas's welcoming meal was considered a feast, then they would be permitted to speak. But until then, the rule of silence applied. In any case, did they really want to let out too much when Thomas was there?

Grace said, they left to go to their various duties. As Anselm washed pots and vials ready for the new batch of medicines, he wondered what they could do. Might it not be better to wait until they saw what the Prior had in mind? But no harm in being prepared. He surmised it would be more of the same – dreams, lights and all the rest of it. Though he doubted that Thomas would stop there.

There was a tap on the door. It was Terence and Peter. He asked Martin to take over, and led the Brothers into the herb garden where they could not be overheard. Anselm seized a basket and a pruning knife.

Terence began, his face now restored to its normal pale pink. "Do I take it that the news does not please you, Brother? No, don't answer. I know how hard you worked in the Spring to stop all this nonsense."

Peter was less circumspect. "The question is, what are we going to do about him?"

Anselm sighed. "Brothers, you know we are bound in obedience to our Prior. I have tried. The Lord knows I have tried. But neither the Bishop nor Prior William will take notice."

"Not even though this could bring our community into disrepute?"

"Not even then, since I and others believe he sees this as bringing great honour to Norwich."

"The man's a liar," said Peter, bluntly. "Yes, yes, I know - none so blind as will not see. Then, what can we do?"

"I believe our only recourse is to protect our younger members and, wherever possible, stop any lies in their tracks. I believe that the Sheriff and his council will support us, as will William's family. And I also have a feeling that the Sub-Prior will be on our side."

"But the Sheriff has no power over us – we are outside their jurisdiction. And Elias owes obedience to Prior William."

"I was thinking more of these unpleasant anti-Jewish rumours," said Anselm. "Those at least can be stopped. And other so-called events can be disproved. But we shall need to be vigilant, so that we have witnesses."

"Brother," said Terence, "It would be a very clever man who could disprove a dream or a vision."

"Agreed. Which is why it will prove so difficult. Let us therefore wait and see what they have in store for us. I shall talk to Brother Dunstan. He is in a prime position to keep an eye on the youngsters."

"And now, I have an excellent tonic that I would share with you."

Terence made a wry face. "Have no fear – it is indeed a tonic, but in the form of an excellent cowslip wine, just come to maturity. Simply known to those not in the know as Aqua Flavum."

And they all laughed.

That was to be the last time they laughed for quite a while.

The next morning it was raining, but that did not stop Prior William leading the community to welcome Brother Thomas. This time he was not on his own, but had his own entourage of six monks, flanking a small cart pulled by a mule.

Prior William walked majestically forward; his arms outstretched. As if greeting the Pope, thought Anselm. Thomas, too, stretched out his arms, and they embraced.

Then they walked together at the head of the procession towards the Priory, followed by Sub-Prior Elias, the community, and a motley collection of citizens who had appeared for the show, all debating as to what was in the cart. They would have to wait a while to be told. A week, in fact. They left disappointed, a few hopefuls pressing their faces to the closed gate.

"Come, dear son," said William to his protégé, his community quite ignored, "let us spend some time in prayer, and then you may give me any messages and letters. I have told the Brothers we shall have meat at dinner in your honour."

Smugly Thomas replied:, "Alas, Father Prior, I have made a vow to eat no meat for a month. But your kind thought is much valued." And he smirked at the Brothers bringing up the rear.

"Did he do this on purpose?" thought Anselm. "Does he realise that the Brothers will now be denied their little pleasure?" If he did not, the Brothers did, to judge from their sudden long faces. But he meant it to be heard by all, he was sure of it.

And now he would doubtless have to deal with more youngsters denying themselves food. He caught Dunstan's eye. He knew exactly what he was thinking.

And there was no talking at dinner. Instead, the usual reading, this time of the Wedding at Cana, although, delivered in Brother Terence's beautiful voice, there was some comfort to go with the bread and soup.

In Chapter the next day, Prior William led Brother Thomas forward.

"I bid you welcome our new Brother, Thomas, who is here to assist me in taking forward our place in the outer community. I have letters of cheer and support from Thomas's former Prior, and on Sunday I shall unveil what they have generously sent us as gifts."

Anselm wondered if the letters of cheer were in gladness that Thomas was leaving. He could not believe that one such as Thomas, always creeping and sneaking around, would have been welcome anywhere. Then, as always, shame for his intolerance crept in, and he promised himself an extra half hour in prayer that night.

But he was not to be left in contemplation for long. The soft slap-slap of flat feet crept up behind him, and a hand was placed on his shoulder. He froze. A recognisable voice. "Brother, may I pray with you?"

He turned, irritated that someone should break the rules in this way. The voice continued: "Brother, I sense that you are troubled. Is it because my presence awakes in you your shortcomings? Your failure to accept the celestial messages I have been privileged to pass on? I will ask my angels to intercede for you."

"There will be no need, Brother," said Anselm as calmly as he could. "Our blessed Benedict has ruled that any Brother may go and secretly pray. As far as I recollect, he did not say that another might interrupt his devotions. Pray take this loving rebuke as from one loving Brother to another, from one who seeks to see Christ in everyone, I believe you have done a wrong thing. Pray leave me to my devotions," and he turned away.

Brother Thomas stood there a while, then left. Luckily, Anselm could not see his face. But he hoped that this would not mean more unsolicited visits to the infirmary.

Later he spent some time in the garden, weeding, pruning, and checking the water butts. The apple trees in the orchard were almost ready for harvesting, following an excellent crop of the summer variety. He would have to check that the apple racks were cleaned and ready. Then there were the pears to consider. Another week should do it. There would be plenty of work for all, novices included. Maybe that would keep them safe from the excesses of Brother Thomas.

And tomorrow he would walk over to Sprowston to visit Lady Alys, now under the wing of Margaret. She must be nearing her time.

XVI

In Sprowston, Alys sat by the fire in the hall, watching her nephews playing one of their interminable games of knights and monsters. It would not be long until she had a child of her own, and she could not help wondering whether it would be a boy or a girl. A boy meant that Revil might keep his distance for a while. But a girl would mean that she had failed in her duty.

She still remembered the cupping and the bleeding, although in the past months, recovering under Brother Anselm's care, there had been no more of that. She smiled as she recalled Margaret confronting her brother in one of her visits to Catton. In fact, the day before, she brought Alys back to Sprowston for the final weeks.

Revil had been in a rare, good mood, having just returned from a visit to the Sheriff's Steward at the castle, to discuss tithes. Anselm had been there at the time, and Revil had not been best pleased. "What are you doing here? I do not want men in skirts around my unborn child."

Margaret intervened. "Revil, were it not for Brother Anselm's medications and advice, Alys would not be in the healthy state she is today. You remember what she looked like last Easter? A puff of wind would have blown her away. After your physician's ministrations, it's a wonder the child thrived."

"Nonsense, my physician knows quite well what he is doing."

"On the contrary, his potions made her sick, she could not eat, and they even gave her bad dreams. I threw them all away outside and look at the result – a blossoming rose. Although I am not sure the plants that received the medication did as well."

Revil was furious but had to concede that Margaret was right.

Seizing the victory, Margaret continued. "I shall be taking Alys and Brangwen back with me this afternoon. Alys will be well cared for until her time comes when, please God, you will have a healthy child. We have both been praying constantly to Our Lady, and we have given a fine beeswax candle in her honour."

He grunted and went downstairs.

Margaret turned to Anselm. "Brother, again our heartfelt thanks for your support. Hugh and

Austin will take me and Brangwen, and we can take you to the crossroads in the carriage with Alys, if you wish. You will have to travel with the kittens who are now very large youngsters. It will be rather bumpy, but it will save your legs and time."

"Thank you, Lady Margaret, but my legs need some exercise. And I need to think. But I will call in on you, from time to time, if I may, to check that all is well. And you will have my constant prayers."

They watched him stride through the yard, then started preparing for the journey. Apart from clothing, there was the large collection of napkins, bonnets, caps, bands and shawls for the newborn. Those days spent sewing during the late summer and autumn had not been wasted.

And two weeks later, here she was, safely in Sprowston.

There was a knock on the door. It was Hugh. She rose.

"No, please, Alys, don't get up. You must rest. Boys, off you go, I have not seen your aunt for a good while, and we need to talk. I am sure you can find plenty of monsters in the garden. Only, don't damage your mother's roses. There are still one or two blossoms left."

"This is a surprise, Hugh. And a pleasant one." She wondered if that was altogether the truth.

"Alys, we need to talk."

"Oh?"

"I will speak plainly. Since last Easter you have been avoiding me. We never speak."

"It is what we agreed."

"No, Alys, not like that. This is something else. There is something wrong, I know there is. It is almost as if you were frightened of me."

Her eyes filled with tears. He put out his hand to wipe them away, and she flinched. He went pale.

"Alys, you must tell me. Anyone would think I were a monster, a murderer even."

She swallowed. Now or never. She had to be honest. "Well, aren't you?"

"What?" He stared at her aghast. "I? A murderer? Whom am I supposed to have murdered?"

"William."

"Alys, what horrible conceit is this? I have never killed anyone. Why would I kill a child?"

"To protect me."

"What from?"

"Revil."

"Revil? From Revil?" He sat down by her side.

"Alys, I have no idea what is in your mind, but whatever it is, you have to say, as I cannot explain what I do not know." He asked again: "Why would I kill a child?"

"Because he found the ring."

They both stopped and remembered.

They had been down by the river, leaning over the wall, and Hugh had taken the ring from her finger to try it on his own. They had both been laughing, and he had kissed her on her nose. Then suddenly, the ring had dropped and rolled over and down the bank.

He had climbed over the wall and scrabbled around in the undergrowth. But there was no sign of the ring, however hard he looked. Alys was terrified. "What can I tell Revil? He will be so angry. What can I tell him?"

Obviously, they could not tell the truth. She would have to hope he did not notice for a while, and then make up some story.

They had walked home that day very slowly, and in silence.

He was the first to speak. "Alys, did you notice anyone by the river? Or rather, did you notice the boy?"

"There were two or three people fishing, but no child."

"Then he did not find the ring. At least, not then. But why are you concerned that finding the ring would put you in danger?"

"Because he went to Revil and said he had found something. Something valuable."

"And you saw this?"

110

"In a way. I had not been able to sleep. I think it was the baby, although I did not know it at the time. I felt very sick. I put on my robe and was going to go down into the hall and into the garden for some air, even though it was cold. But then I heard... I saw..." She stopped.

"Go on."

"Revil was there with another man – I think it was the Sheriff's steward. Revil was shouting at William. He was threatening him. I thought he was going to hit him."

"Then he shouted something like: "For once and for all, nothing has been lost. Nothing. And if you come here with any more of these lies and threats, I shall have you whipped, and your body thrown on the midden. Now, get out.""

"And what did the steward say?"

"I wasn't really looking at him, but he didn't seem concerned. I remember he was leaning against the fireplace and smiling at the boy. Then William tore out of the door, and I never saw him again, because they found his body on Easter Saturday. Later, when they said he had probably been robbed, I thought he must have found the ring and was wanting money for it. For some kind of evidence against me. Against us. That he had seen us. And that perhaps he had also come to you with it. I know Revil could not have actually had the ring, because he was so angry on Easter

111

Sunday."

"Alys, can you remember when this was?"

"Yes, it was the first Monday in Holy Week."

"Ah." He smiled. "Then we may breathe again. Alys, that was the day on which the accounts were drawn up. It is normally on Quarter Day – Lady Day. But this year Lady Day was on the Saturday. I distinctly remember Revil saying that the reckoning would be brought forward a few days."

"But I don't see..."

"Alys, do you remember when we dropped the ring?"

She thought, then her face cleared. "Yes, it was on Maundy Thursday. We had just been to the service in the cathedral."

"Exactly. If William presented something to Revil on the 20th March, then it was certainly not a ring. It must have been something else. And that was probably the reason for Revil's anger. He probably thought it was some kind of jest."

She started shaking, but with relief. "Oh, Hugh, and I have been thinking you were a murderer, and that the child would inherit your violence. And that you might be discovered. And hanged."

She sought comfort in his arms, but he pushed her away. "Alys, we must be very careful. Take care, now. Anyone could come in." But nonetheless, he kissed her, before settling her back in her chair. "And you have been thinking this for the past six months? Dear God. I wish I had known before. It was too much for you to bear. And needlessly."

"Now, if we could only discover who killed that poor boy, we might stop some of these rumours about the Jews."

"Are they still happening? I thought the Sheriff had done something about it."

"The rumours continue. The Sheriff thinks it might be something to do with Brother Thomas in the Priory. He is newly returned from his time away with his previous order, and busy spreading his fantasies."

At that moment, Margaret came in, followed by Brangwen bearing a tray of spiced wine and little cakes, with milk for the boys, and clarea for Alys. She was followed by the boys, and a hopeful Wanda.

He turned to Margaret. "I was just talking about the rumours still spreading about the Jews. From what I can make out, they are encouraged by Brother Thomas, who has just returned. Worse, I understand he is now a permanent member of the Norwich community. Unfortunately, the Sheriff has no jurisdiction over the Church."

"I am sure that will not be the end of it. I will ask Brangwen if she knows more. Her cousin Ardith works for Master Eleazar in the Jewry."

"But let us talk of happier things." She smiled at them both. "It is such a long time since I have seen you both looking so cheerful. You cannot imagine how glad that makes me." And she started filling the cups.

XVII

After Prime the next morning, the community gathered in the Chapter House for the unwrapping of the gifts from Thomas's old house. Bottles of wine for feast days. An embroidered altar frontal for the chapel. And three very large pillar candles – of the best beeswax.

"We shall have these blessed by the Bishop at the appropriate service," said Prior William. "Brother Thomas, did your Prior indicate any special intention as to their positioning? There is nothing in his letter, although I see that one of them is a Paschal candle."

Thomas raised his eyes to heaven and said that he thought that one was possibly meant for the altar of our Lady. Maybe for Candlemas? And he was sure a worthy place could be found for the other, and he glanced meaningfully at the Prior, who took no notice.

Anselm was only too aware of the rumours

circulating among the younger members. How long before there were more lights? More odours? What was wrong with this Brother? And, disloyal though it might seem, Father Prior? When would this madness stop? Never, it would seem, since there had been no support from Bishop Eborard. Who then? The Archbishop of Canterbury? The Pope?

Pope Celestine had died in March after only a year; Pope Lucius had granted several privileges to bishops and monasteries here, including exempting Saint Edmund's monastery from subjection to the secular authorities. He remembered, wryly, that Lucius was on the side of Matilda. He seemed unlikely to see the Sheriff's point of view.

Maybe he was leaping to conclusions. Maybe it was better to wait and see. He drew his consciousness back to what Prior William was saying. Something about a week of special meditations to prepare for the Feast of All Saints. He missed who was to run these; he had a nasty suspicion that the new Brother might be involved. Brother Peter came forward to remind the Brothers that help from everyone would be needed to gather the apple crop. There was also work needed on restoring the wattle fences round the orchard, as the deer were coming in and gnawing the bark. And there was plenty of mulching and weeding to be done. Cabbages would be planted now for harvesting in the Spring. There was plenty of work for everyone. And it would be wise to start collecting and storing wood now, before the autumn rains came. No harm in cutting and drying some of the reeds and sedges, too. And the nuts were probably ready for gathering.

After the Dismissal prayer, they rose, and went to their work. There were no disciplinary reports that morning. On thinking it over, it was a wonder he had not been called to account for discussing affairs outside the monastery, disloyalty, even. But then, maybe the Prior's refusal to act constituted that first warning. He must be more circumspect. It was fortunate that his duties as a physician enabled him to pass freely through the town.

He returned to the herb garden and stood in silent, rather apologetic, prayer for some time, then started gathering and tying up the herbs, ready for drying out.

He went through the garden and gazed across at the orchard. There wasn't any activity there, at least no apple picking. But there was certainly something. A group of Brothers were sitting under the largest tree, listening to someone. It was too far away to see clearly. He did not think it was the Novice Master. Nor was it Peter, giving instructions about the picking, of that, he was sure. He shrugged. He really must stop seeing plotting around every corner.

He would stroll over later. Brother Paulinus kept some of his bee skeps there, and he was running out of honey. By the end of October, the bees would have stopped work for the year. He needed a word.

By the time he was free to visit the hives, it was getting dark. Most of those who had been sitting beneath the tree had left, although a few earnest faces were transfixed by the speaker. And yes, it was Brother   Thomas, who was clutching an apple. Not quite ripe for picking, he noticed. Does he have no sense at all?

"Ah, Brother Thomas. Helping with the apple harvest, I see."

"The harvest of souls, Brother, the harvest of souls. Was it not through an apple that we were redeemed from the sin of Eden?"

"Your reasoning is a little strange, Brother. Was it not through the plucking of an apple that sin entered the garden?"

Thomas smirked as if he had won a point. "Ah, but had that apple not been taken, we would never have had Our Lady as Heaven's Queen. So blessed be that apple."

"As doubtless you are not, for picking an apple that is not yet ripe. Rather like these youngsters here, rather green. I do hope you are not going to try to eat it, or you will be visiting me for a dose of something rather nasty. And are you really arguing that we come to God through sin? That to obtain redemption, we should first deliberately disobey God, pluck that apple and then seek redemption? Should we not, as our Founder says, first seek to be obedient?"

He was not quite sure of his argument, but he could not resist it.

Thomas went rather pink. He obviously did not like being made to look a fool in front of these lads.

"Here, Brother. Let me take that apple. Stored properly and cared for, it will yet delight someone's supper."

And he went in search of Brother Paulinus who was probably already preparing for Vespers. Maybe afterwards, then. He hoped Thomas was not going to report him to the Prior for blasphemy. Or heresy.

The rest of the evening, softened by Compline, was quiet. He caught some sleep, then rose and visited the graveyard before going in to Mattins at midnight. A regular custom these days, that visit. Not a sign of any lights. Just the occasional owl – he recalled young William with a smile. All this furore for one young lad who liked birds. And whistling.

119

The next day passed. And the next. On Sunday the Bishop arrived to bless the candles and the altar frontal and stayed on to break bread with them. This time there was meat, and Brother Thomas could look as sanctimonious as he wished. He had certainly taken advantage of the Service of Blessing, in which he had taken a prominent part, kissing the Bishop's ring, and bearing the candles to the altar.

After the meal the Prior announced that the week of meditation for All Saints would begin on the next Tuesday. Some of the sessions with the novices would be led by Brother Thomas. Brother Dunstan's face was a picture.

Being Sunday, the rest of the day was given over to prayers, readings, gentle work in the garden. It was a blessing to have no more excesses for a while at least. Nonetheless, Anselm thought he would walk over to Sprowston. If anything happened, he would rather not be here. And in any case, it was young Henry's birthday.

The trees were turning, but the sky was still a clear blue, with no sign of rain. Suddenly he heard hooves. He turned. "Step up, Brother. It is young Henry's birthday, and you will be as welcome as the Spring," and a strong brown hand leaned down and pulled him onto the horse. "I am told there is sweet cake as well as some of the last of the plums."

Anselm felt, rather than saw, that Hugh was more cheerful than usual. It was a pity that Alys had married the wrong brother. But then, when did women ever have a choice in the matter? Maybe the child would soften matters between her and her husband.

He was indeed made welcome. A plumper than usual Alys hugged him, and the boys clung to his skirts like young kittens. Margaret and Brangwen were setting out a table, and Luke was in conversation with one of the grooms. There was no sign of Revil. Margaret saw him looking round. "It's a pity that Revil cannot be here, but he has business up at the castle. Come, Brother, take a seat. Here, by the fire."

"First, some plum cordial, some honey, and most important," said Anselm, "something for Master Henry." He reached in his satchel and brought out a monkey that danced on a stick. For the older boy there was a wooden owl, carved by one of the Brothers.

"Ah, I see that you and I think alike," said Hugh, and he handed a canvas bag to Henry. "More for the menagerie." Henry tipped up the bag and two wooden elephants and two lions fell out. He rushed to find the ark, and soon all the animals were lined up on the floor, being batted around by the young cats.

Once Anselm had been settled down with a cup

of wine and some sweet cake, he was badgered for all the latest news at the priory. Obviously, word had got around about Brother Thomas, he thought. Following his resolution earlier, he must try to be more circumspect. So, he told them of the candles, the beautiful, embroidered altar frontal, the plans for the fruit harvest. The planned meditations. The visit of the Bishop. He mentioned the trespassing deer, the broken fencing.

"We have the same problem here," said Luke. "With the cold weather the wild animals forage where they may. And we set the dogs each night to guard the sheep folds. The poultry are not too much of a problem, unless Master Reynard ventures too close. And God grant he leaves us at least one goose for Martinmas."

"We have to guard against him burrowing into the enclosures," said Anselm. "Maybe we should get some dogs. It would please the younger Brothers."

"Why not," said Margaret. "The bitch mastiff has just littered five – all strong and healthy. I'll mention it to Luke."

She glanced around the hall. How beautiful they all looked – healthy, happy. How she loved her family.

Anselm was thinking the same thing, as he sat contentedly, watching. There was a time when his own community was as sunny and warm. Then he remembered that not every community was perfect. Even Eden had its serpent. He thought of Revil.

But the shadow had gone from Alys' face – and for the moment, that was enough.

He rose and stretched his legs. "I must be off, or I shall miss Vespers."

"No, stay a while. Matthew is taking some fruit into his mother, and there is plenty of room behind. Just another half hour."

So, he stayed, and started a game of chequers with the elder boy. Fox and Geese – most appropriate under the circumstances.

At Vespers, giving thanks for the vision he had been granted of serenity and love, he let his thoughts stray to the idea of a dog. Or two dogs. He would have to broach it very carefully. Maybe a word with Peter and Dunstan, before taking it forward. He had seen the pups before he left – healthy mother, healthy sire. Why not?

Talking to them afterwards, they were both in favour. Dunstan wondered if they might not be given to the Priory as a Christmas gift? They could then hardly be refused. Maybe as guardians of the sheep – a kind of symbolic gesture?

"He is learning fast," Anselm thought. They spoke for a while longer, then each went to his own work, before the Office of Compline, and for

Anselm at least, sweet dreams.

XVIII

On Tuesday began the week of meditation for All Saints. Apart from the services, special sessions were led by the Prior and Brother Dunstan, not forgetting Thomas. Anselm had to admit that he found it all very difficult. In the normal run of things, extra instruction and meditation would for him, as for the others, have been as spiritual food. But knowing what he did, he felt uneasy, and worried about the mental health of the younger monks.

But, since obedience was part of the monastic package, he decided that, being blessed in not being called to any of Thomas's classes, he would set to with a will and polish up his soul. In spite of a certain antipathy, Prior William was always interesting, and Brother Dunstan had a disarming simplicity in his presentations, and Anselm often left feeling soothed yet inspired.

There was, of course, the week of fasting. He hoped Thomas would not overdo it; with winter and the colder weather approaching, he really did not wish to see any more half-starved, dizzy-headed youngsters in his pharmacy.

But he did keep a nightly eye on the cemetery. And he was not disappointed.

On the next Friday evening, from his post amongst the laurel bushes, he saw a light. He saw two lights. No, three.

He crept forward. The light from three tapers wavered in the breeze. He could not quite see who it was, but there was the sound of chanting. So, not a heavenly visitation, then. No angelic chorister would sound like that. But what were they doing there? The staging of a miracle? Or something more innocuous, like a nighttime vigil. Nothing wrong with that, except that these were usually led by the Prior as part of the All Hallows prayers.

Well, he could hardly challenge this, although he did wonder whether the Prior knew? The cowled figure sounded rather like Brother Thomas; he recognised his nasal tone. He coughed, to see what would happen next.

The figure then moved off, back into the building, but leaving the tapers, for that is what they were. When he had gone, Anselm crept forward and extinguished the flames. There would be no announcements tomorrow about strange lights.

However, Brother Thomas did announce at Chapter that he had received a spiritual visitation in the night and been led to the Cemetery where he saw strange supernatural lights. There was a gasp from some of the younger monks.

Anselm waited to see what Thomas would say next. He was obviously covering his back with an excuse. He decided to try his luck.

"That is indeed a wondrous thing, Brother Thomas. What happened then? Did you approach the lights? What form did they take?"

"Alas, I do not know, for there was the sound as of a rushing wind (my cough, thought Anselm) and the lights went away from me and up into heaven."

Prior William then thanked Thomas for sharing his vision and moved on to the announcements. Anselm could see that he would now have to continue his vigils to stop any more of this nonsense. He wondered what Thomas would have said, had he not been seen. He sighed, and wondered what the next show would be. And when.

And there was the impending birth of Alys's child. Another visit nearer the time would not come amiss, with receipts for strengthening possets. Maybe after All Souls Day. Please God there would be no more visions or visitations.

But his prayer was not to be granted.

The next few days were spent helping with the apple harvest and storing the fruit on the clean wooden racks in the barn. All around and outside the town similar work took place – ladders propped against laden trees, and heavy baskets carried off for sorting. The smell in the barn was intoxicating, stirring the juices. And the work kept the youngsters busy and their minds on other things, although he had the strong impression that some of them had still been carrying fasting too far. On the Monday, two novices fainted during Prime, and were later reprimanded by Prior William, no less, for overdoing their abstinence.

Anselm glanced at Thomas, but there was no sign of guilt. He wondered whether Prior William would have a quiet word with him? He thought not. But doubtless visits to the infirmary would now increase. Fortunately, it was only for a further three days, although the all-night vigils on the morrow and on All Souls would hardly help matters.

He needed air. After working in his still room for an hour or so, and checking out the latest patients, he went for a walk down by the river. There was something about flowing water that freshened the soul.

He was not the only one there that early afternoon. Wlward was sitting on the bank and seeming deep in thought. He looked up when Anselm sat down beside him. "I was just thinking," he said. "All Souls Day will be very difficult for William's mother. And nothing we can say or do helps. She misses him badly. And the recent attack on the house of Master Eleazar – even if it was just from a known troublemaker and an apprentice - makes her feel that William's murder has, in some way, brought trouble upon the town."

"There has been no repeat of the gossip that she and Godwin used to accuse the Jews?"

"No, thank goodness. Although lies always hang around - like flies on rotting meat. You must come over, Brother. A change of face would help. Godwin has made a little space by the side of the vegetable plot, where she may sit and remember the lad."

"Then I will bring some sweet-smelling herbs," said Anselm. "Maybe a bush to attract the birds which William liked so much. Have you space for a rowan?"

And the conversation turned to gardening, medicinal herbs, and apples, with Anselm wondering whether cider-making might be introduced to the Priory, and then it was time for Anselm to return for the office of None.

All Hallows Eve, the first of the Triduum, started with sunshine. The services were longer, and prayers were said in memory of the saints and martyrs, and every soul who had died in faith. And vigils would be kept in the churches and graveyards, since this was a day of obligation.

Mealtimes were meatless, with no conversation, which added to the general shadowy atmosphere. Tapers were placed in baskets ready to be set round the church and in the graveyard. And, true to expectation, Anselm received not two novices, but five, in his infirmary. He did not question them too closely but gathered that this was indeed a case of excessive zeal in abstention, in spite of Prior William's warnings.

He sighed. He found he was sighing rather a lot lately. It was not his duty to instruct youngsters in the Rule, and wondered what Brother Dunstan would say. It was not long before he found out, as Dunstan came into the room while he was dosing the novices.

He went to his table on the pretext of work but was still in earshot. Dunstan was incandescent, in the way that only an educated man with a taut way with words could be. Anselm wondered what Thomas would have said, could he have overheard. After a ten-minute lecture, the lads were sent packing. "I cannot put you on bread and water, as you are already fasting. Let me remind you that you owe your duty first to the Prior, and then to me. The Prior said quite distinctly that you were overdoing it. Why then did you go against his instruction?"

One of the bolder novices – yes, it was Cuthbert – volunteered the excuse that Brother Thomas had told them stories of saints who had existed on nothing but the Holy Wafer.

"And did he tell you to do the same? Come on, boy, out with it."

"Well, not exactly."

Dunstan looked at Anselm. They both knew how Thomas would have worked. Insinuations.

"Right, boys, off you go. When you are all saints, then you may come to me, and we will discuss the matter of existing on nothing but the Host. Until then, take care you are not sent packing back to your families. And no more of this nonsense."

"But, Brother Thomas..."

"No 'Brother Thomas.' Any problems, send him to me, and I shall deal with him."

And the boys shuffled out off to Sext, with the warning that they were to eat everything that was set in front of them. He, Brother Dunstan, would be keeping a careful watch.

Anselm smiled. He would give a lot to see Dunstan and Thomas in confrontation. Would it be a fight to the death with candles?

Dunstan smiled back. "Do not worry, Brother. I doubt they will say anything to Thomas. And if they do – why then, we shall deal with that when, and if, it happens. I'd take a flask of that purge for handing out, just to keep as a little threat; only I think they would just treat it as some kind of penance."

"And as for those stories about saints and the Host, that is the first I have heard of it."

"Or I. But I think, Brother, that we may well start to hear more such tales – especially if Brother Thomas has anything to do with it."

Anselm quickly put his work in order, then followed Dunstan to the chapel, where Dunstan kept a careful eye on his novices, and on Thomas. But Thomas was far too busy bowing and kneeling to cause any problems.

With dusk, the town people came to keep vigil in the church and the cemetery. Norwich had more than fifty churches, so there was no lack of choice. People carried tapers, and the little lights bobbed along the narrow streets and lanes. Come dawn, the lights had been extinguished, and the weary faithful returned home.

The next morning, All Souls Eve, the bells began their tolling for the souls in Purgatory. Over the next two days, people would visit the graves of their families, and attend the mandatory service, as well as keep another vigil. Among them were Wlward, Godwin and Elviva, supported by Leviva, and William's brother, Robert, only just recently a monk. Anselm wondered what Brother Robert thought about the whole business, indeed, about the so-called sightings. Certainly, Elviva was in a very poor state, and he worried for her. Was it at all possible that Thomas's crazy idea of sainthood for William - and he was convinced that this what was going on - might actually be of some comfort to her?

Late that night, seated in the stalls in the Choir, and praying for the souls of the departed, and for William's family, there was a sudden outburst. A black figure launched itself through the screen and beyond the Holy Cross altar, arms in the air. It turned to face the congregation, but seeming not to see them, its eyes rolling upwards to heaven. And then came the outburst.

"Ah, blessed William. May thy name be praised for appearing to thy poor servant, Thomas. Blessed child, intercede for these poor souls here tonight. Ah, that I could share with them this glorious vision that thou hast vouchsafed to me." And the blasphemy - for that was what it was, thought Anselm - continued for another minute or so, until Thomas fell to the floor in a faint.

The Brothers sat as if frozen, waiting for Prior William to intervene. He, too, looked stunned. Sub-Prior Elias merely looked angry. Anselm rose, and so did Dunstan, and they moved through the screen to raise Thomas and take him outside into the fresh air. Anselm could have sworn he saw Thomas's right eye open – as if to gauge the effect. He chastised himself for this unworthy thought and spent the next few minutes trying to bring Thomas round. From the outward signs, Anselm was convinced that it was all a fraud. If it was, then it was a very cruel one. He had seen Elviva's face. This had certainly brought her no joy.

He looked up to see Prior William.

"Get him to bed," he said. And walked away, followed by Elias.

Anselm and Dunstan missed what happened next, as they were too busy getting Thomas to his bed, first having dosed him with a calmant. The Prior would now have to deal with what was undoubtedly some very disturbed souls, judging from the noise. Perhaps he was already regretting his rather close association with Thomas.

Once the Triduum was over, Anselm decided he would visit Alys and the little family at Sprowston. But first he would need to judge the effect that Thomas's revelations might have had on the community in general, as well as on the town. He had noticed Sir John and his lady among the congregation; he was probably already making mental preparations for dealing with possible trouble.

He wondered what Prior William would have to say at Chapter. And should he also go and visit

Wlward's family? Theirs was the greater need. Alys was safe under Margaret's wing.

XIX

He was up even before Prime, having commandeered some of the more sensible novices into removing spent tapers from the graveyard.

During Chapter, Prior William did not refer to Thomas's putative visitation, and he noticed that Thomas was not looking his usual sanctimonious self. As they filed out, he expressed his concern.

"I trust you are well recovered from last night's collapse, Brother. Perhaps you would allow me to check you over? In these days of fasting, it is all too easy to be over-zealous, and damage the vital forces. I have an excellent potion of nettle, ivy and garlic."

"And maybe a vermifuge, to deliver you from the worms that devour your strength from within? A concoction of wormwood, maybe? You do look rather pale. Grey, even."

"No, thank you, Brother. The Lord will save me

from all evils."

Anselm refrained from saying that maybe Thomas should have a word with the Prior first. He merely nodded and moved on. After Sext and the midday meal, he packed a bag, remembering to include the small rowan bush, and left for Colegate.

On the way, he passed several little groups of people - mainly men – gathered in the streets. There was nobody he recognised, apart from Master Ded. It was a Friday, so he was not sure why these folk were not hard at work somewhere. Master Le Peche came by and waved. And the Constable rode past on his horse.

Wlward and Godwin were glad to see him. From what they said, he gathered that yesterday had been very difficult for them all.

"I have remembered my promise and brought you a rowan. It will need some care for a few weeks as it is still very young."

"Alas, Brother, Elviva was so overcome with last night's events, that she has retired to her bed. Leviva is with her now."

"Then I will not trouble her. But I have brought something to help her sleep - valerian - for no more than three weeks. And some new apples. Maybe a honey-bakcd apple to tempt her appetite?"

Godwin wasted no time. "Brother, what did you

think of last night? Was it genuine, do you think? Tell us honestly."

"Genuine? Well, in Brother Thomas's mind, it may well be. On the other hand, it could all have been show."

"Because?"

"Because he showed no signs of one taken by a fit, a vision. Pulse normal, warm hands, even breathing. I have had to wrestle with my conscience over this one, but I was not convinced. That is why it was so cruel."

"Because you thought having our William declared blessed might have comforted Elviva?"

Anselm stared at him. "Godwin, you and I certainly share the same thoughts. Yes, exactly so. I do not believe Thomas was seeking to comfort anyone. I believe he has something else in mind. And that this is only the beginning. Although, Prior William did not mention it this morning in Chapter, which I found strange."

Wlward added his thoughts. "I saw that Sir John was present last night. And he did not look too pleased."

"Indeed, he did not. And I noticed the Constable in the Town Centre just now. He might have been keeping an eye out for potential troublemakers, although I am not sure what effect Brother Thomas's fainting fit would have had. There were rather more people than usual gathering near the Market, among them Master Ded."

"Come," said Godwin, "Join us in a cup of ale. My wife has been baking Soul Cakes and, since the Triduum fast is over, there is no harm in sharing them."

When they were seated by the fire, Anselm asked after Robert. He did not really know him, and their paths had not crossed in the Priory.

"The boy's happy enough," said Godwin. "But then, he always wanted to take vows, even as a ten-year-old. But as to what he thought about last night, we have no idea, as we have not spoken to him since. But, although he is very observant in his faith, I would never have described him as over-sensitive, as I gather some of the novices have proved to be. However, in this case, this is his brother we are talking about, so you may judge our concern."

They sat in silence for a while, a silence that was broken when Leviva brought in a dish of warm Soulmass Cakes. "Eat up, eat up. These were left over from today's distribution, but I shall be baking more for tomorrow."

She looked at the little rowan bush, sitting by the door. "And that is for Elviva's special place in the garden? You have done a good thing, Brother. God grant it will soon be filled with birds."

Anselm smiled. "My granny used to call it the

tree of life."

"You've never said much about your past life, Brother. Are you a Norfolk man? I wouldn't have said so, from your accent."

"No, I'm from the west country. Below the high moors, two days journey on foot from Exeter. My people were farmers - cattle and sheep mainly, although my granny was what we called a cunning woman. It was from her that I first started to take an interest in simples and cures. And she was also the local midwife."

He stopped. This was the first time he had shared anything of his past.

Leviva beamed. "Ah, so that is why you were discussing the making of cider with Wlward. I have heard tell that Hereford and Devon make the best. Now, don't look so surprised, Brother. We share everything in this family."

The conversation turned to the apple harvest, and to cider, until Anselm had to leave to get back for None. He would have to leave his other visit for tomorrow.

As he passed through the town, he heard shouts, and was passed by several people running. The Constable rode past, too, as did Sir John.

"Get home, Brother," shouted the Constable. "Get home."

"What's happening?"

"Nothing dangerous, just a few nincompoop

troublemakers. We can deal with it, but better you do not get caught up in anything," and he rode off.

Anselm strode home, thinking and wondering. Not already?

After None, there was a gathering in the warming room. He caught Brother Dunstan and mentioned what he had been told. "Of course, it may be nothing to do with yesterday's event, but I wondered whether you had heard anything?"

"No, not a word, which is hardly surprising, really, as no-one has had reason to go outside. And Brother Thomas is either confined to his bed, or else on bread and water in the seclusion cell."

"You don't think that Prior William would really..?"

"No, just a little joke. But as Thomas was not at any of the Offices, I did wonder."

"Maybe I should have called in on him," said Anselm. "The odd thing is, that after yesterday, I might have expected a few of your young fellows in my pharmacy."

"Not surprising, Brother, since I had a very strict word with them all. And checked their plates were clean, with no pieces of bread secreted for discarding later. Trust me. Any problems in the town will be due to those people who attended yesterday's Service of Vigil. By the way, that idea of yours for cider-making. Have a

141

word with Brother Terence. He is very taken. We just need to persuade Father Prior. You know, if we could sell some of it, it could do the Priory finances some good."

"Are they that bad?"

"Well, yes, and no. Of course, I am not the Steward, but as you know, although we are able to have as many as sixty Brothers, we are nowhere near that, and we are a relatively new house. We have only just celebrated our fifty years - although novices do bring certain endowments, and we have generous benefactors, we do not possess anything that would draw pilgrims. No shrines. No saints. No reliquaries. We are self-sufficient in food. We make our own tapers and candles. A few rents. But if we were to rely on the offerings of our congregation, then in the lean years, every day would be a fast day. Which might please Brother Thomas, but not many others, I fear. And one certainly can't eat embroidered altar frontals."

And with a very uncharacteristic wink, he left to check on his charges.

Anselm decided he would check on Thomas but found his bed empty and made up. Maybe he would be at Vespers.

XX

In spite of prayers and meditation, Anselm slept badly. He could not rid himself of a feeling of unease. He rose for Prime, then filed into Chapter, wondering whether anything would be said. No, nothing, and to judge from the Prior's face, it would be a brave Brother who would pose any questions. There was no sign of Brother Thomas.

After private devotions and Terce, Anselm packed a basket, and set off for Sprowston. This time there were no little gatherings, although the occasional man-at-arms bade him good day. It was a good forty-five minutes walk, and he was glad of the exercise. Sitting and kneeling in church eight times a day may have been good for the soul, but it did little for the body.

At Sprowston he found uproar. Almost he decided to leave, but for the fact that Margaret seized his arm, and drew him into the hall. Her normally serene face was angry.

"We have an unwanted visitor. He's up there now. It was nobody's fault. Our gatekeeper let him in, because, well, our Brothers are always welcome, and why should he know who he was? Young Matthew brought him up to the solar because he wanted to see Ardith. How was he to know? And because he just said it was a Brother, we assumed it was you. And by then, it was too late."

According to Ardith, Thomas had called in on Master Eleazar asking to speak to her. On learning that she was not there, he had somehow discovered that she was at Sprowston, where he had just pushed his way in.

"Please, come up. Maybe he will listen to you."

Anselm doubted it.

"I cannot get him to leave. I may be wrong, but it looks like the monk who had a fit during the Vigil. So why was he allowed out?"

Why indeed, thought Anselm, as he followed her upstairs.

There was Brother Thomas, holding Ardith by the arm, shouting that she should come away with him now. A stool had been overturned, and needlework was lying on the floor.

"You are contaminated by the filth of those child killers. Leave now, before it is too late."

"No, Brother, it is you who should leave," and Margaret tried to loosen his arm, while a furious

Ardith scratched at his face.

Behind them, seated on the bed, a white-faced Alys clung to the arm of the midwife. The midwife, who was, in fact, Ardith's aunt Maud, rose to her feet, a strong woman, who would have no truck with such nonsense.

"Have a care, Brother, we have a lady here who will shortly give birth. It is you who should leave." Anselm got the strong impression that she was about to wade in herself.

Thomas took this as another challenge, and tried to get to Alys, his way blocked by Maud. This did not stop him from launching into another attack.

"And you, woman, should beware for giving shelter to this servant of Christ murderers. May your travail be unending and your pains as the pains of hell. Let that be God's punishment." His pale eyes rolled in his head, and spittle ran down his chin.

Anselm stepped forward. "Come, Brother, you are not yet recovered from your fit. Come away."

As he took his arm, which Thomas tried to shake off, the door flew open, and Hugh rushed in, but not before Thomas had reached Alys and pushed her against the large wooden press.

Then, to the amazement of everyone who were used to the gentle, sunny Hugh, Thomas was lifted in the air, pushed into the ingle nook and

145

shaken like a rat.

"Just like Wanda," said Margaret afterwards.

But more was to come. Revil had been called, and he, too, had something to say. Although he said it with more actions. Thomas was dragged from Hugh and received a swift crack to his jaw. Then both brothers dragged him downstairs, out into the yard, and, throwing him into an outhouse, turned the key.

The brothers smiled at each other. They almost, almost, shook hands.

As Margaret said afterwards. "I may hate Revil's violent behaviour, but on this occasion, well, I saw nothing untoward."

Matthew was sent for the Sheriff, and the ladies took care of Alys. Anselm sent Ardith for his basket, and made up a calming potion for Alys, who he really did not like the look of. He gave more to Ardith.

Then he went back downstairs with Margaret, telling the midwife to call him if necessary. "Have no fear, Brother," said Maud, comfortably, "I have delivered more babies than you have had hot meals. Which I hazard is not many, coming from the Priory as you do."

Margaret asked a servant to bring some beer. "I do hope you will stay for dinner, Brother. We shall need our little family round us when this is over. But first, we should wait for the Sheriff."

Anselm took the opportunity of asking her whether there had been any trouble in the town yesterday? He wondered if that was why Ardith was here? Or was she here just to assist her aunt?

"Have you not heard? No, why should you. There were some disturbances yesterday – mainly stone throwing and shouting, I think. Hugh may know more. Eleazar thought Ardith might be safer with her family. Brangwen is her cousin."

Oh, so there was trouble, he thought.

"No, although I did see the Constable, who said there had been some trouble – but he did not say what. Just referred to them as nincompoops. And there were some men-at-arms in the centre earlier today."

"And now, on a different subject. How are your boys?"

"How thoughtful you are. Yes, I would not have wished them to see that. Although, I daresay they would have cheered on their uncles. No, luckily, Brangwen had taken them to gather nuts."

They sat for a while peaceably talking. There was the sound of hooves and voices in the yard. Margaret went to look. It was Sir John and the Constable. She and Anselm went to the door, to keep a discreet watch.

The banging from the outhouse had ceased, and there was the sound of nasal chanting. *De*

147

profundis, thought Anselm.

Revil and Hugh took the men inside and told them what had happened.

"And how is the Lady Alys now?" asked Sir John,

"When last I looked, she was calmer," said Margaret, "Although Dame Maud believes she may well go into labour before her time. Fortunately, it is only a week early. But Ardith was also attacked."

"Brother," said Sir John, "Is there anything known about this monk? Is he sick?"

Anselm was concise. "He visited the order last Easter, and then returned permanently. I understand that Prior William approves of him. He had some kind of visionary fit during the Vigil."

"Ah, yes, I remember. So, it was he. Is he prone to this sort of thing?"

"Not that I know of. Although there was one moment in Chapter when he claimed a vision. Perhaps I should not speak out of turn, since we owe obedience to our Prior, but he does rather overdo the fasting. And has a dangerous effect on the mental health of some of the novices. I feel I can say this, as I am the Infirmarian."

There, he thought, I have said it.

"Thank you, Brother. It cannot be easy, but I needed to know the background."

They went outside.

Revil unlocked the outhouse, and the Sheriff asked Thomas to come out. The answer was not unexpected.

"You can have no jurisdiction over me. I shall remain here."

"That is up to you, Brother. You are quite welcome to this house's hospitality, though I fear it will not run to food and water. And we shall charge the cost of your lodging to the Prior."

There was a pause, and then a far from repentant Thomas emerged. One would never know that he had just been involved in a brawl, thought Anselm. Apart from the cut on his chin. It must have been caused by Revil's ring.

Sir John looked at him. "As you say, we have no jurisdiction over you. You will have to go before an Ecclesiastical court. But you can spend the night in our lock-up and we shall send to Prior William to come and collect you. We shall draw up a full list of charges, which Prior William can deal with as he wishes. But whatever his decision, the whole sorry business will be recorded in full."

"And, before you make any accusations of your own, bear in mind that you were uninvited, and you made attacks on several people. Poor behaviour for a religious Brother."

Anselm noted the smug look that rolled over the monk's face. He's enjoying this, he thought. He's already seeing himself as a martyr, a victim of the Jews; and as if in echo, Thomas began to speak.

"All that I did, I did in obedience to God's Holy Laws. Thou shalt not kill. And the Jews killed the Blessed William. It was my sacred duty to save these women from their vile association with the Killers of Christ. I am willing to lay down my life in the service of God."

"Slander as well, I see," said Sir John. "As for your life, let us pray there is no bad outcome to today's bad work."

And Thomas was linked to the saddle of the Constable's horse, and led through the town to the lockup, to the interest of many passers-by.

And that was that, thought Anselm. Or was it? He wondered what the Prior would say when he received a visit from the Sheriff. But that could wait until tomorrow.

And he cheerfully joined the family around the table.

That evening, returning to the Priory, for Vespers, on the back of Matthew's horse, he mulled over the day's events. Would Prior William say anything? Or would he just deal with Thomas by giving him that second warning? That is, if he ever gave him the first admonition. Tomorrow would be for the Prior. And he himself had work to do. He did wonder whether he should pass on his news to Dunstan and Terence.

Or would that be considered gossip? He would sleep on it.

Brother Thomas had, under the circumstances, a reasonable night, since he was able to turn it to his spiritual advantage and spend the night on his knees.

Sir John had drawn up a list of Thomas's actions, and he sent a copy, together with a note to the Prior that he had Thomas under lock and key, and would value a word with the Prior, before releasing the monk into his care. Relations between Priory and Town had always been good – until now. And he was not prepared to risk any more disturbances. The letter must go that evening.

The Prior did not relish being called from his meal. He was irritated that Thomas had not come to him, as he had been ordered, and the irritation had grown when he realised that Thomas was nowhere to be found. He opened the letter, read the note, and then the list of charges. What was all this? Thomas?

The groom was still waiting. "You may tell Sir John that he may call on me tomorrow immediately after Prime, and we shall discuss this further. You may go."

The groom wondered what his master would think about being summoned in this way.

Prior William read the list over and over. There

must be a mistake. Surely Brother Thomas, a man blessed by God, would not behave in this unseemly manner? It must be some misunderstanding, and they had someone else in the lockup. But who? Thomas had certainly not been seen since Mattins. Of course, Thomas was sometimes overzealous in his search for the truth, he would admit that. Maybe he should have spoken to him after that affair during the Vigil? ordered him not to overdo the fasting, maybe? With his education, his vision, he was far too valuable to lose.

He rose and went into Compline. He rather felt that Sir John had overstepped the mark. He was pleased that he had not obeyed his summons but had turned the situation round. Let him come here. Then we would see.

XXI

A rather disgruntled Sir John arrived at the Priory after Prime. He hoped that the interview with Prior William would be a positive one. He certainly had no wish to stir up problems, but the fact remained that Brother Thomas was a threat to the calm of the city, and he was thankful that he had already been made aware of this man, thanks to Wlward and Godwin. Otherwise, he might have been inclined to send the monk packing, although he could hardly ignore his disgraceful and unbecoming behaviour at Sprowston Manor.

He strode through the gate and was escorted to the door of the Prior's apartment, where he was left cooling his heels for some time. Eventually, Prior William arrived, flanked by the Sub-Prior, Elias.

His attitude was that it must all have been a terrible mistake. And he reiterated his thoughts of the evening before. Brother Thomas was a young man of distinction and promise. With his education, his vision, he was far too valuable to lose. A little over-zealous with the fasting, maybe, which may have had an effect on his mind.

Sir John was having none of it. And he had read the signs in Elias's face – he, at least, did not agree with the Prior. Which was interesting.

"Prior William, the fact remains that he pushed his way into a private house, where he was not welcome; he attacked a young serving woman; he threatened the midwife; he terrified and pushed a delicate young woman about to give birth, so that her husband and his brother had to restrain him. Is that really conduct becoming a man in holy orders? Indeed, of anyone? Whatever your excuse, he needs to be disciplined. Since the summer I have received information that he is behind the voices against our Jewish community. Oh, it's very subtly done, Father, but it is there, nonetheless. And I have to punish the townsfolk involved, whilst your community is outside my jurisdiction. What is that saying, 'To make my sin their door?' Either this Brother is held in check, or I shall go to the Bishop. This will not show your community in a good light, especially if something happens to the lady."

"And there is, of course, the matter of your possible accession to the episcopal throne; I understand that Bishop Eborard is not in the best of health. And, of course, King Stephen, under whose protection the Jewish community lives, does hold the power of veto."

"When I have your assurance that you will take this Brother in hand, I shall release him into your custody." And he turned to leave.

"Wait. Wait." Prior William was all honey and cream.

"Of course I shall discipline him, Sir John, you have my word on that. He is a little hot-headed and, as I have said, overzealous. Leave him to me."

"Thank you, Father. Perhaps you would ask your secretary to pen me an assurance, and when I have that, you may collect your black sheep. I really would not wish to have to go to the Bishop."

And he strode out and down the stairs and into the daylight.

He was about to ride off, when he caught sight of Brother Anselm, on his way to Chapter.

"Good morning, Brother. I was sorry you had to witness yesterday's contretemps. But at the same time, thank you for your support for the Lady Alys and her family. In fact, if there is any message I can take to them, I am making a small detour in order to check on their wellbeing."

Anselm assumed that Sir John had just come

from seeing Prior William. He would like to have been a fly on the wall.

"Thank you, Sir John. Please would you impress on them that they may call on me at any time, although I have great trust in Dame Maud so, please God, I shall not be needed."

As Sir John rode off, Anselm wondered whether anything would be said during Chapter.

After the usual prayers, the Prior made his announcements.

"You may have been wondering about the absence of our dear Brother Thomas. He has been struck by a winter fever, but, once under the care of our Infirmarian, he will soon be back among us once more. Remember him in your prayers, Brothers, for he has suffered sorely."

As have we, thought Anselm, uncharitably.

"And I would remind you, Brothers, of the rule of our House regarding gossip. You will not talk about this matter to anyone, not even among yourselves. As St Benedict said:

'We absolutely condemn in all places any vulgarity and gossip.'"

After the rest of the notices, Prior William rose once more.

"Brother Anselm, perhaps you would come to see me as soon as this session is over."

As Anselm stood outside the Chapter House, he was approached by Dunstan, who raised his eyebrows in query. "Later, Brother, later," said Anselm in low voice. "When you come to me for help with those aching knees of yours." And he gently touched the side of his nose.

As usual, a monk appeared to ask Anselm to wait.

He noted the fire and a dish of plums, which the Prior hastily put out of sight, but not quickly enough.

"Sit down, Brother." So, not an admonition then, but some kind of softening up.

"Brother Anselm, it has come to my notice that you were present when Brother Thomas had his unfortunate attack."

"Do you mean when he fainted during the Vigil?"

He regretted his facetiousness the moment he said it. William narrowed his eyes.

"No, Brother, yesterday, over in Sprowston. Why did you not report it to me?"

"Because it could have been construed as gossip, and it was not for me to judge, although I did try to intervene, as I feared it might sully the reputation of our order."

He rubbed it in. "And, of course, I worried for the health of the Lady Alys."

"I appreciate your thoughtfulness, Brother Anselm. Just as a matter of interest, might I enquire what you yourself were doing there?"

"The Lady Margaret called me in during last Spring because she worried for the health of her sister-in-law. In Christian duty, I could not refuse."

"Of course not. And they have always been generous benefactors. If necessary, you may continue to make all necessary visits." And he stressed that word.

"Brother Anselm, I have an errand for you. Take this letter, and hand it personally to Sir John at the castle. He is waiting for it. Then you are to accompany Brother Thomas back here."

He noticed Anselm's studiously puzzled look. "I am afraid he had to be kept securely for his own safety. But with you by his side on the journey back, he will arouse no idle tongues. And Anselm, as I said in Chapter earlier, there is to be no talk about this."

Anselm rose, bowed, and took the letter. It was sealed. Unfortunately.

"Father, may I collect a few things first?" He remembered the state Thomas was in when the Constable took him away. "He may like to look presentable when we walk through the town."

The Prior nodded, then lost interest, and returned to whatever he had been doing before Anselm's arrival.

An hour later, Anselm was shown into Sir John's study. His Steward rose and took the letter.

"Sir John is over at Sprowston but should be back shortly. In the meantime, he has authorised me to read this letter, and if it is sufficient, to release our prisoner into your care. Pray, take a seat."

He had just finished reading when Sir John entered the room. When he saw Anselm, he smiled. The Prior had been very quick. He cast his eye over the letter and nodded. "He's all yours, Brother. And I wish you joy of him. According to the turnkey, he has kept everyone awake with his chanting, and has refused all food. Would you like someone to accompany you home?"

Anselm thought not, as that really would arouse attention. No, there would be another way. He would work on Thomas's self-esteem.

Sir John went on. "I saw the Lady Margaret and Sir Luke. Everything is calm, but I understand that the Lady Alys is in the early stages of labour. I was assured that they would send for you, if necessary, but that at the moment Dame Maud was in charge, and things seemed to be progressing normally."

They went downstairs into the cells and Brother Thomas was handed over. Since he had apparently been refusing food, Anselm wondered whether he could get back to the Priory without fainting. Then he remembered something.

"Sir John, do you have a cart we could use? Or even a wheelbarrow? I would not want our

Brother to faint on the road from lack of food. People might think he was drunk."

Thomas gave a sudden start.

Sir John understood perfectly. "Of course, Brother. He must not lose his dignity. That would never do. Just what would people think? And there are the novices to think of, too. Word soon gets round."

Thomas gave in. "If you insist, Brother, I will take a little something. But not for myself, you understand, only to save you any concern."

"It will have to be more than a little something, Brother. I have brought some of that calmant that was so efficacious after your falling fit the other night." And Anselm produced the phial and emptied a few drops into the cup of water ignored by Thomas. Then, when Thomas had eaten a piece of cheese and some bread, Anselm produced a comb, and tidied his hair. Lastly, he wiped a damp cloth over his face. He stood back and surveyed his charge.

"There we are, Brother. You'll do. You can face the world again."

And they walked together through the castle gate and down the slope.

"Let's hope Prior William's lost chick does not return here again," said the turnkey, with a grin. "I couldn't stand any more of his dreadful singing." And he emptied a pail of water into the cell, and picked up the broom, ready for the next inmate.

They soon reached the Priory, where Thomas was summoned immediately to see the Prior. Anselm doubted that anything much would be done. He thought that Prior William had his own agenda. In the meantime, Sext called, followed by dinner. What with covering Prior William's interview and the special errand, he had not eaten for almost a day. And, unlike Thomas, he could not exist on air and good thoughts.

During the meal, he caught Dunstan's eye, and signalled to him that they would talk later.

But it was not only Dunstan who visited the pharmacy. It seemed that Terence and Peter had also suddenly acquired ailments that needed urgent attention. Gathering up a basket of jars and vials as a cover, Anselm led the way into the herb garden.

"Brothers," he said with a glint in his eye, "After Father Prior's admonition this morning, I am not at all sure we should be discussing this."

Dunstan said, drily, "This is not gossip, neither is it idle. We just want a few facts. In spite of Prior William's words, some of my youngsters are still disturbed. I caught two of them discussing whether Brother Thomas had been taken up into heaven, like Elijah. Yes, it's ridiculous, I know, when Prior William merely said that he was ill."

Looking round to see there was no-one about, Anselm told them the whole story. They were speechless. And he had never known any of them to be at a loss for words.

Terence spoke first. "There is nothing to be done until we see exactly what happens next. Surely this cannot go on. Surely he must send Thomas away."

Peter said, "But, to be honest, what has he done? That we can actually prove? Had a fit that may or may not have been genuine. Had a vision, for which we only have his word. Stirred up some trouble with the Jews. Rigged up some lights. And caused problems in one of the manors."

"Isn't that enough?" said Dunstan. "Even without the so-called visions, it is atrocious behaviour."

"You know the rule, Brother. A monk should be warned in private by a senior monk. And there is allowance for the monk to be warned twice before any action be taken. Only after that should his fault be made public. If punishment and exclusion is not enough, then he may be expelled. I think we must wait until we see what happens next. At the very least, you can protect the younger brethren, Dunstan. And we can all keep a very careful watch."

The others agreed, over a cup of elderflower wine. They then went for a stroll round the orchards until None. Sufficient unto the day is the evil thereof, quoted Terence, cheerfully.

And for the next few days, Thomas was nowhere to be found.

XXII

The Feast of Saint Zachary and Saint Elizabeth, thought Anselm, on waking from his brief sleep between Lauds and Prime. Maybe today would be a good time to check on the family at Sprowston. On the other hand, he had not been summoned. Maybe some special prayers during his devotions. No news was good news, as they said.

However, at Sprowston, all was not well. After a whole day and night, followed by the morning, spent in a labour that was not progressing, and Alys becoming paler and weaker by the minute, Dame Maud declared herself worried. With each new spasm, Alys shook and shivered, and her body was covered in a cold sweat.

Revil was downstairs tramping up and down the hall. Hugh was not much better. Margaret was insisting that they send for Anselm since Alys was refusing to see Revil's physician. "It is not that we have no faith in your skills, dear Maud, but he might just have some medicines that could help."

She went down into the hall to find Matthew and send him to the Priory, with instructions that he was to bring Anselm back with him at all costs. Revil thundered over and asked her what on earth she thought she was doing.

"We must try everything, brother." She hugged him. "All will be well, I am sure of it, but we can take no risks if you want a healthy child and mother."

She went upstairs again, and gripped Alys's hand as the next wave of pain came. Alys was barely conscious, except to ask, "How much longer, how much longer?" Her screams could be heard downstairs, and the two men took themselves into the garden, it was so hard to bear.

Within the hour Anselm came into the room, holding his satchel of remedies. Maud looked at him doubtfully, but he took her by the hand, saying that they must work together. He had essential oils for Alys's back, hands and feet. And a calming draught.

Maud sniffed. "Essential oils, indeed. What good are they? She needs our prayers, a miracle even."

Anselm smiled. "Nevertheless, we will try them. My grandmother often used them, and it was extraordinary how helpful they were."

"Your grandmother?"

"Yes, she was the midwife in our village."

First Anselm persuaded Alys to drink the potion, then he and Maud set to work with the soothing massage. Together they raised Alys on to the floor and, supporting her, walked her carefully around the room a few times. Then they lifted her back onto the bed and made her comfortable. Time passed, but suddenly Alys gave a great heave. Maud checked her.

"Praise be, the child's head is presenting. Brother, I do not know what you did, but it is indeed a miracle."

"Then I will leave for the moment and leave you to your work. May I fetch you something? You must be exhausted."

"Nothing needed, Brother. Just send me Ardith, and the basket of wrappings for the infant."

Downstairs Anselm sought out Hugh and Revil and encouraged them not to worry. The birth was now imminent. They had only to wait.

Upstairs, all was silent, until, an hour later, a radiant Margaret appeared at the top of the stairs, passing Ardith, who was going up with an ewer of warm water. Margaret came down quickly and again embraced Revil.

"You have a beautiful daughter."

Revil stared as if stunned. Maybe he had been expecting a boy?

"And Alys? How is Alys?" Hugh's anxious face appeared at Revil's shoulder.

"I would not be honest if I said she was fully recovered. After over a day she is exhausted and needs full attention. Sleep is the main thing. The milk will not come through yet, but I will take the precaution of finding a wet nurse. Maud has one in mind, so with your permission, I will send Matthew out again."

Revil was on edge. "Is she healthy? Has she had experience in this?"

"Apparently, she has two children, and is currently nursing a third, and about to wean, so things could not be better. In a short while you may go and kiss your wife. She is very fragile and needs your love and support."

The door opened, and Maud appeared, holding a small bundle. She came down the stairs very carefully and took the child over to Revil. "You may hold the child, sir. But only for a moment or so. She, too, has had a long and painful journey into the world."

Revil and Margaret looked down at the little face, eyes closed, but with a shock of dark hair, damp from the warm water. Suddenly the eyes opened, and a pair of deep blue eyes gazed calmly at the onlookers. Margaret noticed a change come over Revil. He seemed to soften, and he lowered his head to kiss the child on the forehead. Then, as if afraid he would drop her, he handed her back to Maud, who nodded, and returned to the bedchamber. Margaret followed her, first telling the men they should get something to eat. And some sleep. And stop worrying.

She could not say that Alys was still very ill, and the next few days would be critical. But with God's help, and maybe that of Brother Anselm, all would be well.

"Pray join us, Brother," said Hugh. "Some bread and cheese at least. Maybe some soup? We cannot thank you enough for coming."

"That is most kind, but I think, if you do not mind, I should return to the Priory. We have our own problems. But please, if you need support, send Matthew to me. Although I believe Dame Maud is more than competent."

And before anything else could be said, he went into the yard and started the long journey on foot. It was already dark and starting to rain. He might just make Vespers.

Dunstan and Terence were lining up to process in. "How is the lady?" asked Terence.

"You heard, then? Through God's grace, all is well. A beautiful daughter."

What he really wanted to know was whether there had been any more developments at the Priory. There was no sign of Thomas.

Enough of this, he thought. Far better to spend

your time praying for the Lady Alys. And later, some bread and soup begged from the Cellarer would not come amiss. He got his wish and retired to the refectory in gratitude. He was soon joined by Dunstan.

Anselm made the usual gesture of raising his eyebrows, and Dunstan obliged.

"Well, as you have seen, Brother, Thomas seems to have gone into retirement. And my charges have been as good as gold, emptying their plates like good little lambs. I think your pharmacy will remain unvisited for a while. When you have finished, shall we take a walk around the graveyard? Just in case there are any strange lights?"

And happy to say, the graveyard remained as dark and still as it had before the arrival of Thomas into their lives.

XXIII

Alys had slept well. Two days after the birth, and things were not looking so gloomy. The house had been full of comings and goings, with Ysott, the wet nurse, arriving yesterday evening on the back of Matthew's horse, her latest child strapped in a sling.

"Now, remember," Margaret had said, "You are to have everything you need, and we shall reimburse you well, even should your stay be but a short one. We are hoping that the Lady Alys will soon recover and be able to feed the child herself. Baskets of food will also be sent to your family."

Maud had added, "And you will avoid all foods such as spices, onions, duck and beer. But since you will be eating here, that will not be a problem. The child will be fed on demand, and if necessary, I shall bring her to you while you sleep."

Terms agreed, Ysott was led to the little place set aside for her and her son, and then taken to see the child.

The next morning, Margaret and Maud expressed themselves happy.

"She is certainly a healthy-looking young woman," said Margaret. "How old would you say? Thirty?"

"Hardly that," said Maud. "Just the right age. Never you fear, Mistress. I will keep an eye on her, until Lady Alys is well enough to take over. In any case, as soon as my Lady can manage at least one feed a day, the better, as we need to keep the milk flowing. Now, do not you worry. Both of them are in the best of hands. You go and see to that family of yours."

Downstairs, the boys were clamouring to see their new cousin.

"Sorry, boys, but you will have to wait a while. Your aunt is still very tired. Why don't you go and ask the gardener to help you pick some flowers? Come, why those miserable faces?"

"But we wanted to see her wings."

"Whose wings? Your aunt's?"

"No, the baby's. Brangwen said she would fly down from heaven."

"I think you may have made a mistake."

"No, mother, no. She said she was a little angel."

Margaret smiled. "That's just her way of saying that she is very beautiful, and that God has given her to your aunt and uncle."

The boys seemed very disappointed. "When you come back, there are some soul cakes waiting. Now, off you go. And take Wanda with you. I don't want fleas near the baby."

She wondered what she would have answered had they said that the child was brought by an owl or a fox or any of the other creatures favoured by parents as an explanation of where the baby came from.

She turned around to see Revil going up the stairs.

"She was very upset yesterday, Margaret. In floods of tears. She kept saying how sorry she was that the child was a girl, and not a son."

"And what did you say, Revil?"

"I told her not to worry. There was plenty of time. The next one would certainly be a boy. I just want to reassure her."

She sighed. Exactly.

He saw her expression and looked shamefaced. "But the child is indeed beautiful. Not like so many babies which look like little old men." They both laughed. He was learning, thought Margaret.

"Brother, have you made arrangements for the baptism?"

"Yes, Martinmas. The child is healthy, so there is no rush. That gives us four days."

"And the godparents?"

"I have already asked Sir John, and I hope you will be the second, Margaret, with Sir John's wife. And we shall of course, have the feast here, in order that Alys may be present. I am sure she will be well enough to come downstairs for a short while. Talk to your cook about the removes. And I will ask my steward to check the wine cellar and he will send over whatever is needed."

Margaret agreed that not moving Alys back to Catton was most important. "Fortunately, brother, our plans for the Martinmas feast are already in hand, and you and Hugh would have been invited, especially since you hosted us so royally at Easter." What a long time ago that was, she thought.

"Our whole estate can celebrate with us. We are setting up a feast in one of the barns. Will there be any other guests?"

"Perhaps the Bishop, whom I have asked to perform the ceremony."

"And a name? Have you a name?"

"Of course, I had forgot. I will talk to Alys. It might be a pretty compliment to use the name of Sir John's wife in some way."

Margaret said. "What about our mother's name?"

"Ah, yes, yes. Why not? Ermengilde Joane, maybe?"

"Such a heavy load for such a little creature,

Revil. Why not Elizabeth. With Elizabeth Joane Ermengilde for the baptismal font? She was born on the feast of Saint Elizabeth and Saint Zachary, after all. But better to agree it first with Alys."

"Yes, yes, I am sure you are right."

Margaret had never seen him so cheerful. Maybe the possibility of losing Alys and the baby had shaken him from his usual curmudgeonly state.

The door opened and two rather grubby boys came in, followed by a very muddy Wanda. Both children were clutching bunches of late Michaelmas daisies and cranesbill. Margaret could not resist their earnest faces. "Go and wash, and then you may take those up to your aunt. Uncle Revil will wait here for you. And he can take up a jug of water for the flowers. Such beautiful colours."

And that was that for the next half hour. Noises of cooing from the solar room, and the murmur of adult voices. She went up and peeped in. Alys was sitting up, with Revil by the side of the bed. The boys were bent over the cradle, and much taken with the fact that it swung.

"Easy, boys, easy," said Maud. "She's only a little thing."

The cats were sleeping in a basket by the fire, and much objected to being disturbed. The boys decided their cousin was not very interesting and disappeared downstairs in search of the soul cakes.

"Well, sister, does the name of Elizabeth please you?"

Alys smiled. "It is a very beautiful name. But I am just glad that we have a healthy child. And I am feeling so much better, though very, very tired. Have you seen the beautiful flowers that the boys have gathered? Everyone has been so very kind. I have told Revil he must go now. I am well cared for, and he, too, needs his sleep."

"Not before he eats a good meal," said Margaret, and ushered him back down into the hall.

Her mind was busy with the preparations for the baptism. The small carriage would need to be cleaned and swept, and perhaps repainted. Maud and Ysott could travel in it with the baby and Henry. Edward could ride pillion. It was just a little too far for everyone to walk. She hoped it would not rain.

Then there was the decoration of the hall. No shortage of greenery available. The holly bushes were already covered in berries.

Her thoughts were interrupted by the arrival of supper.

XXIV

Martinmas arrived bright and sunny. In the Priory preparations were made for that evening's feast. At Sprowston, last minute checks were being made.

The wooden carriage stood in the yard, its cover in place should there be rain. Maud said with a smile, "Thank you so much for all the cushions, my Lady. My old bones will be glad."

"Not so old, Dame Maud. And I know what these carriages are like Maybe someday someone will invent something more comfortable. But it will do to get you there and back. And here are some rugs to cover you both."

She looked at the boys, in their best jackets, and wearing little nosegays. Bless them, they were so excited, even Henry who had strenuously objected to not being allowed to ride pillion. She had told him that his job was to guard the two ladies and the baby from any danger and reminded him that today was the feast of St Martin, a brave and generous Roman soldier, who had shared his cloak with a beggar. She saw that he was clutching his wooden sword and had not the heart to take it from him. "But mind, Henry. Weapons are not allowed in churches."

When everyone was mounted, they set off, and within a short while arrived at the Priory. Revil busied himself marshalling them into a little procession where they joined Sir John and his lady.

Bishop Eborard welcomed them in the porch and made the sign of the cross three times. After some prayers he touched Elizabeth's lips with salt and commanded the Devil to depart from the child. At a nod, Elias opened the north door, to allow the Devil to escape. Then saying, 'Suffer little children and forbid them not to come unto me; for of such is the Kingdom of Heaven', he invited the Godparents to repeat the Lord's Prayer and the Creed.

Margaret was pleased to see that the boys were very quiet while this was going on. She saw that Henry was still gripping his sword. She also noticed how frail the Bishop looked.

They now went inside and approached the font, where Eborard took the child from Revil, anointed her, dipped her in the water, and named her. And not a whimper. Sir John took her, and

Margaret wrapped her in the white linen chrysom. She remembered Alys making this in the Autumn. After promises were made for the child, they processed outside. Margaret noticed Anselm standing by the main gate.

"Brother, will you not join us for our feast? You would be very welcome." She saw Revil's face and realised that maybe she should not have spoken. Anselm saw it too.

"That is most kind but, you know, we are having our own celebrations here. The Lady Alys. How is she?"

"Recovering every day, and partly thanks to you and your remedies. I hope you will come to visit after the churching, and you will not come only when we need you."

He nodded, pleased.

Then Margaret noticed that Eborard was being helped onto his horse, so she joined the group as it left, waving goodbye to Anselm as she passed through the gate.

In the infirmary garden, Anselm gathered some herbs for the evening's feast. He mused how pleasant it was that there had been no more visits from worried novices, although he did wonder where Thomas was, as he did not attend any services. The initial rumble of questioning voices had died down, and the community had returned to its daily work and worship. He thought he might go and check on William's family and see how the rowan was doing. He doubted they would be celebrating the feast with much joy.

Back at Sprowston the feast was being celebrated by all, although the kitchen servants were kept busy.

As the guests entered the hall, there was a gasp of pleasure. Green branches and berries, with an occasional daisy, covered the beams, the long table, and the window embrasures. Even Revil smiled.

"And who is responsible for all this?"

"I think everyone had a hand in it," said Margaret. "Even the boys." And she pointed to Wanda, who had a ribbon in his collar. "It is a double celebration, after all. When we are more settled in, you must bring Alys down. If she is still too weak, then the Lady Joane will go up and visit," and she passed among the guests, ensuring that both Dame Maud and Lady Joane had cushioned seats and a cup of wine. Ysott had disappeared upstairs with the child, whom all agreed had behaved like a perfect angel. She saw Henry's questioning face, as he was about to make a beeline for the Bishop. "'Like,' Henry, only 'like.'"

Beyond in the fields by the barn, workers had already begun celebrating. A bonfire was burning in the corner, with young men leaping through it, being cheered on by their friends. "That looks very dangerous," said Eborard. "Mind you, I remember doing something similar in my youth."

"And I," said Sir John. "And I burned my boots, too."

There was a gentle cheer as the goose was carried in.

"That's a very large bird," said Hugh. "Master Reynard was kept well away this year," said Luke. "Last year we lost two."

Before the sweetmeats arrived, the boys were sent round with the page to carry bowls of water and napkins to the guests. And not one drop spilled. Henry beamed with pride.

"Young man," said Eborard, "Do you know why we eat geese on this day?"

Henry did not, so the Bishop explained.

"Well, unlike me," and he beamed, "Saint Martin did not wish to be made a Bishop, so do you know what he did? He hid in a pen of geese, and those naughty birds gave him away by their cackling."

"Well," thought Margaret, "that might be rather easier for Henry to believe than thinking his cousin has wings."

"And," went on the Bishop, "As well as being the Patron Saint of Beggars, he is also the Patron Saint of Geese."

Henry did not quite know whether to believe

him or not, but since he had been told that the Bishop was a holy man, he thought it must be true.

"And what happened then?"

"Well, he was made a Bishop anyway. Like Saint Paul, you cannot avoid your calling."

Dame Maud made her excuses and went upstairs to check on her charge, and Lady Joane went with her.

The men started talking business, and the boys clamoured for more stories. Margaret saw that Eborard was looking tired. He also looked rather lonely, she thought.

"Your Grace, would you like me to call for your horse, and have you accompanied home? You did say earlier that you had to be at the Priory for Vespers and supper."

"If you would be so good. My strength is not as it was when I leapt through those fires."

Revil came over and knelt to kiss his ring. "Your Grace, we much appreciate the honour you have done us this day."

"Not at all, Master Revil. It was so pleasant to be included in your celebrations. And a beautiful child. You are to be congratulated. I do hope your wife will soon be fully recovered, and that I shall see her in Church when the forty days are up."

Revil escorted him to the yard and helped him to mount. Then his squire was summoned from the feasting in the barn, to escort him home.

In the distance, the revelries continued. There was the faint sound of bagpipes and shawms.

In the Priory, the Brothers attended Vespers, followed by a late, rather less noisy, festive meal. With the arrival of Advent in three weeks, the fasting season would begin again. The Bishop joined Prior William and Elias at the top table. The whole atmosphere had completely changed over the last week or so. Anselm hoped there would be no more problems.

And so, the weeks passed, with no sign of Thomas. Until the first Sunday in Advent.

XXV

The First Sunday in Advent, with several absences during Prime, due to seasonal coughs and chills.

At Chapter there was a surprise. Had they forgotten about him so soon, wondered Anselm?

The Prior rose.

"Brothers, today, the first Sunday in Advent, seems an appropriate time for me to introduce a new Brother. I say "new", for he has been duly admonished and counselled, and has made due penance for his shortcomings, and he is now ready to come amongst us again." He stretched out his hand towards the door.

"There will be no discussions of this matter amongst yourselves. Be ready to welcome our dearly beloved Brother Thomas back into the fold."

And Brother Thomas almost flew into the hall and threw himself prostrate before Prior William in an attitude of penitence. William raised him, kissed him on both cheeks, and led him to his seat.

Anselm caught Dunstan's eye.

Prior William continued. "As a community we shall take full advantage of our Brother's many talents. He will be writing a history of our community here in Norwich. Under my supervision, of course."

And that was that. Although Anselm did not think it would end there.

Notices followed, and then, it being Sunday, most duties were suspended to be replaced by prayer, reading and meditation until Terce. As they filed out, Anselm noticed that Thomas followed behind the Prior.

He himself returned to the infirmary to check on his patients. They would do. Nothing so serious that warmth and good food could not cure it.

Dunstan called by. He had been to collect goose feathers from Brother Terence. Terence had told him that he had been asked to prepare a larger supply of quills than usual, which he thought must be for the new magnum opus. They had been sent to the Prior's parlour, so he assumed that Brother Thomas would be working in the Prior's office, and not in the scriptorium.

"Do we count that a blessing, Brother?"

"As he has been counselled and admonished, we have to assume that there will be no more unwanted visits, wherever he is."

"Then let us hope so. In my opinion that was a rather theatrical performance earlier. And yes, I know, I will do penance for what I have just said. But I just do not want him anywhere near my youngsters."

"Nor do I want them fainting and coming to me. It has been a very peaceful three weeks so far. Father Prior did not mention that he would be involved in teaching or meditation, so we must be content with that."

And the days passed. Until the Devil paid a visit.

At least, that was the gist of it.

It was the night before the Lady Alys's churching, which is why he remembered it.

Compline had been celebrated, and the Priory was quiet, with all the community tucked up in bed, until they rose at midnight for Mattins. Anselm was already up, as he had needed to check on his patients. Coming from the garden to access the dark entry, he heard a tremendous commotion, and the noise of squealing, then raised voices and shouts. Several of the Brothers had already reached the bottom of the stairs, among them some worried-looking novices. Tapers flickered in the blackness. The Prior strode across the green, his cloak floating in the breeze.

"What is this commotion? Brothers, pray keep silence. Stop this noise at once."

Suddenly past him ran a large, black, snorting, pig, trying to evade those Brothers who were trying to catch it, some of them waving crosses in its face. They had no success, and it barged through a hedge and ran towards the gate, several novices in hot pursuit, others fallen to their knees, praying. One or two were sobbing.

"The Devil, the Devil come among us," shouted a voice. "He smells our sin. He comes by night to steal our souls. His stench is all around us."

Surely not, thought Anselm. Surely not.

But it was indeed Brother Thomas, who stood in a dramatic pose, as if holding back the Red Sea.

"Brothers, you will all calm down. Now. Then file in an orderly manner into your places. There is to be no more of this nonsense. Brother Thomas, see me when the Office is over."

But Brother Thomas seemed to be the old Thomas, the excessive Thomas, the fanatic, the fantasist. At one point, Anselm thought he was going to refuse. However, he lined up with the first person he saw, which happened to be Anselm, and they filed into the church. Anselm noticed that Thomas was muttering under his breath. He several times caught the words: "*vade retro me Satana,*" and his heart sank. He feigned a stumble, and sharply nudged Thomas in the ribs. here was a gasp, and the muttering stopped.

However, he had recognised the pig, from the white spot on its rump. It was Bors, the favourite boar of Boduc, a neighbouring pig farmer. But the credulous would still have to be convinced, and from the hysteria this night, that might not be so easy. He found himself sighing again. During the service he saw Brother Dunstan in his stall opposite. His face told a story. No words necessary.

After Mattins, Thomas left the procession, and went towards the Prior's quarters. The others returned to the dorter, and although speaking was forbidden, Anselm noticed a certain amount of signing, and thought he caught the occasional whisper. He saw Brother Dunstan gather his flock and lead them into a corner of the cloister. He doubted there would be any sleep for anyone, especially with Lauds in another hour or so. He decided not to bother, but made his way to the infirmary, where the inmates still slept soundly.

But if Brother Thomas really were back in circulation, he might just return to his nightly checks of the graveyard.

After Prime came Chapter and an expectant hush. The face of the Prior brooked no nonsense, and even Brother Elias was no longer the serene figure they knew.

The Prior rose. And again, Thomas was nowhere to be seen. How much longer could this go on?

"What I have to say is addressed to you all. Last night was a disgraceful show of hysteria and, yes, lack of faith."

"Brethren, if the Devil – who is always present – were indeed to show himself in his true form, he would have been gratified at your fear. He would have seen souls fit for the plucking."

"It is fortunate for you that last night this was not the case. The Devil did not hide in the dark entry in order to ensnare your souls, although he may have been sniggering in a corner somewhere."

Unlike Prior William to have a sense of humour, thought Anselm. Perhaps that was his way of defusing the situation.

"Brother Dunstan?"

Dunstan rose.

"Brother Dunstan, I saw you take your pupils aside after Mattins. That was well done. Have there been any ill effects?"

"Thank you, no, Father Prior. But we shall pay special attention in the coming weeks."

William looked at the rest of the congregation.

"I hope I have no need to reiterate what I said last month after that other unfortunate business. There will be no discussion, no gossip, no whispering. Attend to your consciences."

Yes, thought, Anselm, but is he going to mention Thomas?

No, he wasn't, and the business of the day continued.

Then something happened to lighten the day. After High Mass, a little group approached the altar and knelt. Behind them stood Brangwen, holding a small bundle. The Prior came forward, saying:

"I prayed for this child, and the Lord granted my request. In all circumstances give thanks, for this is the will of God for you in Christ Jesus.

O God, our every blessing comes from you, and you welcome the simple prayers of those who bless your name. Grant that this mother may live in reliance on your goodness and in thankfulness to you. Give to her and to her child the joyful reassurance that you are always near to protect them. We ask this through Christ our Lord.

May the Lord God almighty, who through the earthly birth of his own Son has filled the whole world with joy, so bless you that the child he has given you will always bring joy to your heart."

And he made the sign of the cross over the mother. Then Revil stepped forward with a gilt purse, and Alys presented the chrysom, as a thanksgiving offering.

After the final blessing, and all had returned to their work, Anselm sped with as much dignity as he could muster to the porch, where Alys and Margaret were waiting for him.

"Oh, Brother, I am so glad you found us before we left."

"It is good to see you looking so well, my Lady. And the child must now be six weeks old."

"Come and visit us soon, Brother," said Margaret. "Do not wait to be invited. And take a closer look at young Elizabeth. So far you have only seen her from afar as a small bundle. If you cannot come before, come at Christmas. The fasting will be over by then."

As he returned to the infirmary, he felt as blessed as Alys in the ceremony of churching. That child had certainly brought joy to his heart.

He would not have been so light-hearted had he been in the market place the next morning. Somehow, the story of the pig had got around. Only, it was not a pig, of course; it was the Devil.

Tongues itched to spread the rumour, but after the Sheriff's earlier intervention, they kept quieter than usual. Ded still had painful memories of his recent stay under lock and key.

And, of course, there was no-one to correct the lies, only Edmund Chepe who described it as the usual scrapings off the midden.

The atmosphere in the Priory quietened down, the novices were duly chastened, and Thomas was kept out of sight once more.

XXVI

Midnight approached, and feet crunched on the frosty path leading to the church.

Adam and Eve Day, with its trees decorated with apples, was almost past. Not only the fourth Sunday in Advent, but Christ Mass Eve, with twelve days of holidays to come. Advent was about to be brought full circle.

The church was lit by flickering tapers and there were candles on the altar, lighting up the branches of greenery.

People were gathered in little groups, with only the elderly seated at the back on the stone ledges.

They were here to welcome the long-awaited Christ Child, celebrated with a mass. Anselm hoped this would start new life in the Priory and the town, which had been troubled by so much unwanted disturbance. There was also hope for what he had begun to call the little family at Sprowston.

As he and his Brothers filed into their stalls, he still saw no sign of Thomas. Surely he would not be denied this, one of the most important days in the year?

His thoughts ran to his infirmary, where he had made up small baskets of remedies and herbs to be taken to the poor, along with the food from the Priory kitchens.

Mass finished, and the Peace was said, and there was a great shout: *"Gaudete. Christus natus est."* People knelt once more on the cold stone floor, crossing themselves, as the Prior processed out, followed by the Brothers. Some stayed for the Mass at Dawn. Others went home. Some might come for the sermon in the Chapter House after Prime.

Anselm thought that after Chapter, he would take time to walk over to Sprowston. If the day turned out to be sunny and clear, then it was a sign that spring would be warm and mild. He hoped there would not be strong winds – a bad year for the rich and powerful.

In the meantime, he would snatch an hour or two's sleep before Lauds.

He had his wish. The morning was blue and clear, with last night's heavy frost still on the grass. Chapter, including a special sermon, had passed without note, apart from a notice about dogs.

A smiling Prior William rose to his feet and announced the arrival of two new members of the community.

"They are a most thoughtful Christmas gift from Sprowston. Apparently," and he nodded towards Brother Anselm, "they learned of our problems with rats and foxes attacking our livestock, and have most kindly sent over a Christmas gift of two young dogs. After this meeting, those who wish may go and be introduced. Brothers Peter and Terence will be in charge, but we hope our younger members will also be of assistance, if they wish."

To judge by the enthusiasm on the faces of the youngsters, they did wish.

After dropping his baskets of remedies off at the Almoner's, Anselm set off for Sprowston.

Margaret, Alys and the boys had returned from delivering baskets of food to the poor and were warming their hands at the fire.

The hall was decorated with bay, holly, ivy. Large dishes of nuts and fruit stood on the table. Even the servants had been welcomed in to share a cup of spiced wine or ale. Elizabeth was passed around among the women, and Wanda pottered about looking for the occasional dropped crumb. Anselm wondered if they would follow the custom of Twelfth Night and bake a bean cake?

Would Revil and Luke become servants for a

day? As had been the custom in his own West country. Since each Brother was servant to another, he could see that it would not be quite the same thing in the monastery. Could Prior William lose his dignity for a day?

But it soon began to grow dark, and he had to leave for None, although they begged him to stay for dinner - fish, a goose, and custards and pies. And he had missed his mid-day meal, too. However, he was sure the cook would have saved him something.

Tomorrow was the Feast of Stephen, with two masses in celebration. It would be a very busy twelve days. He promised to return for Twelfth Night, should circumstances allow.

He saw Brother Thomas in the stalls and was surprisingly glad. Difficult as he had been, it would have been a sorry thing for him to miss the feast.

And so, the days passed, with two masses each day. The Feast of Saint Stephen, the Feast of John the Evangelist, the Feast of the Holy Innocents. He thought sadly of William. And of the Jewish community, too, who were also victims. He knew that earlier that month they would have been celebrating Hanukkah, so he hoped they had found some consolation.

There was a slight echo of those days of hysteria when, just as Compline was about to start, someone reported lights in the cemetery. Brother Thomas was first in the rush from the church, with Prior William on his heels, obviously taking no chances.

They were certainly right, thought Anselm, whoever it was had raised the alarm. In the dark, cold, windy night, lights were flickering in one area. There was the sound of muffled sobbing. With a tight throat, Anselm caught up with them. He noticed that Dunstan was holding back two of the novices.

"Brother Anselm, your help please," said the Prior. "Thomas, you may leave. It is nothing that concerns you."

But Thomas hung around at the back. He need not have bothered.

Anselm recognised the figure. It was William's mother. Between her sobs she explained that, it being the Feast of the Holy Innocents, she had come to place candles and flowers on her son's grave. A small candle lit a little bunch of berried leaves and hellebore.

Prior William was sympathetic. "Pray, rest here as long as you wish. Brother Anselm will remain with you and will accompany you home when you feel ready," and he led the onlookers back through to the cloister. Anselm imagined he could hear him telling them to learn their lesson. And he was right. At Chapter the next day came the now not unusual exhortation to have faith and not succumb to ignorant notions.

Anselm led Elviva back home. He was glad to have the opportunity of talk, as he had not seen any of the family for over a month. As they turned up Colegate, two worried-looking figures came to meet them.

In the lantern light, William seemed to have aged since they had last met. Anselm wondered if his rheumatism had again taken hold.

"Brother, we cannot tell you how pleased we are to see you. Elviva, we were so worried when you left and did not return." Later he was to tell Anselm that they had feared suicide. "Come, let us get you to your bed. Brother, stay and have some spiced ale before you return. Do not refuse. It is a cold night. Just to catch up on the news. And we have so missed your company."

Leviva appeared and hurried Elviva into the house and upstairs.

Anselm was glad to see them again. Godwin stirred up the fire, and they mulled the ale.

"Elviva is safe, but very distressed. She was remembering William on this Holy Innocents Day."

"As we feared. She has been very low, and we cannot seem to help. Christmas was a very sad occasion. It will be worse at Candlemas." He saw Anselm looking puzzled. "William's birthday. He would have been thirteen. Almost a man."

"When will this affair end and peace come once more? It seems never to end. We heard the Devil appeared late one night, and ran about the dark entry, roaring and spreading his stench."

"If you mean Boduc's black boar, well, yes, there was a visitation. But I am intrigued as to how this rumour got about. The community were ordered to stay silent. And we believe Brother Thomas was under the Prior's vigilant eye for the next week or so."

"Just a boar?" Godwin looked grave. "Well, I can assure you, Brother, someone is spreading these tales. And yes, it may only be the usual voices – Master Ded, for example – but where do they get their information? Someone must be talking. Do you think we should approach the Prior? Could it be one of the lay Brothers?"

Anselm thought for a while, sipping his ale. "Perhaps we should wait for a while and see if it dies down. If there is any more of it, then yes. A meeting would be desirable."

He asked after Master Eleazar who, he learned was well, and not at all worried about the little demonstrations. In fact, he had invited William and Godwin to their Hannukah feast. "If only everyone could live in such harmony, Brother. Life would be so much easier."

Eventually, they said their goodbyes, but not

before Anselm had been shown the rowan bush and had promised some more medicines for Elviva and William. Then he set off in the dark for Mattins.

In the following days Thomas was now sometimes to be seen in the scriptorium, writing busily. Many people stopped to look and admire. Anselm had to admit that his script was very elegant. He wondered what he was writing. There was, of course, nearly fifty years to cover since the community's foundation by Bishop Herbert. And there was a different air about Thomas, almost as if all he had needed was some appreciation. Maybe that was the reason for the visions, the dreams. He thought perhaps he should be kinder to him. Then he remembered Thomas's attacks on Ardith and Alys, and the terrified novices.

At the New Year's Vigil and Mass he prayed as hard as he had ever prayed for William's family and for an end to this evil, for in his opinion, that was what it was, through whatever channel it came. The following day the Circumcision of the Lord would be commemorated with two masses. God made man had come among them, but, sadly, no-one was noticing.

Perhaps he would call in on Sprowston before Epiphany. Maybe there would be a Bean King and some laughter.

XXVII

When he arrived, the hall was in a mild uproar. The meal was being cleared by Alys and Margaret, wearing large white aprons. Luke, Hugh, and Revil were acting as butlers, and filling the cups. The boys were riding around on the shoulders of the Sheriff and his Steward. The servants, seated at the long table, might in normal circumstances have looked embarrassed, but too much wine had already flowed.

A sturdy farmer, wearing a straw crown, was ordering everyone around. Presumably the Bean King. And by his side at the head of the table sat his daughter, newly betrothed, and wearing a chaplet of ivy, her affianced at her side. No, he really could not see the Prior taking part in this, thought Anselm, rather enviously.

He took a dish of nuts and caught up with all the news. The story of Boduc's black pig had even reached here. The Sheriff said, "If everyone continues to refer to it in that way, the story will soon die, especially since, as you say, Brother Thomas has other things to keep him busy. We really do not need any more disturbances."

"However, if anything does happen, I shall be straight down to the Priory. Bishop Eborard is not in good health, and the rumours are that he will soon step down, and that Prior William will take his place. Without speaking out of turn, Brother," and he lowered his voice, "Having a Bishop who supports these dangerous fancies is not to be tolerated. If necessary, I shall go to London myself, and strongly object. King Stephen is favourable to our family."

Revil, who was filling the cups, nodded. "Maybe we should be ready to call a Council meeting the moment there is any sign of trouble. Or maybe even a letter to His Holiness?"

"There may be no need. He is currently too busy with the control of the Papal States, the opposition of the Commune of Rome, the South, dealings with King Roger, Edessa."

Revil looked sour. "What is it with these Popes of ours? Celestine was in office not even six months, and now Lucius is involved in politics. So, no support there, then."

Hugh was his usual reasonable self. "It may be that we are concerned for nothing. And, in any case, if it is the Jews you are worried about, they are under the protection of the King, is that not so, Sir John?"

"Indeed, but I'd as lief not have to deploy my men on protecting them unless I have to. There are rumours that a Second Crusade is being mooted. And our country is still not safe. It is no wonder we are sometimes referred to as The Anarchy."

"And would you go, Sir John?"

"To be honest, I have not really thought about it. And it is only a rumour, after all."

Then seeing Anselm near by, he changed the subject, and only resumed it when he saw Anselm making his goodbyes.

On the way home, remembering what Sir John had said about Prior William, Anselm was very thoughtful as he made his way toward the cathedral for Vespers.

The Octave of Epiphany brought rain, good for the garden. As good a gift, in its own way, as gold, frankincense and myrrh. During the Mass, after the Gospel reading, a deacon intoned the date of Easter. It was April 15th, quite late that year. Anselm wondered how people remembered it. But they never got it wrong.

Then came Chapter, with a special sermon. And an announcement by the Prior.

"When the weather is less inclement, Brother Thomas will be sent on a special mission to Bury

Saint Edmunds. One of you will be chosen to go with him."

There was a low buzz of interest.

"Their Prior has announced his intention of a special gift, which we shall bless and present to the church at Candlemas. We are also fortunate in having those splendid candles brought by Brother Thomas from his former community. Let us now say a special prayer for our brethren in Bury."

All knelt.

"We shall also say a special prayer for our community. In spite of my urgings last month, I am distressed to say that the disgraceful story of the pig is still being bruited round the town. Regretfully, my rules were disobeyed, and the lies have continued. Is there anyone here who would confess his sin before the community?"

Nobody moved.

"Brothers, I urge you, by spreading this rumour and staying quiet, you imperil your souls. Remember the Commandment: 'Do not bear false witness.' Very well, then I shall say no more here, but I shall expect to see the guilty Brother in private."

As they processed out, Anselm confessed himself surprised, remembering last night's discussion at Sprowston. Yet he was certain no-one had come from there to speak to the Prior.

Someone else must have spoken to him. And personally, he hoped that, regarding the trip to Bury, he would not be the chosen one. Two weeks in the company of Thomas would indeed be a penance. Fortunately, there was no-one else to look after the infirmary if he were away.

The rain continued, but when the weather looked like brightening up, Brother Thomas's departure was announced for January 14th, the Feast of Saint Felix. Anselm remembered a French Brother telling him that in France that day was also celebrated as the Feast of the Ass, in commemoration of the flight into Egypt.

After Chapter, the Community lined up outside the gate, as Prior William led them in prayer for the safe return of Brother Thomas and his companion, Brother Jerome who, as Anselm recalled, had no specific duties, so could be spared. Except that he had an arthritic ankle from an old fall. For their outward journey, they were to ride in the cart in which they were to bring back the gift. Anselm wondered whether, if the gift were very heavy, the Brothers would have to walk back and save the mules. He thought it was about forty miles, so the travellers should return in ten days or so. His heart sank for Jerome.

In the meantime, he had work to do. The garden was looking rather bedraggled, and his dispensary needed replenishing. Maybe he would plant some herbs early. That did have some advantages. He checked the beds of horehound and chives, decided on sowing the valerian early, and went back inside to attend to his patients, all doing well after a bout of very unpleasant chin cough, which was strange, as usually he only saw that in children.

Martin stirred up the fire, and he heated up some vegetable broth, in which the older monks could soak their bread. Anselm burned some herbal oils – rosemary and basil. And then they spent an hour or so sharing the news about the journey to Bury, and the expected gift. He knew how important these times were. Many of the elderly monks would probably never move out from the infirmary, and they treasured the company. He took every opportunity he could to ask advice on various issues; it was so important that people felt useful, even when they were frail and, more or less, bedridden. And he enjoyed hearing their stories. What would he have to tell when his time came?

He decided he would ask the Prior for some comfortable chairs so that the Brothers could sit outside in the warm sun when Spring came. Brother Martin thought it might even be possible to add wheels.

XXVIII

On 25th January, the Feast of the Conversion of Saint Paul, news came that Thomas and Jerome had been seen on the Wymondham Road, just this side of Hethersett. They were walking very slowly by the side of the cart, so it would be three hours or more.

The cook was sent to bring refreshments and prepare warm water for their feet. Peter made sure there was fodder and water for the mules. The Brothers were told to hold themselves in readiness to greet the travellers, once Sext was over.

And exactly on time, as the Brothers lined up outside the gates, the cart came into view.

Prior William moved forward graciously to take the hands of the Brothers, as they knelt. He gave a prayer for their safe deliverance, and then led them to his quarters for refreshment. And that was that. Anselm looked at all the disappointed faces, as the mules were led towards the stabling. If the Brothers had walked back, then whatever was wrapped up in the cart must be something very large and very heavy. No doubt they would find out tomorrow.

Late at night, as he was passing towards the cloisters in the early hours, he saw two lay Brothers carrying a heavy load into the church, followed by the Prior. He slipped behind a pillar to watch but could see nothing. Although he did hear some grunting and groaning, and the Prior say, "Over here, I think. Just for the moment. You can move it to its proper place at Candlemas."

And during Lauds and Prime, the Brothers had to be content with glimpses of a large, canvas-covered shape, tucked into a little apse to the right of the altar. It looked as if all that impatience would have to be contained for another week. Little reference was made to it during Chapter. Apart from welcoming back Brothers Jerome and Thomas.

Bishop Eborard arrived for the Candlemas Service. Robed in white and gold, he stood before the altar and blessed one of the great pillar candles given by Thomas's former Prior.

"May this candle be blessed in honour of Our Lady and of the Presentation of our Lord. May it bring light to our souls, and to the soul of our dear sister who mourns her dear child, William, who would have been thirteen today. As the Bible says:

'A voice is heard in Ramah, lamentation, and bitter weeping, Rachel weeping for her children; she refuseth to be comforted for her children, because they are not.'"

From the back of the church there was a slight sob. Elviva had been visiting the grave of her son.

"May she be comforted." There was a spontaneous sigh of Amen from the congregation.

The Prior and Sub-Prior lit the large candle and placed it on the altar, saying:

"Approach the altar, all who would have their candles blessed," and a long line formed of townsfolk bearing their precious candles.

Then he turned once more to the congregation, to make another announcement.

"My children. Two of our brethren have recently returned from the Priory at Bury Saint Edmunds to bring us a most beautiful gift."

He turned towards the niche on the right of the altar, where the bundle stood, no longer swathed in canvas, but in a light white veil.

He pulled a cord, and what had been concealed for a week was now revealed. A platform, on which stood a large wooden statue of the Virgin holding a solemn looking Christ Child on her lap. She wore a crown, and her mantle was dark blue over a red robe.

At her feet was a blue jug of snowdrops. There was a gasp of delight.

"We ask God to bless this most precious gift, a fitting reminder on this special day of the Presentation and of God Made Man."

The Sub-Prior took the candle from the altar and placed it in front of the statue.

Then the Bishop, looking even more frail than usual, gave the blessing:

"In the words of Simeon: 'Lord, now lettest thou thy servant depart in peace. For mine eyes have seen thy salvation, which thou hast prepared before the face of all people.'"

After the service, Wlward approached the Bishop. "Your Grace, your words to my daughter, Elviva, will have been of great support and reassurance. It has been a hard year for her."

"My son, you are in my prayers daily." He stumbled, and his Chaplain stepped forward to steady him and to lead him away. As he left, he turned back and smiled at Wlward. "Alas, my son, none of us is getting any younger. Bless you."

On William's grave lay a posy of snowdrops and winter aconite. Anselm added a potted rosemary plant, not yet in bloom. He hoped it would give some comfort to Elviva when next she visited.

He heard a noise behind him. It was Thomas, bearing a small lighted candle.

"The Prior at Bury gave me this, when I had

shared with him the story of the martyrdom of our Blessed William. I thought it would be a kindly gesture to place it on his grave."

At the words "martyrdom" and "blessed", Anselm suppressed a groan. So, it had started again. And not even here, but forty miles away in a different community. He wondered if Prior William knew what had been going on.

"That is indeed a kind thought, Brother. Although you appear to know something that we do not. Has William been beatified? Declared a martyr?"

Thomas produced the old knowing smile. "It will not be long, Brother, it will not be long" and he knelt down to avoid any more conversation.

Anselm returned to the infirmary where he took out his irritation with the pestle and mortar. He decided that some midnight visits to the graveyard would be in order.

Over the next few days, there were frequent visits to the church to pray at the statue of the Virgin. One or two people wondered that she was not more grandly dressed – perhaps a gold crown, a golden mantle. Anselm was standing nearby when he heard this. "Sister, what more decoration does Our Lady require than her own dear son?" He recalled the story of the Roman matron, Cornelia, mother of the Gracchi, but doubted anyone would know what he was talking about. But the speaker was not convinced. And he suspected there would be others.

In less than five weeks it would be Lent, and during Passiontide all statues would be veiled in purple cloth. So, any question of adornment could wait, as could, probably, the matter of speaking with the Bishop. There was certainly no chance of communication with His Holiness.

XXIX

At the start of March, in Chapter, Prior William rose to make an announcement. In his hand he held a letter, probably the one that had arrived on the evening before, keeping the Prior out of sight in his parlour.

"My sons, I have received some grave news from overseas."

"The Holy Father, Pope Lucius, has been killed in Rome. It seems he was injured by rocks thrown at the army near the Forum during a battle, on February 15th, and taken to the monastery near the Frangipani fortress. where he died. He is buried in Saint John Lateran. The news only reached me last night. Alas, his was but a short reign. He died opposing those seeking to split Rome from Papal rule. A Mass will be said for his soul every day for the next month."

"His successor is Pope Eugenius III, who is currently exiled from the Holy City due to the conflict. We shall also pray for him."

"Unless there is any other business, we shall adjourn, and consider these things in our hearts. Go in Peace."

Anselm went into the garden. He needed to think. From the expression on Thomas's face, he was up to something. There was a new Pope, a frail Bishop, and an unsympathetic Prior. Then they must manage the affair themselves, starting with keeping an eye on the cemetery, for he was convinced something would happen there. Then there was the business of Bury and the Blessed William. That was the Prior's responsibility, but what if Thomas had not said anything? What had been in that letter that came with the statue?

He was joined by Dunstan who, when he heard about Thomas and the candle could hardly contain his indignation. "The man is a law unto himself."

"Only if the Prior does not know anything about it."

"You think he does? If that's true, then he must approve, or he would have done something. In a month's time we have the start of Lent, with its Fasting. I really do not want a repeat of last year. And, after what you have just told me, it will happen, I am convinced of it."

"We must try and stop this now," said Anselm. "I propose we keep a vigil on the cemetery each night. Do you think Peter and Terence would join us?"

"Of course, we would need to ask them, but I am sure we could rely on them. It's probably our only hope at the moment. My feeling is that it's likely that something might also happen on the anniversary of the boy's death."

But it happened long before that.

Dies Cinerum passed, although there were no appearances in sackcloth in public penance for open crimes. Any public failings were confessed privately. But foreheads were signed with the sanctified ashes, and Lent began in earnest.

Lent had been underway for a week or so when Dunstan, on one of his shifts in the graveyard, saw some lights. They were bobbing around like large fireflies, although the season for those was well and truly over. He shifted slightly to ease his stiff joints. If he moved, he would be heard, as the leaves were dry from their Autumn leaf fall. He decided to wait for a while, as he could not hear anyone. Whoever had put them there had gone. The bell rang for Lauds, but the lights were still there, although no longer moving. He decided to risk it and crept over to where the lights were now stationary.

Thick tapers, wedged into the ground on William's grave. Well, where else would they be? He leaned forward and blew them all out. They

214

would have burned down in ten minutes or so anyway. Perhaps that was the plan. Fading lights disappearing when anyone came out. He pulled them out, and putting them in his deep pocket, made his way through the cloisters and slipped into his seat.

Anselm must have noticed something in his face, for he raised his eyebrows slightly. Dunstan nodded. They had not long to wait. There was a cry. Very carefully timed, thought Dunstan.

"Ah, Blessed William. I see your face. I see the lights. May your resting place be glorified."

It was as if Prior William had heard nothing.

"Ah, Brothers, let us go even now to visit his grave. I see the angels, I see the saints, surrounding his grave, glorifying it with lights. I see his shining visage."

One or two Brothers rose from where they were kneeling.

The Prior turned.

"What is all this? You will all be silent and remain in your places. Father Elias, will you go and see what is happening. Brother Anselm, get Brother Thomas up off the floor, and to his cell."

And he turned to continue the service.

When Elias reached the grave, he found nothing. No lights. Nothing. Apart from a taper that Dunstan had overlooked. It was still warm. The saints and angels must be economising on their heavenly ventures. Thomas came rushing, pursued by Anselm, who had been unable to control him.

"I had a vision. I had a dream. I am the chosen messenger."

Together Anselm and Elias got him back into the building, and Elias returned to Lauds, which was almost over.

The Prior seemed uninterested. "It was nothing, Father Elias, one of Thomas's waking dreams. As you say, there were no lights."

"But Father, there is this taper."

"Tapers mean nothing. Probably left by William's mother."

"But it was still warm when I picked it up."

"Your imagination, Brother, your imagination."

And that was that. Brother Thomas was absent from the scriptorium for a week, and Dunstan and Anselm were even more convinced about Thomas's intentions. Maybe his foiled plan would keep him out of mischief for a while. Maybe.

Even so, the rumour mill started grinding once more. In fact, it had been grinding since Thomas had arrived at Bury.

"Indeed, Brothers," said Jerome. "They spoke of nothing else. The lights, the visions, the dreams. Even who the murderers were. And I had to stand by and let it go. The Prior even blessed a candle for William's grave."

Jerome was sitting by the fire in the infirmary, where he had gone to have his ankle seen to. "You should never have gone to Bury," said Anselm, as he massaged the swollen ankle before binding it up. "Why did you not tell the Prior about your arthritic knee and ankle? You can take obedience too far. Doubtless you walked those forty miles back on it. As some kind of penance, maybe?"

"Brother Thomas said it would be good for my soul."

"Dear God." But he said it under his breath. And again wondered what the Prior had written on the subject to Prior William.

Wlward and Godwin were also in deep discussion. They, too, had heard the rumours, but had also heard Anselm's version. However, in view of the happenings, as they liked to call them, they were more concerned with William's reputation.

Wlward spoke frankly to Godwin. "I am getting older and these past twelve months have taken their toll. I am past my three score years and ten, and when I am gone, there will be the matter of that ring."

Godwin had almost forgotten, but not quite. He remembered it rolling onto the floor in the infirmary. "What is on your mind, father?"

"We are more than reasonably sure that William did not steal it. We knew him too well.

But I should not like any questions, should someone come across it."

"What do you propose doing? Giving it to the poor? Throwing it in the river?"

"Not at all. It is a valuable piece, and someone paid a fair price for it. No, I have a better idea. In late March, it will be one year since they found the poor boy."

"And?"

"Wait and see. What I am planning to do will soon become clear to you. And only you and I will have the explaining of it. And that will never happen." And he smiled. "But I will need you to come with me."

"Why? When?"

"Anselm is not the only one who keeps a careful watch. On the eve of the Feast of the Annunciation. That should fit in very nicely. And then all shall be well."

"Are you going to tell Anselm?"

"I think not. The more surprise there is, the better," and he went up to bed, leaving Godwin mystified.

The 21st March was the Feast of Saint Benedict, with several masses and sermons. It was Lent, so there were no dispensations during supper, apart from conversation being allowed, after some readings from the Rule.

Anselm laid some flowers at the foot of the

Virgin, not yet veiled in purple for Passion Tide. He had found some late violets, hiding under a rosemary bush, together with lenten lilies whose sap some people believed had healing power. Had they known it, it was, in fact, quite the opposite. But it was a cheerful flower, nonetheless.

On his way back he passed Thomas, busy at work in the scriptorium. True to his rather unenthusiastic promise to himself, he stopped to talk, but he need not have bothered. He was completely ignored, and Thomas took great pains to hide whatever it was he was writing. But at least he had tried.

In the little cell that was the Steward's office, Brother Nathaniel was collating the figures and papers of the last quarter's expenses, no small task, with 47 Brothers to feed, and receipts of income and tithes from Priory farms, all to be reconciled and presented to the Bishop on Lady Day. The daily diet might be modest, but certain items such as high-quality bread and beer, sometimes had to be brought in from outside, the Priory production not being considered quite good enough for visiting dignitaries. Then there were spices that they could not produce in the garden – dried fruits, ginger, peppercorns. And there was no smithy, either. Of course, there was the occasional donation, which might explain Prior William's reluctance to curb Thomas's hagiolatrous behaviour.

He raised his hand to Nathaniel, who looked up from his tables just long enough to nod, and walked back to the infirmary garden, pleased he did not have to produce ginger or peppercorns.

On the eve of the Feast of the Annunciation, Wlward and Godwin came to the church, having paid for a mass for the repose of William's soul, and knelt to pray before the statue of the Virgin. Elviva and Leviva came too, and afterwards, when they had left to walk home, Wlward and Godwin stayed a while. The church was empty, and they did not stay long. But they looked content as they passed through the West Door and set out for Colegate.

XXX

The cathedral was very full that morning for the Feast of the Annunciation. Those who attended different churches were anxious to see the gift sent by the Prior of Bury, and to stare at the nobility and the Bishop, who were all present. Anselm thought that Alys was starting to look pale again, and regretted that he had not paid them a visit recently.

When the Mass was over, and the Peace said, many went to pray at the foot of the statue. Apart from the murmuring, the cathedral was peaceful.

Some people had already left but were halted in their tracks by a loud shout, almost a scream.

"A ring. The Virgin is wearing a ring."

The Bishop and the Prior came back in. The Prior looked puzzled. A ring? He had ordered no ring. What was this?

He went closer and saw a small gold ring on the Virgin's ring finger. It was a wonder it had not fallen off. "What is it? Did you order this, my son?" asked the Bishop.

"No, father. Time enough for that later. Besides, we are in Lent. A time of abstinence."

"I cannot see very well, but it seems to be inscribed."

The crowds were by now pressing round the statue and being held back by Father Elias. Some were shouting that it was a miracle. Had they not heard that there would be no ornaments for the statue? Some even linked it with William, who had been murdered almost a year to the day. Anselm thought he saw Thomas moving in and out of the crowd. Even Revil came forward to scrutinise the ring. But he said nothing.

"Father Prior, are we to think that this has only just arrived, as it were?"

"It was not there yesterday, your Grace. There was a mass for the soul of William, and I was among those who knelt to pray before the statue. So, I confess myself puzzled. But I do not consider it a miracle. People can be very generous. But who it may have been, I do not know."

Eborard turned to the crowd. "My children, go home. This is just a very generous votive offering. No miracle, I assure you."

The crowd reluctantly dispersed.

Later, at Catton, Revil was interrogating Alys.

"I am as certain as I can be, without desecrating

the statue, that the Virgin was wearing your ring, the one you supposedly lost."

"But I did lose it. I did. It must have slipped off my finger. Maybe someone found it, and then felt guilty. Maybe they put it there. I swear I know nothing about it."

"Come, Alys, if it was you, I will say nothing more, except that you caused me a lot of trouble. And extra expense. Maybe you have been praying to our Lady for a son? I would understand it if you had. There is no shame in that."

"Revil, today was the first time I had been to church for a week. I have been too sick."

"Well, then since it was not there yesterday, are we to subscribe to the foolish idea that it was a miracle? Say nothing more. Not to anyone, mind. Loose tongues were muttering that it was in honour of the murdered boy. And we do not want to be linked with that, do we?"

And he slammed out of the room, and down to dinner.

Alys sat, pale and shocked, on the edge of the bed. She knew the ring was genuinely lost. Maybe it was a miracle? No, she did not believe in those anymore. So, who had found it? She must at least talk to Hugh, whatever Revil said. But she must do it without Revil's knowledge. Revil had returned to some of his old behaviour, and she needed to take care.

223

In Sprowston Margaret was also concerned, mainly because she had not liked the look of Alys. She wondered if she were with child. Perhaps she would go over tomorrow. Luke needed to discuss tithes with Revil, so it would not look strange to pay a visit. Once she had seen her, if necessary, she would send a message to Brother Anselm.

Anselm himself was worried, and wondered what Thomas would make of this latest occurrence. He had seen Revil's face as he looked at the ring. It was the old Revil – harsh, dark. But since the ring could not possibly have anything to do with him, it must be something else. But what?

He was not to find out until after his next visit to Sprowston. But in the meantime, he had plenty to keep him busy, not least the chatter, or rather, gossip, in the warming room that evening. And if he were to be called out to Sprowston or Catton, he needed to give Brother Martin some more schooling. He had been rather behind, lately, what with one thing and another. The lad was an excellent pupil, and the elderly monks liked him.

The town was also busy. The next morning, on his way to the castle, Luke noticed more groups of people than usual, all deep in conversation. Then he saw Master Le Peche and stopped him for a moment.

"How are you, Master Le Peche? How is business?"

"Quite good, I thank you, sir. It took a while to train up the new apprentice, but he'll do, he'll do. And I had to let young Ethelbert go, of course. Too much trouble."

"Yes, so I heard. So, he is not involved in any of this latest gossip-mongering?"

"About the miraculous ring, you mean?"

"Well, no, I meant the black pig and some wandering lights.

"Ah, sir, that's old news. The ring is now the topic of the moment."

"Already?"

"I gather the Blessed Virgin is now wearing a miraculous ring, sent from heaven in honour of young William."

From his wry smile, it was obvious that he did not believe a word of it.

"Bless you, don't look so surprised. It's all around the town. I'm not sure who started it, but I noticed that monk of theirs hanging around; you know, the strange one. Brother Thomas, is it? He really should be confined to the Priory."

Luke agreed. "He seems to draw trouble after him, wherever he goes. I'll see if the Sheriff knows any more. Good morning to you," and he headed on towards the mount. Afterwards, maybe he would drop in on Catton. He knew how worried Margaret was about Alys.

Sir John knew nothing more but wondered

about the safety of the Jews. Perhaps, once his business with Luke was over, he would go and pay them a visit.

At Catton, Luke saw what Margaret meant. He had not seen Alys look so sickly since last Easter, when Margaret had whisked her off to Sprowston and called in Brother Anselm. As usual, Revil seemed completely unconcerned.

"It's not men's business, brother. She's always looked like a frightened rabbit. By all means bring Margaret over, if you think it would help. The company might do her good. Now, about those accounts. I think Hugh's about somewhere. And you know the Sheriff's Steward, do you not?"

A tall, dark young man nodded from where he was sitting with the account rolls. Luke had seen him before, but never really taken much notice. He seemed pleasant enough. Tanned, angular face, with warm brown eyes. Elegant. Looked French rather than Norman. He did not quite catch his name. Rolande, was it?

As soon as the business was over, Luke paid a brief visit to Alys. When she heard that Margaret would be coming over, she cheered up. Margaret was right, thought Luke, as he looked closer. Alys looked peaky and, well, frightened. He kissed his niece, embraced Alys, then left to catch the last of the light.

Margaret was angry. "That brother of mine does

not deserve such a beautiful wife and mother. I really thought he had learned his lesson. May I take Matthew with me tomorrow? If I can, I will get Revil to let them come here. It sounds as if he really would not care one way or another."

It was not difficult to persuade Revil to let her take Alys, Brangwen and the baby back home with her, and with the help of Hugh, they were soon safe and sound at Sprowston. There were no kittens this time. Both fully grown, said Alys, and busy catching rats and mice in the various barns; she rarely saw them these days and, in any case, Revil had banned them from the solar.

Margaret spoke to Luke later.

"Honestly, Luke, I have never been in such a dreary house. Clean, polished, but dreary. Lonely. Alys used to try and keep it cheerful with flowers, but there was not one. She seems to have lost all interest."

"What does Hugh say? He has to live there, too."

"Not for much longer. Revil is set on finding him a wife. So, Alys will not even have him for company."

"It sounds as if you think Hugh is not being allowed to find his own wife."

"Who knows. It was bound to happen, anyway. Luke, why don't we have the Easter Feast here? It would give Alys a rest."

Luke agreed. "The boys would like it, too. I'll mention it to Revil when I next go over. It's not for another two or three weeks." As he was passing through the door, he put his head back in. "Would you like me to send for Brother Anselm?"

"Let me talk to Alys first. But thank you. It may not come to that."

She filled a small tray with a little food and some milk and took it upstairs. Brangwen was rocking the baby, and she sent her downstairs for some supper. Alys was sitting in the large, cushioned chair. Margaret thought the scene was almost an exact echo of last Easter, when she had rescued Alys from Catton. This time, Alys was not even doing her usual embroidery.

It took a while, but eventually the sad truth came out. She had thought Revil had changed, had become more mellow. But from what she was able to get out of Alys, he had reverted to his old dark self. When Margaret took Alys's arm, she winced, and drew it back so that Margaret could not see the extent of the bruising. But with Margaret's insistence, she allowed her to wash the arm, and apply some of Anselm's balm. Why had she thought it would no longer be needed?

"Alys, you must let me speak to Revil. How long has this been going on?"

"Not long. Just recently."

"Has it anything to do with the appearance of

the ring?"

"I cannot say, Margaret. Revil has forbidden me to mention it to anyone. But it started earlier than that."

"But surely, he cannot think the ring anything to do with you. Or him?"

"He thinks if we talk about it, we may be linked with William's murder, because some people are saying the miracle is in honour of William, that he is a martyr."

"Alys, let me get this straight. You lost a ring over a year ago. A ring appears on the Virgin's finger. Was it your ring?"

"I don't know. I never saw it. Revil thinks so."

"Does Revil really think you kept it for a year in case a statue was delivered to which you could give the ring? Alys, it does not make sense."

"That's what Hugh said."

Margaret smiled to herself. So Alys had first spoken to Hugh.

"And what else did he say?"

"Only what you said. And that if it were a miracle, the saints must have been hiding it until an opportunity came along. He said someone probably found it, then felt guilty, and got rid of it."

Sensible Hugh.

"Did Revil say anything else?"

"At first he thought I must have been praying to

the Virgin for a son and had kept the ring for that purpose."

"And yet he still hits you?" Alys said nothing.

"Alys, we will wait a few days and see if you feel better. If not, may I send for Brother Anselm?" She was going to ask something, but then thought better of it. Tomorrow would do, if things had not improved.

Alys nodded. She leaned back and closed her eyes. Margaret helped her onto the bed, and quietly left. She needed to plan for the Easter Feast.

At the Priory Anselm and Martin were busy filling jars with various ointments, then sealing them. A stocktaking had been made of the dispensary. They could do with some more cough mixtures, he thought, as he carefully wrote out the labels. In the far corner a novice was busy making ink. He had laid in more supplies of copperas and oak galls, plus gum Arabic. Thomas was now back in the scriptorium. Anselm wondered if this history was going to be illuminated? He would not have thought so. And in any case, it could be quite an expensive process. The main thing was that Thomas be kept busy. In spite of what the Bishop and Prior had said, people were still talking about the ring. And Dunstan, back from visiting the family of the latest novice, said the town was full of it. At one point he thought he had seen Thomas, but might have been mistaken.

But one good thing, he told Anselm. His youngsters seemed to have settled down. No more excessive fasting or bad dreams. With the warmer weather coming, he thought he would restart the outdoor games and exercise. Anselm himself wasn't convinced. Of course, this latest affair could not possibly have had anything to do with Thomas. Where would he get hold of a ring, especially a gold one? But he could certainly take advantage of it. And had, by the sound of it.

XXXI

The morning passed. Even Chapter produced nothing of any note, except the announcement that in a few days time the crucifixes and images would be veiled for Passiontide. But the Prior did say something.

"Brothers, it has come to my attention that rumours are still disturbing the townsfolk over the matter of the gift of the ring. I have every faith that you will all keep silent on this. It is particularly distasteful that it should have been linked by loose tongues to the murder of the poor boy, William. I hope I shall not to have to mention this again."

Dunstan looked sideways and shook his head slightly. So, it was not he who had been to the Prior. Could it have been the Sheriff? Someone must have raised the subject. Well, there was work to be done, and prayers to be said. Sufficient unto the day. But it still did not stem

Anselm's concern.

He passed by the scriptorium and thought he would give a word of encouragement to Thomas. But as usual, Thomas covered his work, and looked pointedly at the way out. Just what was so secret about a history of the past fifty years here in Norwich? He moved on to the dispensary and was soon hard at work with Martin stocking up the shelves and cupboards. He remembered he had been going to ask Prior William about the chairs. Tomorrow would be a good time, he thought.

Prior William was surprisingly receptive to the idea. Anselm had penned a rough sketch, and even drawn up an idea of costs. It would be very little, as it was possible wheels could be attached to those chairs already in use. Maybe some kind of padded cushions and a bar at the back to enable a Brother to push the invalid. Maybe even some kind of couch? He was given permission to approach smiths and wheelwrights in the town.

When he returned to the infirmary, he found Brother Martin waiting with a message from Sprowston.

"Nothing to worry about, Brother, but the Lady Margaret would be glad if you would pay a visit. She said to remind you of the items you brought last time."

Packing a basket, he was soon on his way,

leaving Brother Martin in full charge. No horseback this time, but it was a fine day, with a promise of Easter warmth to come.

Henry and Edward rushed to welcome him, and dragged him into the hall, Wanda yipping round their feet. Margaret poured him out some beer.

"It's not that urgent, Brother, but I wish you would have a look at our dear Alys. She is a little better today, but all is not well. I do not want a repeat of last year."

"May we talk quietly first? Perhaps where we cannot be overheard?"

"Yes, of course. Boys, would you take yourselves outside for a moment? I think it may be some of the old trouble. She finds difficulty in sleeping, although there are no bad dreams. But she is pale, and I found some of your 'blackberries.'"

Anselm looked concerned. It was as he had thought. "And the child?"

"Rosy and thriving. No problems there. And there is still milk for her."

"Then shall we go up?"

Alys was sitting by the fire, and this time she had taken up her embroidery. Anselm noticed some tearstains on her cheeks. Her face lifted when she saw Anselm. I am not a miracle worker, he thought. The problem lies outside the body.

He carried out his usual checks, and laid out the valerian, the balm, the tonics.

"I know you cannot tell me the whole story, so I will not press you. I am assuming that these 'blackberries,' as we called them, are from the same source?"

She nodded.

"I am sure you know how much your family love you and will try to protect you as much as they can. I will ask just one more question, and you need not answer. Is it possible that you are with child?"

"It is possible, but it is a little early to say."

"Whatever the answer, we shall do all we can for you. Take what I have given you - they will not harm the child. And call on me with any concerns," and he patted her hands.

To Margaret, once outside, he said "If she is with child, it may stave off some of her husband's behaviour. That seemed to happen the last time."

"He is going to the King's court shortly, so that may help. Business of some sort. Now, come and eat something before you leave. It may be the season of fasting, but some bread and our own cheese will not go amiss, since I am sure you have missed a meal. Matthew is going into town to visit his sick mother, so he will take you with him. All right, boys, you may come in. Gently, gently, mind."

Anselm wondered why it was that some families were happy and some were not. Yes, he knew that marriages were arranged, and that it was the luck of some dreadful game of chance. But looking at Margaret, Hugh and Revil, he saw such a difference. Now, how did that happen? All from the same root. All from the same nest. And yet.

As he mounted the horse behind Matthew, he asked if he could be of help?

"That's very kind of you, Brother. It's the damp weather. She suffers from rheumatism and painful joints, and sometimes finds it difficult to get around. Anything you could suggest would be much appreciated."

Matthew's widowed mother lived on Colegate, quite near to Wlward. She was delighted to have this unexpected visit and hurried to make her second visitor welcome.

"Please, do not trouble, Mistress Webbe," said Anselm. "I was well-treated at Sprowston and had to keep reminding myself that we are in the season of Lent. But Matthew has told me about your rheumatism. Perhaps I can help there?"

He sat by the fitful fire, and looked at her hands and wrists, which were rather swollen and twisted for someone of her age. He checked her ankles and feet. It was obvious she was in some considerable pain.

"I can send you some balm which will ease the pain somewhat. And something to take which will remove the destructive elements. However, it must only be taken in moderation. It is also rather bitter, and is soaked in vinegar, but I will send you some honey to take with it."

"Thank you, Brother. You Brothers are always so helpful."

"Ah, have you had assistance before? I do not remember calling on you."

"Not for ailments, no, although one of your members said I should pray to the Blessed William for help."

Anselm tried to look puzzled, but he had a dreadful sinking feeling when he heard that.

"And which Blessed William would that be, Mistress?"

"You know, the one who was murdered by the Jews."

Matthew gave a start. He was horrified. He looked at Anselm. "Trust me, Brother, I had no idea. Had I been here, I would not have let him in the house."

"Mother, William has not been declared blessed."

"That's what his granddad says, but I would rather trust one of the Brothers, especially one who has experienced such dreams and visions."

Matthew opened his mouth to say something, but saw Anselm shaking his head, so said nothing,

"Mistress, will you believe me when I say that there is no evidence that William was a martyr or

237

that he was killed by the Jews. These are just malicious rumours. I am not sure whom you spoke to" (well, yes, he was) "but it is likely that he is unwell. Our Prior has denied this rumour, so has the Sheriff, and so should you. I beg of you, please do not bruit this about."

She looked very doubtful, but agreed she would not discuss it with anyone. It was just that he had looked so saintly and trustworthy.

"Try not to worry about it, Mistress. There are unsound apples in every barrel, and it may be that this man was not even part of our community, even though I am sure he told you that he was." May God forgive me, he thought. "When I come again, I hope to hear that you are much better, and that you have had no more dealings with this man. I know that is difficult but if you wish, I will ask Wlward and Godwin to keep a look out for you."

"And now, I think I will leave you to enjoy the rest of the day with Matthew."

Matthew let him out, but was still shocked, for he knew the trouble that had been caused. "Truly, Brother, I had no idea."

"I know, but coming here today was a good thing for me, because it enabled me to see just how far this thing has spread. I will send the medicines to your mother, and then follow them up with a visit."

And he strode out thoughtfully into the night. He turned towards Wlward's house and rapped on the door.

Leviva opened up with a welcoming smile.

"May I speak very briefly with your husband? Or your father?"

"Godwin came out. "Of course. Always glad to see you, Brother."

"I cannot stay very long, as I have already been away from the Priory for a good while, but I wanted to ask for your help. I have just been to visit the mother of Matthew, who works at Sprowston. It seems the rumours about martyrdom and the Jews have now reached even her. She says she was told by a Brother that William is the Blessed William, and she was told to pray to him to ease her rheumatism."

"Dear God" and Wlward sat down heavily on a stool.

"Nothing to be done, but if you could keep an eye on her. She is a widow, and I doubt would be strong enough to send Thomas (for that is whom I think it must have been) away with a flea in his ear."

"Yes, we know the lady well. We shall certainly look after her. It is only when these things get near home that one realises how far it has gone. Call in on us when next you are up this way – you are always most welcome."

And this time, Anselm really did go home. He wondered if he should ask to speak to the Prior. He did not think he would get very far. When he later discussed it with Dunstan, he was of the same mind. For some reason, Thomas did not seem at all chastened. He also seemed to have free access to the town. Why had he visited Matthew's mother? He was not the Almoner. He was not the Infirmarian. Why was Prior William not more strict with him?

He busied himself packing a small basket of medicines for Mistress Webbe, and asked Martin if he would like to deliver it in the morning. He deserved an hour or two outside the Priory walls, and his presence might cheer up the lady. And another pair of eyes and ears might be useful.

XXXII

Martin was like a child with a toy, as he set off for Colegate, and, as Anselm had thought, Mistress Webbe was very pleased to see him, and fussed over him as if he were her own son. She must be lonely, Martin thought, with her son over at Sprowston, and all her other children moved far away.

He sat and talked with her for well over an hour and made sure she knew how to use the various cures. He hoped Anselm would not chide him for spending too long away.

On the contrary, Anselm was pleased with the lad's thoughtfulness. And also, with what else Mistress Webbe had had to say. She was not the only one to have received a visit from Brother Thomas who, it now seemed, spent a good deal of time away from his work in the Priory. Mistress Webbe thought he had been talking to people about the murder, and about what they had seen.

"I think she no longer believes the Jews were responsible, but that is because of you and the boy's family. But others do. This morning, when she tried to tell two of her neighbours the truth, they refused to believe her, even when she said she had been told the truth by several people in authority. One man apparently called her a 'mad old besom'. And now she has become frightened that they will attack her house as they did that of Master Eleazar. I told her to let it go. Some people cannot accept the truth, and that's all there is to it. You and the Sheriff would deal with it, if need be."

"I am flattered, Brother," said Anselm with a smile. "But you are right. However, the Sheriff cannot take everyone under his protection."

"Brother, there was one thing."

"Oh?"

"You know the way everyone seems to know everyone else. Well, she mentioned that Thomas had visited the maid that worked for Master Eleazar. Apparently, she knows the maid's cousin."

"Go on."

"Well, she didn't know what was said, or what happened, but there was a bit of an argument."

"She didn't happen to say when this was, did she?"

"About two or three days ago. Mistress Webbe

said it wasn't the first time, either."

What a useful little gossip you are, thought Anselm. It must be that knack you have with older patients.

"Brother, you are not angry with me?"

"Angry? Goodness no, Martin. Quite the opposite. Tell me, would you like a little task, every so often - say once a week? Mistress Webbe is obviously lonely, and I think she would appreciate your company, especially if you were able to do the odd chore for her. I know that Godwin Sturt will drop in on her every so often, but you are young. It can make a difference. And I am sure that it would take a load off Matthew's mind."

Martin's eyes glowed with pleasure. "Indeed, Brother. Anything I can do. Tell me when you want me to go again. But, will Father Prior allow this?"

"If I say it is on charitable work, then I am sure he will. Oh, and that idea we had about wheeled chairs seems to have struck a spark. We have his permission to go ahead with investigating how wheels and a hand bar might be affixed. We shall have to visit the smith and the wheelwright. That is something we can do together."

Although Anselm and his Brothers kept a nightly watch on the graveyard, there were no more lights.

However, that was not the end of it.

On Palm Sunday there was a disturbance. The green branches of yew and box had been blessed, and people were processing around the church, when there was the sound of running feet, and a man, babbling incomprehensively, hurled himself at the foot of the Holy Cross altar. "A miracle, a miracle. I have been healed."

As Infirmarian, Anselm left his seat in the choir, and came through the screen to the nave. A concerned Elias was bending over the man, while some members of the congregation were begging him to desist. "He is lame, father. He cannot walk."

But the man rose to his feet and knelt at the feet of Prior William. "It is a miracle. I am cured. The Blessed William has healed me."

Anselm wondered what he should do. He recognised him. The man was a well-known fraudster, although the Prior was not to know, nor were those people in the congregation who had spoken out. Probably others did not know, either. He sat in the market place every day until moved on, and at night was usually to be seen in one of the low-class alehouses spending any coins dropped at his feet by credulous passers-by.

He wondered how the man could now continue begging, if everyone thought he had been cured. Perhaps he had not thought of that.

The Prior glanced at Anselm. "Brother, take him into the infirmary, and I will come to him later."

He turned to the congregation. "The service will continue, my children. Please remember you are in the presence of the Lord and calm yourselves."

In the infirmary Limp Hamon, as he was nick-named, sat hugging the fire. Anselm folded his arms and looked at him sternly.

"Hamon, are you going to repeat this story to Prior William?"

"It is not a story. I am cured, I tell you."

"Then in that case, you will now be able to find work, will you not?"

There was a shocked silence, but before Hamon could make any sort of answer, the Prior entered.

The silence continued. For a moment, the Prior said nothing, just observed.

"I gather your name is Hamon? Come, Hamon, now tell me, how did you come to lose the use of your leg – just the one leg, was it, in the first place?"

"It was an accident, your honour. Ten years ago now. Lost the use of my right leg. Broke it in a fall."

"And did you report it to anyone at the time. No? Did anyone see this accident? No? How very unfortunate. Brother Anselm, would you examine Hamon, please."

"You won't find nothing, father. It was all healed this morning, you see. That Brother said I should pray to the Blessed William, and he would heal me. I slept on his grave all night, I did."

Anselm stifled a gasp at the enormity of the lie. He had been on cemetery watch, and if Hamon had spent the night there, then he had been invisible.

He lifted Hamon's leg and rolled down the stocking. Apart from looking as if it hadn't seen water for a year, there was no sign of any damage. But then, he hadn't expected to find any. "Father Prior, may I have a word with you in private?"

"Yes, Brother Anselm, when we have dealt with this man."

"Hamon, you will understand that if nobody has seen the early injuries, we cannot claim a miracle. I am sure you will understand that."

"But sir, people saw me limping. They saw me limping."

"I am sure they did. But that in itself means nothing. So, I would suggest you go away. Now." And he opened the door and watched Hamon slink out.

"And now, Brother, I am sure you can shed some more light on this."

"Yes, Father. It is true that Hamon has pleaded a gammy leg for years. It is also true that at night he can be seen, perfectly fit and well, in any of the lower taverns in the town. As to sleeping on the poor boy's grave, I was out there myself last night. I like to check that nobody is desecrating the area and with this talk of lights, I like to be sure."

"That is very responsible and praiseworthy of you, Brother Anselm. And it has certainly helped to correct the man's lies. Obviously, he took advantage of Brother Thomas's charity."

Anselm said nothing.

"Tomorrow, I shall make another announcement about discretion. I understand that someone has been talking in the town. It needs to be stopped," and he strode out.

It would need more than a few announcements in Chapter, thought Anselm. Someone was determined to spread these lies. It was amazing that Brother Thomas was always seen as a blameless innocent. He had a feeling that there would be more miracles before long.

But surprisingly, things were fairly quiet, apart from the odd murmurings among the brethren. This was in spite of Prior William's announcement in Chapter. The problem was, thought Anselm, that Prior William did not tell the whole story. He just let it be known that the man was a fraudster. But there was nothing about Thomas's suggestion that Hamon should sleep out on the grave and pray to young William. Of course, there was only Hamon's side of the story, but on the other hand, no-one knew what the Prior had said to Thomas in private, for surely he must have questioned him about the affair? What would Thomas's explanation have been, he wondered?

Over the next few days, as he passed through the town on his various errands, he noted that Hamon was still sitting in his usual place, asking for money. But this time he was not limping. Godwin told him that he was asking for alms in fulfilment of a promise to the Blessed William who had healed his leg. The money would go to his altar.

"What altar? There is no altar," said Anselm. He wondered if the Prior knew what was happening? Did the Sheriff know? With Hamon spreading the story of his so-called miracle, the rumours would soon start again. What was more dangerous? Sin? Or stupidity?

On the Wednesday before Easter, the purple veils were removed from the altars and images. Late that night Tenebrae was sung in anticipation of Holy Thursday. The Tenebrae hearse, with its twenty-four candles, had been set up, the candles being extinguished one by one as the service continued. Just one light was left burning, the Light of Christ. The service would be repeated on the mornings of Good Friday and Holy Saturday. Anselm always found these rituals strangely comforting.

On the Thursday, in the middle of Mass, Bishop Eborard washed the feet of twelve poor men, and, for some strange reason, Anselm was reminded of Hamon. That same ceremony would take place that evening in the priory, with Prior William washing the feet of twelve Brothers.

Anselm in his prayers asked for humility. He was conscious that he had been all too ready to condemn. He would be kinder to Brother Thomas. Sometimes he did not like himself very much.

The Triduum passed slowly. There were no masses on Good Friday, but the story of the Passion was read from St John's Gospel. Again, the hearse was lit, and as the candles were extinguished one by one, darkness fell upon the whole congregation. Anselm felt the sadness of the absence of light, as he chanted the Miserere. Most of the congregation would not know Latin of course, but they would be aware of its meaning.

He thought about how many people had been affected by the murder. William's family, the Jews, the Brothers, the novices. Even Lady Alys. He reflected that so many had been affected by the mendacious actions of others. It had been a year now. He prayed that light be shed upon the whole business, and that a page could be turned on the whole sorry chapter.

XXXIII

Bishop Eborard stood before the Holy Cross altar and gave the final blessing.

"Cristus resurrexit. Surrexit vere. Alleleuia. Ite, missa est."

There was a resounding Amen, and people knelt and bowed their heads as the Bishop and the other priests and servers processed out. Easter was late that year. The fasting and darkness had taken their toll.

Outside the porch people greeted each other, shook hands, stood and stared at the gentry. Anselm reached there in time to greet the party from Sprowston.

Alys was not so pale, but nevertheless, he thought there was still cause for concern, and this time he knew it could not be placed at the door of the murdered child. He asked after the baby. "Not such a baby now," he smiled. "Five months, I think?"

Alys smiled back. "She had her first tooth last week. Thank you for sending the camomile infusion; it was most thoughtful. Why did you not come yourself?"

"Duties kept me here. Maybe with the better weather, our older Brothers will recover a little."

He strode over to Brangwen, to see the baby Elizabeth. "Indeed," he said, "a very healthy and beautiful child. Such eyes." Brangwen preened as if it were her own. "She knows she is loved, Brother. That is the best food of all."

He did not mention the story of the miracle, but doubtless that would have reached as far as Sprowston, if not through Matthew, then by some other way. He watched, as they rode off. There was no sign of Revil in the party. Maybe he had not yet returned from his visit to King Stephen. He had seen him ride through the gates a good two weeks ago, accompanied by the Sheriff's Steward and his Reeve. Business, Margaret had said. No doubt the King needed more funding to protect the realm from possible incursions by supporters of Matilda.

He stood enjoying the April sun. Time to start thinking about those chairs for his patients. The next day he set off to find Baldwin the smith, whose brother-in-law was a carpenter. He hoped they could work together. Their enthusiasm was immeasurable, and within minutes they were making chalk sketches on slate tablets. "How many would you be wanting, Brother?" Baldwin's face, burned ruddy from the fire, beamed with pleasure.

"We thought three to begin with. We thought that maybe you could adapt what we have. Maybe add some wheels. A ledge for their feet?"

Giles looked disappointed. "Well, we can have a look at what you already have, but it would be a real challenge to build something special. Something for the purpose, as it were. A real challenge. Maybe we could come down and take a look? Say this evening after work? I'll bring my son."

Anselm wondered what it would all cost, but that could wait.

"Then come this evening after None, and before Vespers. You can talk to some of the older brethren. I shall be in the infirmary as usual, along with Brother Martin, my assistant."

Back at the Priory, he and Martin carried some of the more infirm Brothers out into the garden and settled them in chairs in the sun. The infirmary was swept, dusted and swabbed, medicinal oils infused, and the shutters opened.

He decided he would start on his promise of being kinder to Brother Thomas. He had seen him hard at work in the scriptorium and wondered why he had not come to the refectory for the meal.

Brother Thomas was anything but welcoming. "What do you want, Brother? I have work to do," and again he covered his work.

"I saw you were not in the refectory, so I have brought you a little strengthening drink."

"There is no need. I have taken a vow to continue my fasting."

"Then I shall leave you to your work. I am sorry to have disturbed you."

"It won't be for much longer," and the pike showed its teeth.

"How do you mean? Are you leaving the community?"

"No, you are." Anselm was speechless. What was this?

"And how do you know this?"

"I have been informed by the highest sources."

Anselm turned and went back to the infirmary by way of the Steward's office, still clutching the cup. Maybe Brother Nathaniel would like it.

Brother Nathaniel did like it. "It's very thirsty work bent over these records," he said. "And, by the way, I am sorry to hear that you are leaving us. When did you decide?"

Anselm wondered what to say. "As far as I know, I am not leaving, Brother. Where did you hear this?"

"Oh, I can't remember, really. Probably in the

warming room. You mean, it isn't true?"

"Well, I would not like to say, but I have been told nothing. Maybe I should go to the Prior."

"Let us pray it is just rumour. We would be very sorry to lose you."

Anselm was rolling bandages when there was a tap on the door. It was Dunstan. "Have you a moment?"

"Of course, how can I help?"

"Is it true you are leaving?"

Anselm did not know whether to laugh or cry. "I will tell you what I told Brother Nathaniel. It's the first I have heard of it. And surely the Prior would have said something? I suppose you heard it in the warming room, too?"

"Well, no, I didn't. It was one of my novices. Young Benet. He was very cagey, but I got the strict impression that he had heard it from..."

"Brother Thomas."

"How did you know?"

"Because he took great pleasure in telling me that I would be leaving. It came from the highest sources, apparently."

"What are you going to do?"

"Ask the Prior, of course."

"Is that wise? It is probably just malicious gossip."

"But I have to know, Dunstan. I have to know whether I have done anything wrong? Or whether

I have been given a mission somewhere. I will go tomorrow. I have some business to see to tonight."

His patients were delighted to hear about the proposals for the chairs.

"It's not that we don't value how much you look after us, Brothers, but it would take a load off your shoulders if we could just be wheeled out. And left. And this afternoon was such a pleasure."

He thought perhaps he could find some way of involving them in the discussions. After all, they were the people who would be using the chairs.

When Giles and Baldwin arrived, the whole infirmary was astir with anticipation. Measurements were taken of the current chairs; Brothers were asked to sit down in them. Then Giles brought a footstool over and raised the legs of one Brother onto the stool. "There, how does that feel, Brother? Is it comfortable? It doesn't pull on your back, does it? How about if we raised your legs along two widths of a stool." And he added another stool.

"There, now you could take a little nap in that."

"Yes, and their legs would not swell so much," said Anselm.

"Then I'll tell you what I propose, and Baldwin agrees with me. We'll make them from new. My son here" – and he indicated a fresh-faced fifteen-year-old – "can take it on as an apprentice piece – under my supervision, of course."

Baldwin added, "I'll fit a larger wheel each side, and two small ones. Plus a push-bar."

"And there will be a long wooden piece at the front that can be raised, to support their legs. Once in place, two concealed legs can be brought out to steady the chair. What do you think?" and Giles looked very pleased.

They all thought it was very ingenious.

Anselm though that now was the time to discuss cost. The Prior hadn't actually mentioned a limit.

"And there'll be no charge," said Giles. "Nor from me," said Baldwin. "Our families have had great support from you and your Brothers on the occasions they were sick. It will be a pleasure to give something back."

There were bright faces all around as Anselm escorted the men to the guest refectory for some ale. People were so generous at times. Indeed, God saw everything that he had made, and behold, it was very good. A pity about the serpent. Although he supposed God had made that, too.

The next morning, at the end of Chapter, Prior William asked Brother Anselm to come and see him. Anselm caught sight of Brother Thomas, who seemed to be smiling. So, was this to be his removal?

Apparently not. Prior William wanted to know about the progress of the chairs. He must have seen Baldwin and Giles leave.

"All is going well, Father Prior. The smith and the carpenter have already taken measurements and drawn up detailed plans and are starting work tomorrow. The chairs will have a hinged end that will support the invalid's legs. They were also able to talk with the Brothers in the infirmary, and the atmosphere after they left yesterday was very cheerful indeed. Sitting out in the sun really does do them good. And I think they appreciated being involved in the designs for the chairs."

"Then that is very pleasing. There is, of course, the small matter of cost."

"Giles and Baldwin would like to make a gift of the chairs to the Priory, in acknowledgement of the help they and their families have received over the years in times of sickness. Father, I did not even have to ask. They offered it freely."

"That is splendid news. How very generous. When the chairs are ready, we must have a special ceremony and have them blessed. Is there anything else?"

"Just one thing, Father, if I may. I don't quite know how to put this."

Prior William looked defensive. "Go on."

"Father, if you were going to send me away, you would let me know?"

The Prior looked puzzled. And relieved. I

wonder what he thought I was going to say, thought Anselm.

"Send you away? What put that into your head?"

"Several people have mentioned it."

"But as it is not true, they cannot possibly have anything to say on the matter. Tell me, where did they hear these rumours?"

"Oh, just general talk. In the warming room, for instance."

"Gossip, you mean?"

"The first person to tell me said he had it on the highest authority."

"And may I know his name?" He saw Anselm hesitate.

"No, well, I realise that you, at least, are not succumbing to the vice of gossip. Will you just accept my assurance that you are not to be sent away. Far from it. Your work here is far too valuable. And this latest initiative with the chairs is most laudable. I will say something in Chapter tomorrow. We must put a stop to all these rumours."

He stood up. "And now I have an appointment with the Bishop."

Anselm opened the door, and the Prior swept gracefully out, passing Thomas who was coming up the stairs. Anselm followed him and beamed sweetly at Thomas as he passed.

He mentioned it only to Dunstan and Nathaniel, as well as Martin, who had also heard the rumours. He hoped the Prior would do the rest.

He did indeed.

"Brothers, you may have heard that Brother Anselm is leaving us."

There was an intake of breath, and a surreptitious turning of heads towards where Anselm was sitting.

"Fortunately, I am able to give you the happy news that this is untrue. What would we do without him?"

"But I am sad to have to remind you, once again, that I will not tolerate any gossip. This story about Brother Anselm is another such example. Those responsible should hang their heads in shame."

Anselm tried to see whether this was having any effect on Thomas, but had no success. The Prior was continuing.

"I am also delighted to praise the work of Brother Anselm and his assistant, Brother Martin, with a new initiative to help our frail and elderly Brothers. I am happy to add that it also involves two esteemed citizens of the town, who are giving freely of their time and artistry. I cannot say any more at the moment, but when the work is complete, we shall celebrate it with a special service of blessing."

Outside Anselm was surrounded by smiling Brothers all wishing to show how happy they were that he was not leaving. He also noticed Brother Thomas slipping upstairs to the Prior's parlour. Why did it have to be like this, he wondered. It achieved nothing. What was the purpose of that particular rumour?

He spent the rest of the morning tidying up his shelves, then set off with Martin to make some deliveries, leaving his latest assistant, Jerome, to look after the invalids.

First, they visited Mistress Webbe, and he left Martin talking to her, in order to go and see Wlward and Godwin. It seemed Elviva had taken to her bed.

"It's these latest rumours, Brother. We've tried to persuade as many people as possible that the Jews had nothing whatsoever to do with William's murder. But it's nigh on impossible. And now we are hearing stories of Limp Hamon's so called cure, when everyone knows he's just a fraud. But Elviva is starting to believe them herself. Yes, even the stories of the Jews."

"It's almost as if she needs William to be some kind of martyr," added Godwin. "As a source of comfort."

"How wise you are," said Anselm. "The tragedy is that God and his blessed Son seem to be insufficient for their needs. But maybe that's because a beatified human being is nearer to them than divinity, even God made Man. But please, do not give up. These rumours have to be stopped before something bad happens."

And he told them about Thomas's latest exploit. "Such a little thing, but it soon spread around the community. And I do not even understand what the purpose of it was."

"Maybe he thought you were getting too close to the window into his soul, to his ultimate aim."

"Which is?"

"Norwich's own personal saint and martyr. With maybe Thomas as his sacrist. Possibly supported by your Prior. Who knows? From what you have said, he certainly seems to have taken him under his wing. Of course, that may just be to control his worse excesses. But at the moment, we are more worried about Elviva."

Wlward added, "We pray for her daily. Add your prayers to ours, Brother. And come and visit when you can."

"I will do both. Gladly. And next time I will bring some calming medicines with me. Tell Elviva I called. She does not deserve this."

His next visit took him through the market. In the distance he thought he saw Thomas but decided that could not be. Someone in a Benedictine habit, certainly. He really must stop this nagging obsession. But was it an obsession?

As he knelt to anoint poor Rolf's swollen ankles and feet with a balm of mint, lavender and marjoram, again, he and his wife were full of the stories. It was as if any contradictions had had the opposite effect. and just fired up their belief in the miracles. Would they believe anything he had to say? He had his chance when Eda asked, "You must know him well, Brother. What do you say?"

Know whom? Hamon?

"Why the Brother, of course."

"Which Brother do you mean? There are more than forty of us. Apart from the Prior."

"*The* Brother. The one who has been granted dreams and visions. The one who sees the lights on the Blessed William's grave. The one who saw the Devil. The one who was imprisoned because the Sheriff does not like him."

With a description like that, maybe they should be promoting Thomas for sainthood.

"Yes, I know him quite well. But it is not as you say."

"Then what is it like?"

"My children, I cannot be too specific because there is such a thing as loyalty to one's family. And our order is a family. But let me just say that Hamon's miracle was a fraud, the Devil was Boduc's black pig which had escaped from its pen, and the lights were somebody praying."

He couldn't really add that Thomas had been thrown into prison for attacking a lady in labour and insulting a maidservant.

"And the Sheriff, Brother?"

"Let us just say that the Brother in question had done something he should not and was put in a cell to quieten down. I cannot tell you more under the rules of my order. And I hope you will keep this to yourselves. We have known each other for some time, so I hope you will trust what I say. When next I come, I hope you will help me by telling me if you have heard any more of these stories."

He looked at their downcast faces. "Please, I hope I have not upset you. I am just so glad that you told me. Now, continue with that balm – here is another pot – morning and night. It is quite slippery, so let it sink in before you put your feet to the ground. Then wear a sock to avoid slipping. Broken bones would be a lot more difficult to deal with, I can tell you. Oh, and before I forget. Some of our own honey."

He was thoughtful as he walked to his last patient, Godric, and hoped he was not to find the same farrago of nonsense. No, indeed. Not quite the same. This time a little spice had been added, in the name of Theobald of Cambridge. Who was Theobald of Cambridge? Godric did not quite know, except that he was someone who knew something about the murdering Jews. Brother Thomas had said so. And Brother Thomas must be right. Anselm did not even bother to discuss it. He would have to make his own enquiries.

He caught up with Brother Martin at the Priory gates.

"I am glad you were able to spend some time with Mistress Webbe," he said. "How was she?"

"As you will see, Brother, much better. And expecting Matthew on Sunday. It must be very lonely for her."

"That is why our ministry of healing should not just be balms and tonics. I think you have the true gift of healing, Brother. Come, let us see how Brother Jerome has been getting along."

The next few weeks were busy, and Theobald of Cambridge slipped from his mind. Thomas was to be seen in the scriptorium every day, and there were no events of note. In the middle of May, Anselm received a request from Sprowston.

He was glad of the invitation. The weather was warm and sunny, and he had spent far too much time huddled over his retorts and pans. And the day after that, he would call in on Baldwin and Giles to see how the chairs were coming along. Maybe take Martin with him. With the warmer weather, they would be most welcome. Some of the Brothers were quite heavy.

XXXIV

Martin was delighted to be left in charge. And with the help of Brother Jerome, all should be well. Jerome was an interesting man, thought Anselm. He was not as old as he had seemed with that painful knee. Maybe in his late thirties. His wife had died in childbirth, along with the baby, their first, and he had joined the order a year or so afterwards. It seemed nobody had even asked what his skills were, which is why he had been sent to Bury with Thomas. He was considered dispensable. And yet he was skilled in animal medicine, having come from a farming family, and seemed to have an internal calendar for the tasks and seasons of the year, the phases of the moon.

He would ask Prior William if he might be seconded to the pharmacy. And maybe assist Peter and Terence with the dogs. He was also an adept carver. It was he who had carved the little

265

owl that Anselm had given to Edward. And this had given Anselm an idea.

As he strode up the grassy road towards Sprowston, he wondered about Alys. He had packed some balm, and some tonics, but hoped the balm would not be needed.

The boys must have been on watch, as they came rushing towards him. Not for the first time he felt a thump in his chest. He wondered what it would have been like to have had a wife, a family. He would never go back on his vow, but it did not stop him dreaming. They were followed by the ubiquitous Wanda, and then Margaret, probably having heard the commotion and the barking, came out to greet him.

This time Alys was not confined to the solar. She was sitting in the garden in the sun. Elizabeth was on a rug under a tree, trying to crawl. Brangwen, who seemed to have taken on the offices of nurse, sat darning hose so small they probably belonged to the two boys. In the distance could be heard the shouts and singing of the farm labourers. If the fine weather kept up, they would be haymaking in five weeks or so.

"Do you mind me asking how you are?"

"Quite well, thank you, Brother. The invitation was from all of us. In a way, just to see how you were."

He smiled. "So, the patients look after the

physician. But that is good news. Is your husband returned from the court?"

"Yes, a while back, but these days he spends a lot of his time at the castle."

Margaret came out with a tray of drink and titbits. "There is a rumour that there will be a second crusade. But it is only a rumour."

"Would your Brothers join it, do you think?"

"I do not know. Although this is the fighting season, as they call it, farms do not run themselves. In a month it will be haymaking. We could not spare any of our able-bodied men, even supposing they knew how to use a weapon. Especially as things are still not totally calm as regards Matilda and her son. Then, so Luke says, those rumours about the Jews still pop up now and again. We are rather out of things here, so we are fortunate. And it is not as if we are at war with another country."

He looked at the two women, Alys in blue, and Margaret in green, and the plump baby, and thought they looked like some wall painting of saints, although much more cheerful. He hoped that was not blasphemous. He noticed that Alys was wearing a little gold ring and remembered the ring that had appeared on the finger of the Virgin, the so-called miracle, if Brother Thomas were to be believed. He remembered the time when the loss of the first ring had caused so much anger and fear. Had things really changed? Alys looked like a rose; he suspected there might be another child before Christmas.

As usual, they were keen to hear his news, so he told them about the chairs, and Brother Martin's great gift with the sick and elderly. He mentioned the possible service of blessing when the chairs were finished. He told them how well the dogs were doing. Great ratters, and the foxes seemed to be keeping away. He did not mention Limp Hamon or William's rise to Blessedness, or even Theobald – whoever he might be. He supposed, out here, they did not hear the gossip or experience the busy noise of the marketplace. It was the same in the Priory, although he knew some of the Brothers did go out and about on various duties.

Soon it was time for him to leave. As Margaret saw him to the gate she told him, in a low voice, that Alys's child would be born around late November, but Alys had not wanted to tell him.

"The last time was so painful and frightening for her, that I think she is trying to blot it from her mind. The only good thing – if I may be a little indiscreet – is that for the past two weeks or so, Revil is again a changed man. I think he has his mind set on a son."

Then she looked abashed. "I should not have said anything, because there is such a thing as loyalty. But you have always been so helpful, I thought you should know."

"Indeed, there is," and he thought of the loyalty to his order and to the Prior. "But you must not let it affect you. If I am ever to help, I must know these things. Promise me you will send for me, if necessary."

She nodded. And he set off back to the Priory and Vespers. How very pleasant it was to walk back through the countryside in the daylight and see the workers in the fields. Tomorrow he would call on Giles. He wasn't sure whether to mention his idea to Jerome, or wait and see what Giles had to say. Probably better to wait.

After Chapter the following morning, he and Martin went to see Giles, whose face filled with pleasure to see them. He enthusiastically took them to his workshop. "As you see, Brothers, almost finished, although the armrests need some work still. We now just need the wheels and the handlebars. But I was wondering. It seems to me they are rather plain."

"But the craftsmanship is superb. Just look at the polish on that grain. It positively glows. And the curve of the backs."

"I had my son work on that. He has a good eye. But I was wondering if we might not add something more – in celebration, as it were?"

Anselm smiled. "You and I think the same way.

In my case, it was not that the chairs might be rather plain. When has that been a problem – there is great beauty in simplicity. No, it was just that we have a Brother who is an expert carver. I wondered whether he might be able to add something. On the armrests, say? Animals? Flowers? What do you think, Martin?"

"Why not send Brother Jerome along. He is the expert."

"In that case, we will hold up the work until all is decided. Would he need permission?"

"I am certain he would not, as the Prior is most enthusiastic and very grateful. We will come tomorrow, if that is acceptable? I will then leave you and Brother Jerome to discuss any ideas."

The Prior was indeed enthusiastic. "I had no idea you were so talented, Brother Jerome. Had you any ideas for what might be carved?"

"It will be a surprise, Father, but I had thought – maybe little mice, or roses in honour of Our Lady, or perhaps cats chasing the mice. Fish?

"Why not a dog?"

Anselm saw that one of the dogs from Sprowston was lounging in front of the fire. So much for its duties as a guard dog. Perhaps the foxes were on holiday.

Prior William saw him looking and looked rather embarrassed. "Yes, I know, being kept from his duties. He sometimes drops in to keep me company for an hour or so."

Anselm thought this was yet another side to Prior William. He really was an enigma.

"Maybe each chair could be different. But whatever you, Anselm and Martin decide. It is, after all, your project. Let it be a surprise to us all. And Jerome, you have my full permission to be absent from the Priory after Chapter, and until Vespers, as I imagine you will need to work in Master Giles's workshop. Are you content?"

They were, and bowing, they left the parlour to return to their work, passing Thomas on his way up. Anselm greeted him, but to no avail. There was still no warmth there.

Jerome spent the next two weeks working in the town. Each time he returned home there was a new glow in his eyes. And he flatly refused to share any information on what the carvings were to be. Surprises were surprises, after all.

Meanwhile, with the arrival of Rogation Sunday, and then Rogationtide, in the three days before Ascension Day, prayers were said for the fertility and protection of the crops, and each parish, each manor, had its processions and prayers for the Beating of the Bounds. Small children upended onto boundary stones, or tapped on the head, or lightly dipped in a stream, to ensure they knew the boundaries of their parish, usually with a small gift afterwards. Provided their elders were not too rough, it was, in its way, a holiday.

Following the Pentecost Vigil and the day itself, the Brothers were surprised when the Bishop rose and stepped forward at Chapter.

He raised his arms. "My children, this is an announcement I never thought to make. At the end of the year, I shall be stepping down from my duties, and entering the Cistercian order at Fontenay. I do not have the final word in the election of my successor, but in the meantime, I recommend to you your Father, Prior William. He will be taking on some of my lesser duties. I need hardly stress that this is in strict confidence."

"However, today I have one very pleasurable duty to perform. After our mid-day meal, we shall gather before the altar for a service of blessing of a most worthy project effected by Brothers Anselm, Jerome and Martin."

After the Brothers had filed into their stalls, the Bishop entered, followed by the Prior and the Sub-Prior. Three novices pushed the new chairs, each with an elderly occupant. Anselm, Jerome and Martin followed on behind, together with Baldwin, Giles and his son.

Trying not to be too obvious, some of the Brothers tried to gain a glimpse of the arrivals.

The service was short but cheerful, the church decorated with greenery, and benefiting from the

Ascensiontide red altar cloth. Eborard praised the thoughtfulness of the Brothers, and in particular, the generosity of the craftsmen who had helped make this possible.

"What a blessing is the sun and the warmth it brings. What a joy there is in the song of the birds, the scent of the flowers, the green of the grass. Yet to those who are not so agile as the rest of us, access to these is often denied. With the use of these beautiful chairs – and some of our sturdier Brothers to act as drivers – our older brethren can now enjoy these gifts of God to the full."

"Let us thank our Lord for the gifts and kindness of Baldwin, Giles and Wilfred, and may his blessing be bestowed on these his children, and on our dear Brother Jerome, for the fruit of their labour. May God bless us all."

"And now, let us give these splendid carriages their first airing, with a short walk round the town."

As they all lined up outside, Brothers crowded round to touch and admire the carvings on the arms. There was a plump kitten about to pounce on a mouse. A cheerful-faced dog with its tongue hanging out. A frog seated on a lily pad. A scaly open-mouthed fish. A rose. A goldfinch. Who would have thought that the hands of quiet Jerome could have created such beauty?

All the novices were vying to push the chairs, so

much so, that Dunstan told them they had to take turns. The oldest monk, Bartholomew, asked the Bishop if he would like to take his seat. Eborard even looked as if he might accept the offer. The novices were open-mouthed at such daring.

There was a general air of festivity, and Dunstan had to warn his charges that this was not a race, even though the passengers were egging on the youngsters.

People came out of their houses to cheer. Small children ran after the cortège. Was there was ever a better way to celebrate Pentecost, thought Anselm. What a beautiful summer it was turning out to be.

And continued to be. Soon came Saint John's Eve, celebrating the everlasting flame with the lighting of the three types of fire – the bone fire, the wake fire and Saint John's Fire. Young people played games. Anselm remembered his home village where people had placed bread and cheese as well as beer, on small tables outside their houses for any traveller who came past. With the warm, dry weather, on his recent daily travels, he often saw teams of mowers swaying in the fields, wielding their heavy scythes to cut the grass ready for hay making. Doubtless at Sprowston and Catton they would soon be preparing for the shearing. He smiled as he remembered Henry and Edward, and their enthusiasm for sheep.

But much more important, this warm weather ought to put a stop to all those coughs and colds. He had visited far too many dark little houses, with their smoky and damp rooms. The poor would at least be spared that for a few months.

As Anselm tidied up his worktable, he suddenly recalled what Godric had said about Theobald of Cambridge. Or rather, what he had not said. Just a name. He had meant to have made enquiries, but what with one thing and another it had quite slipped his mind. There had been no more happenings, so he supposed it was not that important. These days Thomas spent all his time in the scriptorium, although it was Anselm's personal opinion that he might benefit from some fresh air and sunshine. He looked as pale as when he had first come to Norwich, all those months ago.

The day following St John's Day, Thomas received a visitor. A tall, thin, saturnine man in a long black robe. Anselm and Jerome were returning from visiting some sick townsfolk, and although Anselm was interested because he had not known Thomas to receive visitors before, Jerome gave a start.

"What is it, Brother?"

"That man. I am sure he was at Bury. I had nothing to do with him, but Brother Thomas spent a lot of time in his company. From what I overheard, he is rather a strange man."

Anselm turned to watch the two figures walk towards the Prior's lodging.

"Do you have a name, Brother?"

"I am not sure, but I think it was Theodore. No, Theobald. That was it. Theobald."

Was it wrong for Anselm to feel a sudden cold breath at his back?

"I don't suppose you know anything ese?"

"Only that like us, he, too, was a visitor. Why do you ask?"

Anselm wondered whether to say what he had heard. "It was just that a month or so back, one of my patients mentioned a Theobald in connection with these lies about the Jews."

"Ah. So that was it. Master Giles said that someone was spreading some tale about a prophecy or was it conspiracy? I can't really remember, but Giles said it was just idle gossip, and he didn't believe a word of it. He thought that sort of thing was dangerous."

"Brother, would you mind coming with me to pay a call on Master Giles? In confidence, there have been far too many of these sorts of rumours and, like Giles, I truly believe they are dangerous and could cause trouble."

The next morning they set off to see what Giles had to say.

Giles was forthright. "Indeed, Brother, I am

276

sorry to have to say so, but it is one of your community who is spreading these lies, for that is what I believe them to be. Unfortunately, too many people are starting to believe them."

"Can you be more specific?"

"Well, given as I was not involved directly in any of these janglings, as far as I can gather, every year Jewish leaders supposedly hold a meeting in France – Narbonne, I think was the name, but I could be wrong as I don't know the country - and then plan to find a Christian boy and sacrifice him on a crucifix every year at Easter. Last year it was the turn of the Jews of Norwich. Something to do with a prophecy and regaining Israel. That's the gist of it. The information apparently came from this Theobald, although nobody knows who he is, except that he is supposedly a Jewish convert."

Anselm was appalled. And this man was now in the Priory.

"Master Giles, would you be prepared to come and speak to Sir John about this?"

"Indeed, I would, Brother. As soon as you like."

"Give me time to seek an audience with Prior William. At the moment, it may just be a chance remark blown out of proportion, although from what you say, I think there is more to it than that. But I need to ascertain the truth."

"Anything I can do, Brother."

As they walked back, Anselm told Jerome that he need not become involved. In fact, it was probably better not. He wondered if it would be in order to call on Master Eleazar. Perhaps he had better do that first, in case Prior William forbade him getting involved. He left Jerome at the gate and turned back toward the Jewry.

A young man asked his business, and on hearing that he wished to speak to Master Eleazar, he bade him wait. Eleazar's son came out and reassured the servant: "It's all right, Reuben, this is not the troublemaker. You may go back to your work. Pray, come in, Brother, You are most welcome," and he led him into the parlour and asked him to be seated.

Master Eleazar was intrigued. "It is not often we receive members of your community. In fact, I can remember only one," and he smiled wryly. "Now, how can I help?"

When he heard what Anselm had to say, in all its lurid detail, he was silent for a while, thinking.

"I can honestly say that this is a farrago of lies. I do not know who this Theobald of Cambridge is. There is no Jewish community in Cambridge. And as to this Council of Narbonne, and the so-called prophecy, neither exists. In fact, I have business associates in Narbonne, so I could always write to them, although it would take some while for an answer. If this is something to do with the rather strange Brother that called here last year, and attacked and insulted our maid, I am not surprised. In fact, he is still occasionally making a nuisance of himself. What do you wish me to do?"

"Nothing, Master. I will approach our Prior to find out more. At the moment this Theobald is a guest in our Priory, so our rules of hospitality could make things difficult. But in the meantime, I would urge you to take great care."

"You are kind, Brother, but we trust in King Stephen's protection. I hope we do not have to call upon it. But your thought for our welfare is most warmly appreciated. We have many friends in this town, and it is good to know that your Church is also on our side."

As he saw Anselm to the gate, he begged that he would keep him informed.

Anselm reassured him. "Have no fear, Master. Whilst I have a loyalty to my Community, I also have a duty to the wider community."

He spent the afternoon seeing to his patients, who were benefiting greatly from the chairs, now situated under the trees in the garden, and extended for maximum comfort. He smiled as he saw Brother Martin chatting to one of them. They were in good hands. There was a cat sleeping under a bush, and one of the dogs was wandering round.

Shortly before None, Prior William appeared in the garden. He had come to find out how the patients were finding the chairs. He was followed by Thomas and Theobald (if it was Theobald).

"Just taking our visitor on a tour of the Priory," he explained to a surprised Anselm. "This is Master Theobald of Cambridge, visiting Brother Thomas."

Thomas smiled smugly. Theobald seemed not in the least interested.

"I thought it might do the Brothers good if Brother Thomas were to pay the occasional visit."

Anselm thought that was not the cure he would have suggested. If Thomas put one foot in the infirmary, he would ensure he was told first, so that he could be there to pick up the pieces.

"Father Prior, I wonder if I might have a word with you?"

"Certainly, my son. Why not here?"

"In confidence, if I may."

"Of course. Come to see me after None."

XXV

Anselm was not quite sure how to begin, He thought he would start with Giles and Rolf, and then go into detail.

He watched the anger rise in Prior William's face.

"Brother Anselm, this is nothing more than idle gossip and slander against Brother Thomas and our guest Theobald."

"Then I humbly beg your pardon, Father. But these rumours are spreading, and there is the question of the safety of the Jews."

"As regards the Jews, that is what they are. Jews. Heathen. They must look after themselves."

"And the story, Father?"

"I know the story. The person who told me is a scholar and a Christian. Furthermore, he was once a Jew, and is therefore in prime position to know the truth. I now know that young William was indeed a martyr, murdered in the same way as was our Saviour."

Anselm held back his retort, but only for a moment. "Father, William was not crucified. He was hit on the back of the head by some kind of spiked weapon."

Prior William looked pityingly at him.

"Anselm, you are a valuable member of our community, but sometimes your naiveté gets the better of you. Obviously, the boy was removed from the cross and left in the woods."

"But Father, the day of his murder was Sabbath eve. The Jews do nothing after sunset, in order not to break the Sabbath. How would they have been able to carry the body to the woods? And there were no nail marks on his hands or his feet."

"Ah, Anselm, Anselm. Credulous again. If the Jews could murder our Lord, they could equally murder a young Christian boy and break their own Sabbath rules. I think we are done here. You may go."

"Yes, Father." No answer to the question of the nails.

"And I trust you to stay well out of this. I am most grateful to Brother Thomas for introducing me to Master Theobald, so the matter is ended."

Anselm bowed and returned to the infirmary. He did, of course, drop in on Dunstan and the others, just to keep them informed. They reacted exactly as he had thought they would. Dunstan added his own thoughts.

"And if Thomas starts interfering in my work, I shall tell him where to go. Very politely, of course. But I want him nowhere near my young lads. Nor his lying friend. Obviously, we cannot all go to the Sheriff, should you decide on a visit, but you have my full support."

Back in the infirmary Anselm impressed on Martin that he was not to admit Thomas or Theobald.

Martin looked reassured. "Brother, could you possibly come and have a word with Brother Felix? He seems rather worried about something, but he won't tell me what it is."

With Anselm, Brother Felix was more than ready to speak out.

"Brother, I overheard Father Prior saying that Brother Thomas would be calling on us here. Is that true?"

"Well, yes and no." He saw Felix's face drop. "Yes, it is Father Prior's suggestion, but he will only be allowed in on my say so. I will say no more, but I think you get my meaning."

"Then I hope you will refuse, Brother. We are all rather weak and walking away has been impossible."

"You sound as if he has been here before? But I have never let him in."

"No, Brother, because he comes through the

little garden gate at the end. Ask the others. Nobody wants him here."

Anselm looked thoughtful. "What does he talk about?"

"He tries to get us to undergo extra fasting. He says we will be doomed to extra years in purgatory, if we don't, especially Brother Udo."

"Why does Brother Udo get special treatment?"

"Well, you know he used to be a soldier before he took the cowl, and he sometimes forgets himself. Brother Thomas got sent off with a ripe oath or two," and he smiled at the memory.

"And not only that, but we also get all this dreadful gossip about young William, the lights, the Jews. It's not right. Please keep him away; he ruins our day every time he comes here."

"I wish I had known this before. Why didn't you tell me?"

"He gave us the impression it was your idea."

Anselm looked grim. "The very first chance I get, a lock is going on that gate. And a bell. If he wants to come in, he has to ring in a civilised manner. Or knock on my door. And either I, or Brother Martin or even Jerome will deal with him."

He smiled. "And I doubt any of us will even hear the bell. It will be a very small one."

Felix seemed relieved and settled back in his chair, leaving Anselm to go round and discreetly

284

reassure all the other patients.

Brother Terence found a lock and chain, and the next morning Jerome was sent up to the smithy to commission a very small bell.

On the way back he noticed Theobald and Thomas talking to a large group of mainly men in the marketplace. He could not hear what was being said, but there were grim faces and nods. As soon as he returned, he mentioned it to Anselm, who decided he would visit the castle the next morning.

But by then it was too late.

XXXVI

In the late evening, a group of men carrying flaming torches marched on the house of Master Eleazar. Others ran to join them. By then it was getting dark. Red faces, some fuelled by drink, shone in the torchlight. Open mouths gaping black. There were shouts, some like the roar of animaols, the others clear enough. "Christ killers. Murderers. Kill the Jews." Stones were hurled at the gates. Other houses were attacked. Servants rushed to close and bar the shutters. Someone rode for the Sheriff, others alerted the watch.

Further down in the town those that had come to their front doors rushed back inside. Others joined the mob, either to watch, or else to gather more stones. Flaming torches were thrown at the heavy wooden doors.

Word reached the Priory, and the order went out to keep indoors and bar the gates.

As the Sheriff arrived, accompanied by armed

guards, Revil and Hugh rode up, both armed, fearing an insurrection.

"Get back, get back." The men-at-arms beat at the mob with staves, driving them towards a timber yard, where some of the wood caught fire. Residents rushed out with buckets of water or beat at the flames with rush mats. Women screamed. Dogs barked.

Under the Sheriff's well-organised band, some of the men were corralled into a group. Others ran off. Within the hour those under arrest were marched to the castle and thrown into the cells, to await judgement in the morning. Sir John then sent messengers to summon the Council for the following morning and paid a visit to Eleazar and his community.

Inside Eleazar's parlour, he sought to reassure Eleazar that he and his community were under the full protection of the King. Space would be found for them in the castle, and they would be well advised to take it, at least until the hearing was over. He wondered if Eleazar knew what had caused this latest disturbance.

Apart from what Eleazar had learned from Anselm, he was able to add nothing more. Sir John looked grim.

Reluctantly the women and children, and a few elder folk, gathered some belongings and set off under armed guard. Eleazar and the other men decided to stay. Sir John posted guards at their gates and front doors, although he felt that the violence was contained for the time being. As he left, he impressed on them that the moment they felt insecure, the guards would escort them to the castle and safety.

In the castle the Bailiff was taking down the names of the rioters. Sir John himself was at a loss as to what had started all this, but he was determined to get to the bottom of it and find the ring leaders. He had spotted one or two well known faces among them. His wife and some of the servants were making some comfortable space for the little families, and the cook was asked to provide food, first having checked on dietary requirements. The hall was prepared for the morning's meeting. Nobody slept much that night.

In the hall, Sir John sat at the long table together with Revil, the Bailiff, and the leading citizens. His Bailiff had drawn up the charge sheet. But first, he wanted to hear what the rioters had to say.

He nodded to the Bailiff who went to the door and shouted: "Bring them up."

Into the hall shuffled all those who had been unable to escape arrest. In total there were about two dozen of them, unwashed, unkempt, and many playing the righteous citizen. The names were read out. There were apprentices, several labourers, a woodsman, an ostler, a potman, and yes, who else but Aelward Ded and Ethelbert, not forgetting to mention Limp Hamon. They lined up before the table, Sir John surveying them with contempt.

"I trust you are all ashamed of yourselves. Such brave men, such heroes, attacking a small community of honest men, not to mention women and young children. I will hear your defence, one by one, but first, I want to know who is your ringleader. Someone started this; it did not just blow up like an untended bonfire. Come now, who was it?"

There was a silence as they all looked at each other and shuffled their feet.

"In that case, I will hold you all as ringleaders, and I trust you know the penalty for riot? No? Then let me tell you. Fines, flogging, loss of a hand. In the case of at least two of you, whom I have had to deal with before on such matters, your punishment will be even more severe. In the case of all of you, it may even be constituted treason since the community that you attacked is under the protection of King Stephen. Treason is punishable by death."

There was a shocked intake of breath.

A wavering hand went up. "Yes. Your name, man."

"Aelward Ded, Sir John, an honest citizen."

"Ah, yes, honest citizen Master Ded. Again. What do you have to say for yourself before I bring you before the judge to commit you to the gallows?"

"Sir, it weren't no riot, Sir."

"Then what was it? A maypole dance?" Someone sniggered.

"Sir, we were defending our faith, Sir. Our faith."

"In what way?"

"The Jews, Sir. They martyred the Blessed William. On Good Friday, Sir. Last year, Sir. We wanted to kill them for this evil deed."

"Master Ded, and you others, I am not going to spend my morning telling you where you are wrong, deluded. If you have proof of what you say, then you come to me, you do not behave like animals. Have you proof?"

"Well, Sir, he told us the truth. About the Council, Sir."

"Who did? What Council?"

"In France, Sir. In Arbon. A plot to kill our Blessed William. Last year, Sir. Norwich was the place."

"And who told you this? You do realise, all of you, that you have been completely misled? There is no Council of Narbonne, which is the place to which I believe you are referring."

"The monk, Sir. Brother Thomas. And his friend, Theobald. From Cambridge, Sir. A scholar, Sir. A Christian. He knows the truth. They told us. Yesterday, Sir."

"Then it looks as if I shall also have to arrest Brother Thomas and his friend for incitement to murder. Is Brother Thomas here? No, of course not. Or Theobald? I see."

"Before I consult my fellow citizens, has anyone anything else to say in their defence, apart from this little tarradiddle? I should also add that you have caused me and numerous others a lot of extra work, and loss of sleep, so your excuses had better hold water."

There was no excuse. So, they were sent back down while discussions took place. Some members of the Town Council had not heard the story of Narbonne; others had, which showed just how far the lies had spread.

Sir John gazed at the sorry-looking spectacle before him. Then the sentences were read out. Two days in the cells on bread and water. All would be fined, unless they were apprentices. All would give a half day a week for six months to cleaning the streets, emptying the cess pits, labouring in the fields, and, more to the point, repairing any damage. And Ded and Ethelbert would have extra labouring duties in Master Eleazar's garden.

"Count yourselves lucky. This should at least keep you out of the taverns. You have escaped lightly, since it seems the real ringleaders may be hiding down in the Priory. They will be dealt with." How, he did not know, since they were under Canon Law. But something could be attempted, at least.

The Clerk finished writing the sentences, all rose, and the Council dispersed.

Sir John seized a quick breakfast, called in on his guests, then set out for the Bishop's Palace, on the way there debating how best to approach the Bishop.

The gates were still locked, and he had to ring the bell. A worried looking porter come to let him in.

"It's all right, Brother. The riot has been put down and the perpetrators will be punished. I am hoping to have an audience with his Grace. I will wait, if I may." He dismounted and tethered his horse.

Ten minutes later he was walking up the stairs to the Bishop's parlour, where Eborard was seated at his desk. "He looks frailer every time I see him," thought John.

"Welcome, my son. How can I help?"

"I am not sure whether the news reached you, your Grace, but we had a serious disturbance in the town last night. But maybe your people did not wish to disturb you, possibly because they felt it did not concern you."

"No, I have heard nothing, Sir John. Perhaps you could explain more."

Sir John briefly explained the situation, omitting Theobald and Thomas, but alluding to the gist of the rumour.

"If that is so, I am not sure why you have called here. Surely it is a matter for the town."

"I am sorry to have to say that this rumour was deliberately spread by one of your Brothers and a guest of the priory, and credulous citizens were incited to violence. My enquiries have proved the story completely untrue, and yet lives of innocent people were threatened. Indeed, I had to take them into the protection of the castle. Even now, two dozen or so rioters are in the gaol. Since the Jews are under the protection of the King, it is possible that such incitement could be classed as treason. I am sorry to have to say all this, but I think you can see my point."

The Bishop sighed. Again, John thought how tired he looked.

"If, as you say, the culprits are under our roof, then it is for the Church to punish them, since you have no jurisdiction here. Pray, Sir John, take a seat and I will ask the Prior to come, and we will see what we can do."

He rang a bell on his desk, and his secretary

was sent to summon Prior William. Prior William was immediately on the defensive.

"Sir John, Theobald of Cambridge is, in my opinion, an esteemed scholar and, being a Jewish convert, can be trusted to tell the truth in this matter. And Brother Thomas is equally respected. I have no reason at all to accuse either of them of lying. If anyone lies, then it is the Jews."

"Master Eleazar is a respected member of the community and under the protection of King Stephen. For members of the Church to incite people to violence is completely unacceptable."

Bishop Eborard looked from one to the other, completely perplexed.

"Who is this Theobald, Father? I know of Brother Thomas, who has always struck me as deluded but completely harmless, and as a member of our community, in need of our protection."

"Theobald of Cambridge is a guest and is assisting Brother Thomas in his history of our Community here. Would you doubt the word of a Christian, your Grace?"

"So, Sir John, if you have a problem, might I suggest that Master Eleazar and his neighbours be challenged to take part in Trial by Ordeal to prove their innocence of the murder. We shall then soon see on whose side our Lord places his hand," said Prior William, triumphantly.

"Father Prior," said Sir John, "I do not wish to cause a split between our communities, but, as His Grace has said, the crime was a secular one, therefore the ecclesiastical court has no jurisdiction over the Jews, since they are not Christians. So, there will be no Trial by Ordeal, and they remain under my protection. Put clearly, I will not allow the Jews to answer such inventions of the Christians."

"And, just a suggestion. If Brothers Thomas and Theobald feel so strongly that they have to incite to murder, maybe it is they who should be undergoing Trial by Ordeal."

"We are done here, I think. Good morning, Your Grace, and thank you for your time."

He bowed and turned to leave. A sudden thought struck him.

"If I find any of your Brothers committing further incitement, Canon Law or not, I shall have them arrested and returned to you under guard. Make of it what you will."

He was untethering his horse when he suddenly realised that if Bishop Eborard died or stepped down – and he was looking very frail – he would possibly have to deal with William de Turbeville as his successor.

As he rode through the gates, Baldwin the smith passed him. "Good morning, Sir John. Just here with a little parcel for Brother Anselm. That was a bit of a riot last night. Glad you got it under control."

Sir John smiled and waved. Thank heavens for good, solid citizens like Baldwin.

Good solid Baldwin was making his way to the infirmary, where he gave his parcel to Anselm. "I wasn't quite sure how small you wished it to be. At first, I thought it was some kind of jest, as Brother Jerome said something about it being almost inaudible. I thought maybe you did not want to disturb the older monks."

"That is exactly it, although not quite in the way you have understood it. Come through, and I will show you," and he led the way through to the garden, where Baldwin was welcomed by the Brothers enjoying the new chairs. "We thought the bell might be hung just here, so that those wishing to enter could ring first. The gate is to be kept locked, you see."

Baldwin did not quite see. "Well, if you are sure, Brother," and he produced the bell and hung it on the gate.

"Quite sure. Sometimes we have unwanted visitors, who are incapable of understanding that they first need to apply to me or my assistants. This will save my legs, as I shall be quite unable to hear when they ring. And that is a very pretty piece of engraving. I like the idea of a titmouse."

Just at that moment, quite by chance, Brother

Thomas appeared in the distance, purposefully making his way towards the gate. Baldwin looked at Anselm, and a wide grin spread over his face. "Ah, Brother. Brother Reynard has nothing on you, if you don't mind me saying so."

And they turned and went back to the pharmacy, where some cowslip wine was produced, and Anselm caught up with the news, which hit him and his assistants like a hammer blow. Through the shutters he could see Thomas shaking the gate like a madman and ringing at the bell. All good.

Baldwin had him tell the whole story, and he had just got to the point where he had met Sir John leaving, when they heard angry knocking at the door, and a voice yelling.

"Your gate is locked, Brother."

"Yes, it is. Did you not ring? That is the courteous thing to do."

"There has never been a bell there before."

"That's right. Then did you ring?"

"Yes. But no-one came."

Baldwin had turned his head away and was obviously trying to contain his amusement.

"We must have been busy. So, your business here? Some ailment, maybe?"

"I am here at the agreement of Prior William, to offer spiritual succour."

"That is good of you, Brother, but now is not the

time. There was some disturbance in the night, with our gates having to be locked. Some villains inciting the townsfolk to violence, Master Baldwin tells me. The Brothers had very little sleep and they now need to catch up on their rest. So, if you will excuse me, I will show you out."

But Thomas took no notice and tried to barge past. "Brother Thomas," said Anselm, scandalised. "Please."

At that moment, Jerome passed through carrying a pan of boiling water. Whether by accident or intent, Anselm was never quite sure, but as Thomas tried to push through, Jerome slipped, and the water covered Thomas from waist to foot. There was a howl of pain. And the next thing that happened was that he slipped on the wet paving and hit his head on a dispensary.

Anselm helped him to his feet, and sat him on a bench, where he inspected his feet, which were bright red and very badly burned. He dried him off, then asked Jerome to find the burns ointment, which he lathered over Thomas's feet, first having immersed them in cold water for a few minutes.

"You see, Brother, that is why you should never visit unannounced. I fear your walking is going to cause you considerable pain in the next two or three weeks. Maybe, with Father Prior's per-mission, you should remain in the scriptorium, and keep those feet up. I will deal with any blistering, which I fear will be considerable. I will bandage them for the time being, in order to prevent any putrefaction. Come back and see me in two days. Try not to put foot to ground in the meantime."

Ten minutes later, Thomas hobbled out and back to whatever it was he had been doing before he decided to make the lives of the older monks a misery.

Once Thomas had gone, Baldwin let out a tremendous roar. "Glad I could help, Brother. And there is no charge for the bell. Quite made my day. Just wish Giles had been here to see it, too." And he passed out into the cloisters, still chuckling.

Anselm thought his little plan had worked very well. And even if Prior William took Thomas's side, it would be quite a while before Thomas came anywhere near the garden again. Maybe a little celebration was called for. He took a tray and added some cups of wine, which he instructed Martin to take to his patients. It just remained to be seen whether Thomas would manage to experience a sudden miracle, and be up and about again with hours. He doubted it.

The days passed. Harvests were gathered in. People's minds were now more centred on harvest suppers and general thanksgiving, rather than imaginary Jewish plots in France. And those that had escaped the Sheriff's men kept a very low profile indeed. Sir John even changed his mind about writing to King Stephen. The Jews returned to the Jewry, and all was calm for the present. But the reminders were there, in the teams of malefactors seen swabbing the cobbles, emptying the cess pits and weeding the streets. Only the low alehouses missed their best customers for the next six months. Bring on New Year.

At Michaelmas, Bishop Eborard made public his decision to step down from office in the New Year, although he told his congregation that he would probably leave for Fontenay before the autumn storms made sailing difficult. However, he would still be their Bishop until a replacement was chosen, and Prior William would cover his duties in the Diocese. He hoped they would remember him in their prayers.

The news of his departure was received with sadness but also with concern in certain quarters. Sir John could not forget his reception after the riot and knew that he could count on no support from Prior William, even less should he become Bishop. But he also wondered where the two monks who had instigated the riot had gone to. He did not believe the Prior would have sent them away, so maybe, like the other rioters, they were keeping out of sight. Anselm could have reassured him, since he had himself seen Theobald leave the Priory the day after Sir John's visit. Thomas, however, was very much in evidence, ostentatiously hobbling in and out of the scriptorium, leaning on a large stick. The burns seemed to be taking longer to heal than he had thought, but as Thomas no longer visited the infirmary, he had no way of telling.

His concerns were shared by Wlward and Godwin.

"Did you know, Brother, that Prior William has gained permission from the Bishop to move our William's grave nearer the cathedral? Maybe, even inside? Or at least, the Chapter House."

"No, I did not, but the community would not be asked. Do you know when this was?"

"About a week or so ago. They are going to have a short service, and we were asked to attend. But it won't happen until after the Bishop has gone."

"Were you asked for your permission? He is, after all, your grandson and nephew. How about Elviva?"

"No, Brother, not a word. I think Prior William considers our lad the property of the Church. Mind you, Elviva is pleased. She is starting to believe that lie about the Jews and thinks that young William really is a martyr. We can't change her mind. She has her heart set on being the

301

mother of a saint. Blunt, I know, but there it is."

"It must be some comfort to her, I suppose."

"Indeed, Brother. But it isn't right, all the same. Let us keep in touch on this, since I do not believe it will go away now. It has gone too far."

October that year was dry and sunny. Work finished on the tree pruning in the orchards, and the fields saw the last ploughing of the year. Fruit was gathered in. Just as we have the Church's year, so we have a country year, thought Anselm. All souls, like the fruits, to be safely gathered in.

There was an elaborate service to say farewell to Bishop Eborard. In general, he had been well respected, even loved, and the cathedral was full. Then he was led in solemn procession through the town and sent on his way with many blessings. Who would be his successor, many asked themselves. Not necessarily Prior William. It would depend on his fellow prelates. In the meantime, the Prior behaved as if he were already elected. Anselm was told he had moved into the Bishop's office on the evening of his departure. And Brother Thomas was frequently seen hobbling backwards and forwards on various duties.

But on the whole, life was peaceful. There were no more sightings or disturbances, the youngsters played games in the fields, and the patients enjoyed the last of the sun and warmth.

November was a different scene entirely, and not just because of the All Hallows Triduum, with its accompanying rain and cloud. At the end of October an announcement was made.

"Brothers, after careful thought and long discussions with His Grace, it has been decided to move the body of William into the Chapter House. It was felt more fitting that this innocent child should receive more shelter than our humble graveyard can offer."

"This will take place with a special interment on All Souls Day, after High Mass, with a very simple ceremony."

Very tactful, thought Anselm. No mention of miracles or lights, or even Blessedness. Just the fact that it had Eborard's approval. As Dunstan said afterwards, "That's not the end of it, of course. Do you think they will invite the Sheriff?"

XXXVII

On the morning of All Souls Day, after High Mass, a solemn group gathered in the Chapter House to lay to rest the body of William. The little slab was gently placed over his resting place, and a blessing was said by the Prior. Elviva came forward with some flowers – hellebores and rosemary. Then after prayers, led by the Prior, the little group passed out into the fresh air once more. Although it was a private ceremony, some people had stayed to watch from a distance. Again, nothing was said about William being blessed, but it would not be long before the rumours started again, thought Anselm, as he walked with Wlward towards Colegate.

They did not speak much. Wlward and Godwin were still angry about William's body being moved, even though it was a comforting thought that the boy was under the shelter of the cathedral complex. They were all too well aware of what the outcome might be. Elviva was now convinced of the Jews' involvement. Anselm stayed briefly. They wanted to be alone.

Anselm had seen the Sheriff and his wife in the parvise after Mass, but there was no sign of Revil or Alys. He supposed she must be near her time. Maybe another three weeks. Today was Friday, so perhaps he would walk up to Sprowston. Maybe take some of that oil.

When he arrived, somewhat damp, as there had been a slight shower and the grass was wet underfoot, he received the usual warm welcome, with Margaret hanging his cloak near the fire, and producing mulled ale.

Alys was resting, she said, but she had been in good health, and Dame Maud had been asked to call. Revil was never around much, so Alys would remain for the birth. Anselm gave them the latest news, including that of William's removal to the Chapter House.

"Brother, is there any news of who will be our next Bishop?"

"Not yet. Of course, Bishop Eborard is still, strictly speaking, in office, although Prior William has taken over many of his duties. We may know late in the new year." He saw that she was looking worried.

"It's Alys. For some reason she seems to have taken against Prior William baptising the new child. Yes, I know, she has no choice, and last time it was the Bishop. But, nonetheless."

"Do you know why?"

"I can't quite get to the bottom of it, but I think it's a tangle of the rumours, the recent riot, Brother Thomas, and the fact that it seems Thomas is supported by the Prior. She has not forgotten what happened here last year."

"Margaret, a baptism is a baptism. It is the sacrament that it is important, and our God who gives. The person who carries out the ceremony is just a channel, a tool, if you like. I do not think she could choose. And, in any case, she will still be confined until after the forty days. Try and reassure her. And call on me, if needs be. Although I am sure Dame Maud will be quite enough."

He had a sudden thought. "Of course, any Priest can baptise. Had you thought of a different church? Your own, for example?"

"Revil would never allow it, especially if it is a boy."

"Then nothing more to be said. Prior William is a good man. If he has taken Brother Thomas under his wing, it is probably not for me to question it."

He thought this conversation was getting difficult, so he changed direction slightly. "And if it's also a question that the Lady Alys worries that

Thomas will pay another visit, that will not happen. Sir John paid a visit to the Prior and Bishop, and I think I can say with certainty that Brother Thomas will not be permitted to visit you. Yes, I know the traditions are that doors and windows should be kept open during a birth, but you have Matthew and your brothers and husband to bar the way; I don't think even Brother Thomas will risk another crack on the jaw. And now, I fear I must be going."

Again, she gave him a spontaneous hug, and he left, smiling.

Such dismal days. His patients could no longer spend time in the garden, although they had frequent permitted visitors. Brother Dunstan had suggested that his youngsters might pay occasional calls, to talk or to play chequers. He told Anselm that he rather feared some of the older monks were inspiring the lads to bad habits with reminiscing on what they had got up to at the same age. But he smiled as he said it.

"Have no fear. It is the reminiscing that is important, the memories, the feeling that they are still young at heart, listened to, needed. Your proposal was a good one, and it is having such a good effect; the infirmary is a really cheerful place these days."

"And Brother Thomas and his homilies?"

"He has not been back after his little accident,

which has kept him indoors for quite a while. Whether he is completely healed, I really could not say, as he has not even come in for me to change his bandages. But as long as he does not have any more of his visitations, then I am content." He did not add, 'as are all my patients.'

Over the next week or so, he kept an eye out for Thomas, who was sometimes seen working in the scriptorium, again in a very secretive manner. Anselm's offers of salves for his feet were ignored, and with Prior William spending most of his hours, when not in Church or Chapter, in the Bishop's Palace, there wasn't anywhere much that Thomas could go. The rainy weather helped, too, as there weren't any groups hanging around on corners or in alley ways. And those that were out and about, those condemned to street cleaning and gong collection, would hardly be sweet companions.

However, nothing lasted for ever.

XXXVIII

Passing through the cloisters early one morning he noticed a small crowd outside the Chapter House. He caught the words he had hoped never to hear again. "A miracle, a miracle! The Blessed William has cured me." Should he fetch the Prior? Or could it be sorted out right now?

He did not recognise the man. He looked dishevelled, as if he had been sleeping out all night. Another Limp Hamon? He walked over to the crowd, then saw that Brother Thomas had got there first. Nothing wrong with his feet, then.

"Cured, I tell you. I am cured." The man was babbling on. Actually, he did look familiar. Anselm had seen him somewhere, but where? Then he remembered. A year ago, maybe less, scribbling in a side room near the Sheriff's office.

"Come, child." Brother Thomas was at his most sanctimonious, since the man was about forty. "Pray. Tell us your story."

"I had the most dreadful toothache, Brother, a worm gnawing away in there. The stone cured me, it cured me. The pain has gone."

Anselm looked at his face. It was swollen on one side. He had his own ideas. "You say the stone cured you. In what way?"

"Come, come, Brother," said Thomas, officious- -ly. "The man is cured, and what is more, by the Blessed William. What more do you need?"

"It was the stone of William's tomb," the man insisted. "I slept with my cheek on it."

"Would you mind if I looked?" Anselm asked. "I will be very gentle."

The man opened his mouth. There was a large rotten tooth on one side. The cheek was swollen, as was the gum. His breath was putrid. Of course, there would no longer be pain. He now had an abscess. Sooner or later it would burst. In fact, it looked as if it already had. Should he say anything? What was it his granny used to say? "They must learn it for themselves."

He smiled. "Come to me later, if you need help," and he walked away, wondering how long it would be before there were dozens more people queuing up for a cure. Plenty of teeth available. This was the result of listening to fantasists and the credulous – and he did not just mean honest townsfolk. He remembered the verse in the Bible about the innocent and millstones.

In the distance he could still hear Thomas asking if he had seen anything. Any lights? The Blessed William himself? If he hadn't seen anything last night, he certainly would have now. He thought he should maybe go and check on his supplies of cloves, henbane, leek seeds, alum. Although, if what he suspected regarding the clerk's toothache, a large pair of pliers might prove more useful.

In the days following, except for the early morning gathering, he tried not to go too near the Chapter House or the main gates. People were starting to dribble in – two this day, three the next. They left flowers. And always, Brother Thomas hovered in the background, ready to give spiritual succour, or to spread the lies of the tooth or the leg. And the lights. Even though the story of Limp Hamon had proved Thomas a fraud. It was almost as if he had appointed himself the Sacrist of a shrine. Did the Prior know?

One thing was sure. Should Prior William be elected Bishop, then his successor, Father Elias, would have something to say about all these comings and goings. Although, of course, what the Bishop wanted would always take precedence.

Anselm continued to take advantage of the calm, and clean out his dispensary, ready for the winter. However, he could see that the situation might very well soon mount to hysteria. Really, Prior

William needed to intervene.

On the 19th, news came that Lady Alys had gone into labour. All was going well, said Dame Maud, and to thank him for the oils. They really had a most helpful effect. There was a verbal post scriptum. Please would he keep that dreadful Brother Thomas away from Sprowston.

Anselm thought he would not even have to try very hard. Brother Thomas was far too busy elsewhere. He hummed to himself as he refilled his shelves, and wondered what he could take as a little gift to the new child.

At Chapter the next morning, Prior William made an announcement. Following a little miracle by William's grave, they were seeing extra visitors in the cathedral. Brother Peter would therefore be requiring help in keeping the area of the Chapter House clean, and any extra attention to the cathedral itself. Some people were not too careful where they dropped their litter. "And we would not like to frighten them away from the House of God by being too strict."

Brother Peter's expression was a picture. He contained himself until he had a chance to come into the infirmary. Anselm saw his face and poured out a drop of the cowslip wine. "Calm down, Brother, calm down. This will do no good."

"Anselm, it is not my job to play the part of Martha; my work is in the gardens and orchards.

It's not that I feel the work is beneath me, but it is entirely unnecessary. All due to the fantasies of one person in particular, God forgive me. We all know there were no miracles, even little ones. Why doesn't Prior William step in and stop it? If it goes on like this, we could be like a Roman circus within weeks. There'll be food stalls in the cloister, holy badges at the gate. Maybe the Sheriff could be persuaded to hand the cleaning job over to those wretches who caused that riot."

"Peter, it won't happen, and we know it. All we can do is limit any damage. We just have to hope that if Prior William becomes Bishop, he will be too busy to get involved. Bishop Eborard has not been on his visitations for years, due to his ill-health, so Prior William will have a lot of catching up to do. And Father Elias will stand no nonsense."

"Hmm. And another thing. I'd dearly like to know what's in that book that Thomas is writing. He covers it up whenever anyone goes past. I'm sorry, Brother, anger is a nasty thing, and I regret that I brought you into my rant. It's a shame, because this place has been so much happier since you organised those chairs, and Dunstan got the youngsters involved. And your idea about the cider. Come and see what we have done with the new cider press. What a good idea of yours. The cider should be ready to welcome in the new year. Maybe a little earlier than I would have wished - six months would have been best – but drinkable, nonetheless." And looking more cheerful, he returned to his work.

That evening, Matthew came to his workplace with the good news. The Lady Alys had been delivered of a boy. Both were well, and Lady Margaret would welcome a visit.

The next day, once his work area was put to rights, Anselm packed his usual rush basket, gave Martin his instructions, and set out for Sprowston. The house was calm. He remembered the uproar a year ago. He knew for a fact that Brother Thomas had not left the Priory for days – he was far too busy welcoming visitors and praying with them, though he noticed that he did not pick up any litter.

The child was large and healthy. Black hair and blue eyes, like Elizabeth. Revil was in the hall, talking to Luke, and this time he did not say anything about skirts. "Have you a name?" asked Anselm. "Stephen," said Margaret. "I think my brother had it ready and waiting."

"And the matter of the baptism?"

"I think there can be no argument. The Prior will officiate. Revil is determined. It is to be on Sunday. But enough of this, do give us your news. Has there really been another miracle?"

"Just one poor wretch with a gum boil, who will

probably soon need an extraction, since a burst abscess will only produce temporary relief. But they come in their twos and threes, drop their apple cores and nutshells, and keep Brother Thomas well and truly busy."

"Not sweeping up?"

He smiled at the thought. "No, just acting as an unofficial sacristan."

She laughed. "From what I have heard, he should be among those people ordered to clean the streets and empty the cesses."

"So, news does get through. Have you heard anything else? Did Ardith come down to help her aunt?"

"She was not needed. The birth was very easy – if one can use that word. All being well, Alys will not even need a wet nurse. Dame Maud says the Jews were kept safe but are now all returned home. Thank the Lord for a strong Sheriff who stands no nonsense. Brother, I am being very inhospitable. Pray, will you take something to drink?"

"That is very kind, but today is the Feast of the Presentatiom of the Virgin, so I should put in an appearance at the special service."

"I have never quite understood how you manage to get out and about so much, Brother. I thought your order was very strict."

"Well, it is and it isn't. Although we are in the

world, we are not of it, but that does not stop us helping in the wider community. Not everyone can afford a physician. And my craft is very much in demand."

"Then I will see you to the gate. And have no fear, Brother. If Brother Thomas feels like widening his ministry, he will find our gates tight shut. It is a long way away, and the Advent Fast is almost upon us, but I hope we shall see you over Christmas, if not before."

As he had so often thought before, visiting that little family was always so energising. He h hastened on his way back for the service, and got there just in time to wash and join the procession. He did hope that any visitors to William's grave would stay for the service, and not just treat the occasion as a fairground show.

From what he could see, there was indeed a larger congregation than usual, and he was glad to see that Cuthbert and his friends had brought in the older monks in their chairs.

He remembered the affair of the ring. Since they would be praying at the altar of Our Lady, for a moment he wondered if that had anything to do with it the larger numbers. Were they hoping for another little miracle? Or maybe it was just the novelty of William. Who knew?

Young Stephen was baptised on the Sunday, with Prior William officiating. Margaret held the child, who, unlike his sister, complained loudly. Either it was the Devil leaving his young, rosy body, or else Prior William did not have quite the same way with babies as Bishop Eborard. The party then left for Sprowston, but caused little interest among the six or seven people eager to visit William's grave. He noticed the Prior bypassing them and going back to the Palace. So, unlike Bishop Eborard, he had not been invited back to Sprowston.

All in all, apart from the visitors to the grave, December passed without event. Alys came to church to give thanks on Christmas Eve, amid the scents of the bay and the apple-decorated trees; then Midnight Mass celebrated the breaking of the fast, and over the next week Anselm was able to find some time to visit Sprowston. Jerome had made a small cross, similar to that which Anselm had given Alys a year ago, and there was a wooden puzzle for the boys, and a wooden doll for Elizabeth, who was now walking. He also had a small flask of the cider for the men.

All was not totally cheerful, however. Sir John had not made his customary visit, laid low with some affection of the lungs, which he had refused to acknowledge. According to Revil he was planning to visit London. He was just about to say more, when he remembered that Anselm was present, and changed the subject. Later Margaret explained in confidence that Sir John was going to argue against the election of Prior William as Bishop.

"You will probably guess why, Brother, so I need say no more. Except that he has been very concerned for the Jewish community and puts the disturbances down to one of your Brothers."

Anselm nodded. "Have no fear, I shall say nothing. But should Sir John be making the journey in this weather, in his condition? I would offer help, but since I am not supposed to know anything..." He thought he would send up some soothing tonics and balms. "When is he going?"

"I am not sure, but around now, so that he can petition the King after the Christmas Feast is over. Revil will go with him, so he will at least have some support, which should reassure Lady Joane."

"Then it will do no harm for me to send something – as a gesture of goodwill. Especially if I send some cider with it."

Hugh and Luke came over. "What are you doing over here in this corner? You look just like Henry and Edward when they are up to something. And that cider is excellent. I think we must do the same at Catton."

"Just catching up on the news. Yesterday we heard that the Holy Father has been allowed to return to Rome and can now be consecrated there."

"And no more miracles, Brother? We were expecting at least half a dozen."

He saw Anselm's face.

"My apologies, Brother. It is no joke. I should not have spoken out of turn."

"It was very understandable. Let us hope that the New Year brings an end to all this. For the sake of all the community."

He refused a ride with Matthew, who was off to visit his mother. He needed a walk. He thought he would send Martin up tomorrow with the medicine and the cider. He could visit Mistress Webbe at the same time. And deliver some more embrocation to Rolf and Eda. It would get him away from all the chatter about William and the miracle. He would have sent Jerome, but the streets were too icy for his sore knee.

A message came back from the castle to thank the Community for the cider, and for the medicines.

"Did you see Sir John?" asked Anselm. "How did he look?"

"He and his lady were in the solar. To be honest, he did not look at all well, and I think Lady Joane was worried. He had a hard dry cough. He did mention his journey, although he just said it was on urgent business. He is leaving tomorrow early. At first light, I think."

"And your other errands?"

"Eda and Rolf were grateful for the visit, as was Mistress Webbe. Rolf said the oils were working very well, and he did seem rather more nimble on his feet."

"Then let us hope he remains so. And that Sir John's errand is successful."

"Errand, Brother?"

Anselm realised he had said too much. "Perhaps I should have said business. It is not the season to be setting out on a long ride – it will take at least four or five days. May the weather keep calm for them."

As soon as Lauds was over, he snatched an hour's rest then set out for the castle, aiming to be back for Prime. The weather was fine, with no sign of rain. He reached the mound as the small party were setting off – Sir John, Revil and two men-at-arms. They were pleased to see him, but in truth, Sir John looked very ill. As they continued on their way, Anselm said a quiet prayer, and thought, had it not been for this trouble with Thomas, the Sheriff would still be recovering in his warm bed. Indeed, he might not even have caught that infection.

He passed Master Eleazar, out for an early walk with his wife, who was seldom seen. He was looking well, as was his wife, even after her sojourn in the castle. They exchanged greetings and wished each other a good New Year, before Anselm hastened back to Prime, passing the street sweepers on his way.

There were again more people than usual at the service for the Epiphany, heralding the next octave of celebrations. Please God, Sir John would be back safe and sound by the time they had ended. He seemed to recall someone telling him that as a feast, Epiphany was even older than Christmas. In the Chapter House he saw that someone had put flowers on William's grave.

XXXIX

The following morning, shortly before Prime, Anselm was passing through the cloisters when he heard a commotion. "Praise the Blessed William. I am cured. A miracle, a miracle!" His heart sank. There was the sound of rushing feet. Brother Thomas. Was that man always on the watch?

A rather large, red-faced man was pulling himself to his feet. Like the clerk with the toothache, he seemed to have been out all night. Thomas was too busy embracing him and shouting alleluias to notice that Prior William had arrived.

"What is all this noise? Brother Thomas, we are due to start Prime in a few minutes. Pray get back to your place."

"But it is a miracle, Father. Another miracle. Let the man speak."

"Oh, sir. I was so ill. A dreadful ague. My guts

ached so bad I thought it must be the side sickness and I would die. And no-one around to shrive me. And a pain like nails in my head. I must have fainted here, and when I woke, I was cured. It must have been the Blessed, Blessed William."

"What is your name, my son?"

"Magnus, your honour. Magnus Woode, Sir."

"And did you see anything?" interrupted Thomas.

"Indeed I did. Visions of hell, sirs. Monsters. Such as you have never seen."

"Nothing else? No visions of the saint?" That was Thomas again.

Anselm thought, the man has slipped up. No vision, no miracle.

"Oh, that too, Brother, that too. of course. I forgot to say. All in white, Brother, just as you said the other day."

"Father Prior, may I speak in private?"

"If you must, Brother Anselm."

They passed into the corner. "Father, I have seen this man on Elm Hill. He is a frequent drinker, often to be seen staggering home the worse for wear. This is not idle gossip. Others will tell you. There is still the smell of drink on his breath. I would suggest overindulgence on Twelfth Night, nothing more."

The Prior looked at him shrewdly. Was he going

to believe the truth, or was he still under the impression that Anselm was wildly jealous of Brother Thomas?

"Do you know, I believe you are right, Brother."

He returned to the man. "Master Magnus, it is quite clear you are still under the influence of a heavy night out. I am shocked that you should have brought yourself in this state to the grave of a young child. Now go, and later confess your sins and make penance. Come, Brothers. I am beginning to regret my original decision to lay William's body in the Chapter House. Leaving him in the cemetery would have caused far less of this excessive behaviour."

Brother Thomas's face was a sight. He opened his mouth, but nothing came out. Anselm left him there, as he walked to join the others, thinking, 'It will make no difference. This will be yet another miracle to add to Thomas's collection.' If you counted phantom lights and dreams, he was almost losing count. He wondered what had originally induced Prior William to place William in the Chapter House. He must ask Dunstan.

Dunstan had the answer. "I think you may have missed that particular bit of flummery. It was when all those rumours about lights were going around. According to one of my lads – yes, I know, gossip - Thomas had another one of his dreams, in which Bishop de Losinga appeared to him and said that William must have an honourable place of burial in the Chapter House. To be honest, I dismissed it at the time, it seemed so ridiculous, and we all knew what Thomas was like. But surprisingly, Prior William seems to have taken it seriously and must have persuaded Bishop Eborard to agree."

"It's beyond me, Brother. But as long as my lads stay calm and devoted to their calling, I try not to get angry."

As the weeks passed, Anselm started wondering about Sir John. The weather was bad; he doubted it would be any better in London. Even so, surely he should have returned by now. He passed the Bailiff in town and asked him if there had been any news.

"The news is not good, Brother. Sir John's sickness worsened, and on his return, he turned off towards Mileham."

"But that is miles from here, towards the north-west. Why would he do that, in his state of health?"

"I know no more than that, Brother, only that Lord Revil says his brother William de Chesney has a manor there. Between you and me, Sir John is not well, not well at all," and shaking his head, he rode away.

On 30ᵗʰ January, there was an announcement

in Chapter, but given by Sub-Prior Elias.

"Brothers, yesterday we received news from London. Our Prior, William, is to be the next Bishop, taking over from Bishop Eborard who, as you know, resigned, and is now in Fontenay. There will be special prayers today, and a Mass of Thanksgiving – the day still to be announced. Bishop William will be ordained on Easter Sunday, but will be travelling down to London in the next day or so. In the meantime, I have been told that I am now your Prior." He knelt. "In humility, I ask for your prayers."

There was a subdued murmuring. Elias was well-liked, a no-nonsense kind of man. Sadly, it seemed that Sir John had not succeeded in his mission, thought Anselm.

On the next day, it was announced in Chapter that Sir John had died at Mileham. There would be masses said for his soul. His brother, Sir William de Chesney, would be the next Sheriff. Anselm wondered if the community had lost its champion against the anti-Jewish element? Or was this why John had turned off to Mileham in the first place? Had he wished to make sure Sir William was fully briefed? He had paid dearly for it, and so had his widow.

Candlemas, and William's birthday, arrived, and people brought their candles. Flowers appeared on William's grave, whether they were all from Elviva, or from other people as well, one could not know. His heart was sore for the little group, whom he could just see through the screen as they filed past with their candles for blessing. He thought Wlward was looking tired. He must go and visit them – maybe take some of that cider. He remembered when they had discussed cider-making all that time ago. It was a very sad time, when really, they should all be celebrating the light of the world. Elviva was mourning her son, Lady Joane had lost her husband. And in just over two weeks the Lenten Fast would begin.

One good thing. Since the affair of Magnus Woode, there had been no more happenings. Could it be because the Bishop-elect was absent, so could not be swamped in tales of dreams and visions? Or was Thomas a little in awe of Elias? He doubted that would stop him.

XL

Anselm was prevented from making his promised visit to Wlward because of a couple of new admissions to the infirmary, and because the weather suddenly worsened, with heavy downpours. It had to wait until the following day, although even then, the streets and lanes were full of deep puddles.

Leviva admitted him. Elviva was at the cathedral. She visited William's grave every day now. Wlward was in bed. Anselm went through to the back, where Godwin was in the garden.

"He is not at all well, Brother. Nothing I can put my finger on, but things seem to have got to him. We pray, we talk, but the heaviness will not lift. There is a weakness there, and his appetite has gone. See what you can do."

Wlward looked exhausted. He smiled weakly. "Good to see you, Brother. I am sorry you see me like this. Cheer me up. Tell me some good news."

Anselm took his hand. "There is really nothing to add. As you may have heard, we have a new Bishop, and poor Sir John has died."

Wlward looked defeated. "Will that mean that we have lost our support in Sir John? If I were well, I would go and see the new Sheriff. Just to warn him, as it were."

"It is possible that he already knows. I believe that is why Sir John turned off to Mileham. Taking precautions in the event of his death."

"Let us hope you are right." He smiled. "What have you got in that flask, Brother?"

"I thought you might like to try some of our first cider. It should now be at its peak." He poured out a little into the cup by Wlward's bed.

Wlward drank a little, then started coughing. "That's a good strong brew, Brother. If that does not clear my chest, and lift my spirits, then nothing will. Apart from prayer." He sank back against his pillows.

"Thank you for coming. Your presence is cheering, and I really think I begin to feel a little better."

"Let us hope so. Your congregation must be missing you."

"They have Godwin. And Alexander is now a deacon. If the date for Bishop William's coronation is still Easter, then I pray to be better by then. If not, find me a place in your infirmary.

I hear those new wheeled chairs are very comfortable."

"You might just have to put up with the youngsters rushing you over the cobbles in a race."

"Yes, I saw that. But the passengers seemed quite happy about it. Perhaps we should all become as small children. Enjoy life a bit more."

They talked for a while longer, until Anselm saw that Wlward was falling asleep, so he went downstairs to speak to Godwin.

"I will send up some tonic which may help. And I will call in as often as I can. You know that you are all ever in my prayers."

But as he walked back, he knew in his heart that Wlward would soon be passing on. It must be painful to leave your earthly home feeling that you had not done all you could. Or not trusting in God to do what was right. Probably even worse was to leave Elviva believing a lie. Had Wlward lost his faith? He hoped not. He was probably just old and tired. It would be good to achieve some positive result, but he had little hope that it would happen soon. Maybe the new Sheriff could assert some influence.

It was some days later that Hugh came to the Priory gates asking for him. He was puzzled.

"Excuse this visit, Brother. I know it may sound strange, but the new Sheriff is asking if you could call at the castle, Godwin and Wlward too. I have already spoken to Godwin – Wlward is too ill to move. Do you think you might need the Prior's permission to do this? I do not know what he wishes to speak about. Would you need permission?"

Anselm was taken aback. "I could ask the new Prior, Elias. But since you have not told me what the subject is, maybe there would be no disloyalty. Certainly, Godwin would have no such obligation. We must be honest in our dealings. I will go now. It might just be to do with illness, although I am not sure why Godwin would be asked. Or Wlward either."

"Then I will wait."

Prior Elias seemed surprised. "Do you really not know what this is about, Brother? Of course, I am very keen that the town and our Community should be at one, but then, there was that business of one of our Brothers being arrested, and the riots. I would have thought he should have approached me, rather than you."

Anselm looked embarrassed. "It is probably because I was there on the first occasion that he might just wish to bring himself up to date. Sir John died unexpectedly, so probably had no chance to fully hand over."

"Then go, Anselm. I have every trust in you. I know you are not one to chatter. Report back to me."

To save time, Hugh took Anselm on the back of his horse. They passed Thomas returning from some errand or other. He hoped it was not 'other.'

Sir William was a slightly younger version of his brother, but with an expression that seemed less easy-going. He welcomed Anselm, who joined Godwin on the settle.

"I will get right down to business, and I want to reassure you that I mean no disloyalty to your Community. My brother died before his time, but he did try and bring me up to date on the events leading to the attack on Master Eleazar and his community, and the anti-Jewish feeling that has been whipped up, as well as all these strange cures and visions. I am not asking you to be disloyal, but if there is anything else you could add, I would be grateful. He or I may have missed something."

Anselm looked at Godwin. "Perhaps you first? As young William's uncle?"

"Sir, both Anselm and I were in at the start, as it were. As Brother Anselm will tell you, there was absolutely no indication that my nephew had been murdered in some kind of crucifixion, which is the story now being bruited about. Indeed, my father-in-law and I were, and still are, even more so, disquieted about William being transferred to the Chapter House. It has affected my sister-in-law very badly. She is even starting to believe the rumours."

"Ah, this I did not know."

"Of course, I know that these events concerning Brother Thomas are a matter for the Church, and not the town, yet since they are having an effect on certain members of the populace, I can see your concern."

Anselm added. "I hope I am not speaking out of turn, but the Brother involved is of a rather unstable disposition. I am not in a position – indeed, I do not think anyone is – to be able to say whether his visions and dreams are genuine. That is between him and God. Although I do have the odd suspicion. Since you have no jurisdiction over the Church, I do not see what you can do. Apart from being forewarned. Our, that is Godwin, Wlward, I and a few other Brothers, main worry is for the Jewish community, although I should add, in passing, that one of your own clerks claimed a miracle, which personally, I felt I could disprove. Nothing more than a gumboil, with a burst abscess, which relieved the pain for the time being."

"Would that be Gaufridus? If so, as you have said, the whole thing blew up, and our farrier pulled out the tooth. He really should go to a physician for help, but I suppose that would disprove the miracle." And he smiled. "Try not to worry, Brother Anselm, Master Godwin. We shall keep a good watch. I just wanted to be certain of all the facts. I will say goodbye, but if you have any worries in the future, please call on me. I know my brother was concerned for Dame Elviva, so please, remember, she will continue in our care."

Anselm refused a ride back, because he wanted to clear his head. Who would have thought that the new Sheriff would have called on them. He was clearly concerned for the Jews.

They walked alongside Hugh for a while, before he turned off for Catton.

"Well," said Anselm, "It's not much, I know, but this should give some little reassurance to Wlward." Anselm was also able to reassure Prior Elias, who seemed relieved.

Ash Wednesday came and went, and the Lenten fasts began, but Anselm kept to his promise to visit Wlward, taking tonics and embrocation for his chest. These, plus knowing that Sir William was on their side, seemed to boost him a little. Bishop-elect William returned from London, but was seldom seen, except sometimes to speak in Chapter. Prior Elias ignored Thomas's occasional outbursts, and life was, on the whole calmer.

Bishop William officiated on Passion Sunday, then again on Palm Sunday, which was the anniversary of young William's death, and the blessing of the palms. More devotional items had started appearing on his grave – mainly flowers. The following day, the Feast of the Annunciation, crowds huddled around the statue of the Virgin. Were they hoping to see another ring, thought Anselm?

Lady Alys and Sir Revil attended all three services, warmly welcomed by Bishop William, whom Revil took the opportunity of congratulating. Alys seemed happier, thought Anselm. People were gathering in the churchyard. Possibly to catch sight of Bishop William. Alys tapped Revil on the arm, and then came over to speak to him.

"Brother, it is too long since we have seen you. Will you not call in on us at Catton? My husband is frequently away, and it would be good to see you. Our babies are now very much thriving. Elizabeth has been walking for the past three months." She was joined by Margaret and the boys. "And come over to us, too, Brother. There is much catching up to do. Have you met the new Sheriff?"

She must know that he had. Or maybe Hugh and Revil had not said anything. "Yes, he was most welcoming. I think he will make an excellent Sheriff. He reminds me very much of Sir John. Tell me, how is Lady Joane?"

"She has returned to her parents. She and John had no children, you know. She has taken her husband's death hard. Understandably. And so young, too. Oh, look, they are waiting for us. We must leave. Remember to call. Don't forget."

The Bishop-elect arrived for the Maundy service, and took part in the Washing of the Feet, giving a homily on the virtue of humility. The next three days culminated not only in the Sunday Easter service but in the ordination of the Bishop when, invested with mitre and crozier, he was invited to sit on the *cathedra*.

The cathedral was packed, lit by dozens of candles, the altars decked in white and gold. It had been many years since the last investiture – just a few weeks short of 25 years. Anselm suspected that an added attraction might well be the new Sheriff. And there was, of course, William's grave. He hoped that Bishop William being now fully confirmed in his post would not be a signal for more happenings; he absolutely refused to call them miracles.

Outside, Margaret and Alys came over once more and reminded him of his promise to visit. "If you were to come next weekend, or in the week following, Brother, you could kill two birds with one stone. Revil is working at the castle with the Sheriff and his Steward, so Alys is coming over to Sprowston. Now, don't forget." He promised, and then looked about for Godwin, whom he thought might have come to the Ordination. But there was no sign of him, so he decided he would call in on them the following day.

The next morning he was walking through the cloisters when he heard raised voices coming from the Chapter House. There was a light on William's tomb, and three people, two of them arguing. One was Brother Thomas. The second man he did not recognise, but the third was, to his surprise, a very annoyed Prior Elias. He drew near but kept out of sight.

"Just what is all this? Brother Thomas, are you responsible for this? The candle? The carpet? May I remind you, this is a grave of a young boy, not a solar chamber."

"But a saint, Father. A saint, nevertheless. Saints must be honoured."

"He is not a saint, Brother. Who are you to even dare to presume the child's sanctity? Remove these fripperies this instance. Only a saint may have a cloth placed on their tomb. And who is this man?"

"Master Clement, a dealer in wool, Father. I came to sleep at the shrine to be cured of my ague. My men kept watch outside."

"And?"

"He said I would have a dream, Father, in which

the Blessed William would appear. He said I would be healed, and I should then donate a large candle. So, I bought one of the best, and your Brother here placed it on the cloth."

"Master Clement, I fear you have been misled. Your dream was possibly the result of a disordered mind due to the ague. Brother Thomas, remove these items at once, then come and see me."

"You are heinously wrong, Father. I owe no obedience to you. And no, I shall not remove the items. It would be an insult to the Blessed William. I shall speak to the Bishop." Thomas was shouting now.

Elias took up the candle and pinched it out. "Then if you will not, I shall." Thomas seized the candle from Father Elias. It fell to the floor. Anselm came forward and picked it up and handed it to Elias.

"Ah, thank you, Brother Anselm. I wonder if you would very kindly remove that piece of carpet and bring it to my room. And escort Master Clement out. Master Clement, I know you meant well, but the Brother you spoke to has no authority in this respect, so I return to you your very splendid candle. I sincerely regret this contretemps. Oh, and did you see William?"

"Well, no, I didn't, but your Brother said it was probably because I did not have enough faith."

"I see. And were you cured?"

"No, I still feel very weak. I think I would like to go home now." He did sound very sorry for himself.

Elias turned to Thomas, who was still fulminating in the corner. "You will come and see me after None, when we shall discuss this further. This is gross disobedience. You are turning this place of prayer into a raree show. I am only sorry that your behaviour was experienced by another Brother, not to mention an esteemed citizen."

And that was that, thought Anselm, as he escorted Clement to the gates, waving him off, but not before offering him some remedy, if he thought it would help. But the wretched Master Clement was so embarrassed he joined his servants and went home.

Anselm made his way to the Prior's room. Thomas was nowhere to be seen. He knocked gently. "Come in," said a rather weary voice. "Ah, Anselm, a lighted candle in this naughty world. Come, sit by me. Oh, put that thing over there, if you would. I am sorry you had to witness that. But I know you will be discreet. How did Master Clement seem?"

"I offered him some remedies for his ague, but he refused. To tell the truth, I think he was very embarrassed. He just wanted to go home."

"If it were me, I think I would have felt the

same. I do not wish to speak out of turn, but you are the Infirmarian, so if you have anything to suggest as regards our errant Brother, it might prove helpful."

"Father, I do not think Brother Thomas would accept our help, since he sees no problem. And I believe Bishop William has him under his wing."

"Indeed, and our obedience is to him. But it would be helpful if we could put a stop to all this. Bishop William has a heavy load on his shoulders, although, as you say, he does treat Brother Thomas as his protégé. I believe he is writing a history of our order here. Would it be indiscreet to ask if you have read it?" And his eyes twinkled conspiratorially.

"No, Father, Thomas keeps it under lock and key."

"As I feared. Then let us hope these extremely suspect miracles do not find their way into it, or we shall be a laughing stock. But I am sure Bishop William will keep a firm hand."

"Anselm, I was going to ask whether you would mind me occasionally visiting the infirmary? Yes, I know as your Prior I have the right, but I was thinking perhaps in a more sociable way – perhaps talk to your patients, play chess, reminisce. I am told that the idea which you and Brother Dunstan had about the novices is proving very successful. And I have felt – I do not think I am imagining it – a lightening of the atmosphere, a joy even, in these past few months. Let me share in this."

Anselm smiled broadly. "You would be most welcome, Father. And, speaking of visiting, would you mind if I made more visits than usual to Wlward and Godwin and their family? I have been visiting in the past, with counsel and remedies, but Wlward is not at all well. This business with the grave and the riots has caused Elviva to believe the Jews responsible, and Wlward in particular finds this very distressing. In the normal way I would not ask, but I would like to visit every day, if I may."

"Brother Anselm, that is a kindly thought. I might even pay a call myself, if you think that might help. Let me know if that would be welcome. And now, I think I have kept you long enough. I have other people to see."

If he was referring to Thomas, thought Anselm, that was unlikely. Although if Thomas really were considering running to the Bishop, he might have quite a long journey, since when last seen, William was setting off on one of his Visitations. And he wondered about Elias asking if he had seen the manuscript. Was that a gentle hint? Surely not. He had to admit that after Brother Peter's remark, he had certainly considered it, on more than one occasion.

He packed a satchel with some embrocation and tonics for Wlward and set off for Colegate. A quick glance at the scriptorium showed no sign of Thomas. He wondered if he had gone to see the Prior?

Godwin was glad to see him, and Leviva made him comfortable by the fire. Wlward was now mainly sleeping. He had little appetite these days, but appeared in good spirits. Godwin thought this might be because he knew the Sheriff was supporting them. Anselm wondered whether he should mention the latest outburst, but then thought that they had the right to know that the Prior, too, was concerned. Godwin was shocked but not totally surprised.

"Your community has our sympathy, Brother. His behaviour does not put the Priory in a good light. Mark my words, the story will get round. Stories always do. I won't mention it to Wlward. He still worries. But it is a kind thought of your Prior to pay us a visit. Let us go up in a minute or so. Wlward is probably awake by now. If the weather were more clement, I would settle him in the garden, near the rowan tree, but at present it is too cold for him. Maybe in a week or so."

Wlward was awake and pleased to see Anselm. He took the tonic and allowed Anselm to massage his poor swollen ankles. Godwin was right; he seemed more positive than before. But to

Anselm's eyes, he had not much more time on this earth.

Later, as he was leaving, Anselm lingered in the doorway for a last word with Godwin.

"This pain and disquiet, these damaging rumours, all due to one unexplained murder of an innocent child. If we could only find out the name of the murderer, would it change, do you think? Would the pain go away?"

"Sometimes, Brother, I think that in some people there is a fault – the need to look at someone and say – you are worse than me. An anger that requires a shout, a stone. Making our William a saint will only encourage that, will encourage these lies. By disproving that the Jews were responsible, William could certainly no longer be regarded as a martyr. But I doubt the inner anger of many would disperse. They would find some other target."

He embraced Anselm. "Come again, Brother. It is good to be able to discuss these things. Wlward is now too weak. And some subjects are too deep for homilies in church. Maybe it would be something to discuss with Prior Elias. Tell him he would be most welcome."

Anselm did report back to the Prior, who seemed very pleased at the idea of some deep discussion. As he returned to the infirmary, he again wondered whether Thomas had reported to

343

Elias. Then he chastised himself. Too much gossip. But he liked the idea of the discussions. And in a day or so he would stretch his legs and walk to Sprowston.

XLI

Wednesday ten days later was the day chosen. It was dry, breezy but not too cold. And there was some sun. Good weather for harrowing and sowing. Chapter had produced some interesting information.

The Holy Father had once again been forced out of Rome. Not all the news had filtered through, but it seemed that since he had refused to give his name to a treacherous agreement against Tivoli, he had been forced to leave. When last heard of, he was in Viterbo.

Thomas was still nowhere to be seen, not even in the scriptorium. Indeed, he had not attended Chapter since his argument with Prior Elias. Dunstan was of the opinion that he was in seclusion. He and three of his pupils had been passing by at the time of the argument, and he had hurried them away and told them not to say anything. "After such a disgraceful display,

345

Brother, the Prior could not in all honesty turn a blind eye. But as long as he is not meddling in my work, I am content."

Sprowston was as lively as ever. The boys were out in the fields, watching the sowing. Alys and Margaret were sitting in the garden, under an arbour.

"That's new," said Anselm. "I don't remember seeing that."

"It was Luke's idea," said Margaret. "He thought it would be a shelter, whilst affording fresh air, especially to the children. Hugh helped. The little birds like it too. Several are already nesting."

Anselm thought they might do something similar in the garden for the older monks.

A young girl came out, carrying a tray of refreshments. "This is Brangwen's younger sister, Godyf. With all these children, we now need some extra help. I cannot expect Brangwen to watch them all, especially as she is now nurse to Elizabeth and Stephen, and usually lives at Catton. So Godyf has joined our happy family."

He looked at Margaret. Was she? She was certainly blooming. He wasn't going to ask. She would tell him if she thought he needed to know.

"Now, sit down, and bring us up to date."

He told her everything, even about the fracas in the Chapter House. He told her that Wlward was not expected to live long, that Prior Elias was well liked, how much the new Sheriff's support was appreciated. He told her about the Pope in exile. She had something new to add.

"Brother, is it true that there is to be a Second Crusade?"

"I know it was bruited after the fall of Edessa, but I know nothing more. Why do you ask?"

"Hugh said that the Sheriff's Steward had heard that St. Bernard was offering indulgences, such as those offered during the first Crusade. And that the King of France and his wife and all the court knelt at his feet to receive the pilgrim's cross."

"No, I had not heard. Certainly, Prior Elias did not mention it. But then, being monks, we are forbidden to bear arms."

"The news only came through yesterday. Brother, what were those indulgences?"

"I am not completely sure, but roughly it went like this. The Pope at the time, Urban, forgave all penance to those who took part in the Crusade. I also heard that later, if you couldn't attend but gave money to the cause, you also received them. And I believe it got you some time off Purgatory."

Luke had come in at that point. "It could sound rather like pennies for forgiveness, Brother. But I am just an old cynic, so what do I know."

"Not so old," said Margaret, giving him a kiss.

"But why all this interest?"

347

"As I was telling Brother Anselm, Hugh says the Sheriff's Steward is considering going on the Crusade."

"Well, Sir William won't like that. His Steward – Rolande, by the way – is a hard worker, competent, and well-liked. He won't care for him going off when he has only just become Sheriff and is still learning the ropes. Although your brother spends so much time at the castle these days, he could probably take over."

The idea of Revil keeping account books made everyone laugh. Not that he did not keep a careful eye on farm and manor expenses, mind.

Luke went on. "It's not only Sir William that would be hard hit. How would we run the farms if everyone went off? It's sowing and harrowing now, then ditching and ploughing. Odd, I would not have seen Rolande as a soldier – far too elegant. But who knows what is in a man's mind. I must admit, I don't really know him. It's only Revil he has anything much to do with."

They talked on until it started to cloud over, and Anselm said he must get back. As he left and set out for the track homewards, they made him promise not to leave it too long until the next time.

The Priory was peaceful, with a few Brothers finishing off the last of the work in the orchards while the light held. Some of the novices were playing a game of Choule, watched by a smiling Brother Dunstan. Anselm wished that every day was like that. And indeed, the next few days proved so.

Wlward slowly faded into the distance, supported by Godwin and some of his parishioners, who came to sit with him. Anselm was glad he never became aware of what happened next.

A Thursday. The Feast Day of Saint Mark. And an event that was to wrench the hearts of many.

She was often to be seen in the streets, occasionally wildly dancing, like a kitten chasing a moth, to her own inner music, sometimes running from some imagined monster, or stopping men to talk. She was not a prostitute, nor was she anyone's mistress. Just a strange, thin creature, long pale hair, fluttering vague blue eyes. On that Thursday she came into the Chapter House, dressed in only a thin linen smock, dancing and singing, and carrying candles. Thomas tried to stop her, then backed away at her touch, obviously finding her behaviour unbecoming, but she pushed past him, and fell upon William's grave. This time Thomas called the Prior, who gently raised her and asked what she was doing there.

By this time a small number of people had stopped to gape and stare at the poor disturbed girl. Some even laughed and sniggered, but were sent away by Elias, saying that they should be ashamed.

She was all too ready to tell her story. It seemed honest enough. Everyone had seen her odd manner in the streets which was due, or so she said, to an incubus, only she called it a man monster, who hardly ever left her, not even at night, Indeed, at night it was worse, and she feared to go to her bed, lest he should come and lie upon her, and breathe his hot breath into her face. But someone had told her to bring the boy candles. And now she knew that the nightmare had left her. As soon as she came into the church, it ran. It ran right away. She was safe. She knew it would be so when she heard the Brother talking in the Marketplace about the boy martyr, and saying people should visit the grave and bring candles. No, she didn't know what a martyr was, but she was safe, so did it matter? And she took up her dancing again.

Elias would have left her to pray, but she did not even know how to do that, so he asked Brother Anselm to escort her to her sister, who had the care of her, humming and smiling as she went. Was it a miracle, wondered Anselm, as he wrapped a blanket round her like a mantle? Or merely a poor distressed creature who was easily led?

Her sister was relieved to see her. She was a comfortable looking woman, with two small children hanging on her skirts.

"I cannot always be looking after her, Brother. She just slips out. She's not a bad girl but has these fancies. My husband is a carter, so is away from home a good deal."

She looked at the girl, who was standing smiling in a corner.

"Now, away to your bed, Frideswide, and we'll talk about this later. You had me fair worried."

"But Audrey, I am healed. The martyr has chased away the dream monster." Audrey looked doubtful. "He has, he has. I know it."

Audrey looked at Anselm. "We shall not know until she has passed a peaceful night," he said. "How long has she been like this?"

Audrey looked embarrassed. "Since she was quite small. She was a good girl, but always a bit, well, odd. But the bad dreams came later. She was about thirteen. We cannot tell, because she would say nothing, but we thought maybe she was attacked by someone. Since then, there have not been many nights when she hasn't woken us all with her bad dreams. I tried taking her in with me, and my man slept downstairs, but it made no difference. If the saint really has wrought a miracle, then this household is truly blessed."

"As I say, we shall have to wait. If the dreams

come back, send for me. Sometimes calming potions can help. She will not be the only one," and he thought of Alys and the novices.

As he walked back to the Priory, he chastised himself. On the one hand, it seemed that Thomas was still at work. On the other, who could begrudge a poor child release from such a burden. He just wondered what use would be made of this latest event.

That evening, a message came from Godwin. Wlward would soon be receiving the Last Rites, and he wanted Anselm and Robert to be with him. Permission from Elias was freely given, and they set off in the dusk towards Colegate.

Wlward lay there, pale and drowsy, with candles at his feet and head. Every so often he came out of his sleep. He seemed worried about something and kept enjoining Godwin to protect Elviva and to keep the secret safe. Godwin looked at Elviva and the others. "Have no fear. I have reassured him. Wlward has made a confession and will go to his Maker with nothing on his conscience."

They all knelt, not just the family, but all those parishioners who had loved him dearly, and who had come to say goodbye.

"The Body of Christ" and Wlward responded as firmly as he could "Amen."

After the Viaticum was administered, with

Alexander, his son, assisting, Godwin gave the blessing, including everyone:

"May the Lord Jesus protect you and lead you to eternal life."

And Wlward accepted the hands of all those present, kissed them all, and slipped away into the night, like a breath.

Prayers continued, and then people left one after the other, leaving Godwin and Robert to comfort a distraught Elviva and Leviva. The funeral would be held in their Parish Church, and invitations would be sent to Elias, and to the Sheriff, whose brother had been of such great help.

"And we hope you will also attend, Brother. You have been of such support over the affair of young William. We regard you almost as part of our family. I hope you will continue to call." And they embraced.

The next few days were sad although, as Anselm said to himself, Wlward would surely find a place in heaven, but of course those who were left behind would miss him. If a man or woman were unloved, there would be no-one to mourn them. He remembered the story of the poor man, who was not allowed to lean down from heaven and warn his rich brother. He fantasised: What would Wlward have to say about the true story of his grandson's murder? Whatever it was, he would probably know by now.

XLII

The days lengthened, the fields grew greener by the day, and the hedgerows blossomed. Nesting birds darted here and there. On his occasional visits to Sprowston, Anselm refused offers of travel on the back of a horse, such a joy was it to see the labourers in the fields and smell the green-scented countryside. The haymaking passed, and the second ploughing, and at Sprowston, all were busy with the shearing. There was no more news about another crusade.

Bishop William was seldom seen these days, his duties in the diocese proving heavy. Brother Thomas was seen out and about, more often out than in, although he could occasionally be seen in the scriptorium. Anselm wondered if he just followed his own writing path without Bishop William to advise him. He must need some advice, surely, else how would he know the events of the past fifty years? He also wondered what had happened to Theobald after he left the Priory. He wondered, because that so-called prophecy was still being quoted.

Wlward's funeral had been and gone. It was attended by many, including the Sheriff and Prior Elias. Wlward had been greatly respected and loved, and stories were shared of his great kindness and, yes, great common sense.

He was surprised that there had been no more events since Frideswide. Had Thomas learned his lesson? He doubted it, even though it was generally believed that Thomas had been secluded after his outburst. What was it that Benedict said? He thought, and those particular passages came into his mind:

"A monk should be warned privately by a senior monk if he was found to be at fault and he allowed for the monk to be warned twice before any action was taken.

Only after that was his fault to be made public. If he still went his own way, he was to be punished. This punishment might be a beating, or it might be exclusion from the common life for a while..."

He could not quite see Elias ordering a beating, especially as Thomas would probably welcome it with open arms as an offering to the Lord. And in any case, the outburst had been seen by so many, it was hardly private. Time would tell. At the moment, the Priory was calm and, it appeared, so was the town.

However, he should not have spoken so soon, for not long after there was to occur one of the ugliest events of the past ten years.

It wasn't clear who found the body, but soon everyone knew about it. In its way it was as nasty as the murder of young William.

It was an older man, well dressed, long dark hair, bearded. He was soon recognised. It was Master Eleazar, his back pierced by several sword wounds. The horror was immediate. Someone summoned the Sheriff and the Bailiff called hue and cry, although the Sheriff wasn't confident in finding the murderer. The body had been found in the woods, but several hours had passed. Townsfolk flocked the streets and lanes and were told to return to their homes. Soldiers were already scouring the paths and roads. Whoever he or they were, they were long gone. His horse was found wandering in the woods.

The inquest was held in the castle council room. Because of the Jewish customs, the body had to be washed and prepared for burial within the day, which rather rushed matters. But William had seen enough, as had his Bailiff.

The hall was full. Master Jacob and his brother

sat on the front benches, as did the Bailiff and the watchman.

The watchman spoke first. He had seen two armed men ride out just after dawn, taking the Wymondham road. No, he did not recognise them. They were not that well accoutred. Bodyguards? Hired assassins? Sir William agreed. They were definitely sword strokes.

Master Jacob was asked whether his father had any enemies.

Jacob nodded. "On the whole, sir, he is, was, well respected, and people pay their debts. There are no business rivals. However," he hesitated.

"Yes?"

"There is one person who has a bad debt and refuses to pay. It is possible he has not the money, but my father had not pressured him, just said that he expected to receive the money soon. His man arrived a few days ago. There were words."

"Can you explain?"

"The debtor didn't come himself. Apparently, he was too busy. He sent his squire, who not only insulted my father, but threatened him, and said he could whistle for the money. His Lord wasn't paying any money to a... He was very insulting."

"I understand. Master Jacob, do you feel inclined to give us this man's name? If he had a squire, then obviously not a poor yeoman."

"The man is Sir Hugh de Novers, and the debt

was considerable, much too large to wipe off."

Sir William looked grave. Things could prove difficult. Hugh de Novers was a tenant of the Bishop.

Master Jacob continued. "The man came back yesterday. I am not sure what happened as I was in the yard, but I supposed Sir Simon had changed his mind, and sent his squire to fetch my father to collect the debt. I saw them both ride off."

"We shall have to investigate further, although I doubt we shall get anywhere. Sir Hugh will probably deny it, and if his hired men were involved, they will be long gone. Since Bishop William Turbeville is his Lord, it is there we shall go for redress. Unfortunately, he is away at the moment, with business in Christchurch, visiting Dean Hilary. I believe he is also intending to visit Salisbury. It could be weeks before we receive any reply."

"You and your community deserve the rights of a citizen, so I shall certainly take this further. I am truly sorry, Master Jacob. Your father was a worthy citizen, and much respected by many, my late brother included, who spoke well of him. Almost his last words were that you and your community should receive our protection."

He spoke out loud, as if he wanted his audience to be quite clear of where he stood.

"I know the traditions of your religion, so I now officially release the body of your father into your care. I shall be in touch when I know more. In the meantime, please receive our sincere condolences."

"Thank you, Sir. My father will be escorted to London, and buried there, in our graveyard in Cripplegate, just outside the city wall."

"Then may I offer you armed escort? It is the least we can do. Come and see me when this sitting is ended."

Jacob nodded. "That is most kind. I will let you know when. Probably in a week or so, after we have sat Shiva. Normally that would occur after the burial, but under the circumstances…"

Sir William addressed the company.

"This inquest is now over, but there will be further enquiries. If anyone saw, or has any knowledge of, this heinous deed, we ask them to come forward. Notices to this effect will be cried in the Market Place."

The Bailiff announced: "All stand," and Sir William and his Council left, followed by Master Jacob and his brother.

Anselm had been at the back of the hall. He had noticed Aelward Ded, but realised that Sir William would not have known who he was, so could not warn him off. Then the Bailiff returned and came over.

"Master Ded. I did not embarrass you at the time, and quite frankly, having you where I could keep an eye on you was better than having you outside causing trouble. I warn you now, that if there are any repeats of your disgraceful behaviour over the past months, you will be among the first to be arrested. You have been warned." And he stayed to watch as Ded shuffled out of the hall, muttering under his breath.

Anselm stayed for a while to let the main crowd descend, then followed. As he walked down toward the town, he saw Ded holding forth, surrounded by a group of men. So much for the Bailiff's warnings. Or was he being over suspicious. No, he wasn't, because he distinctly heard the words: "Just what those Jews deserved. Kill the Blessed Martyr, and you gets your come-uppance. I drink to those that done it," and there was a ragged cheer, although some did look around to ensure they were not observed.

Should he say anything? Should he tell the Bailiff? At the moment, it was only words, and the Bailiff had given a warning. Better to wait for the time being.

Had he known it, the Sheriff was already debating whether to write to the Bishop. He thought it would probably be a vain exercise, as William was on his travels. However, in consultation with the Bailiff, he drew up a minute of the proceedings, together with an announcement for the Crier, which included a stern warning against anyone who caused trouble. He then asked the Constable to check the work rotas for his men, so that at least three would be available for the return trip to London – slow because of the hearse, but quicker on the way back.

The news had by now reached the Priory, and Anselm was able to reassure Prior Elias, and some of the senior Brothers. Prior Elias did ask whether he had seen Thomas that day. He did not say 'in the town' but that was probably what he meant, thought Anselm. When he heard that he was not in the scriptorium, or indeed, anywhere else in the priory, he looked grave, but said nothing.

"For two pins," said Dunstan, afterwards, "No, make that one, I'd break into Thomas's cupboard and take a look at that book. But that would not be Brotherly, and I have no wish to spend longer in Purgatory than necessary. Who knows, I might even meet Thomas there. And that would never do. But just what is he writing? Every time I pass by, he covers it up. A lot of secrecy for a history of the Priory. Must be something else. Some strange heresy? Love poetry?" They both laughed.

What with keeping an eye on his patients, teaching Brother Martin, drying herbs, and stocking up his medicine dispensary for the winter, not to mention his visits to Godwin, Anselm was kept very busy. Where he could, he helped out in the vegetable and fruit gardens. On his occasional trips to Sprowston, he saw the haystacks standing neat and tidy, covered against any rains, and by the start of August, the harvest was well and truly gathered in, with the usual feasting and merriment, to keep some people's minds off the anti-Jewish rumours, not to mention the miracles. Which was just as well, as another unpleasant and very distasteful incident had occurred three months earlier, in May. He did not witness it himself, and was glad he had not, it was so cruel.

XLIII

It had been very early in the morning, ten days or so after the inquest on Master Eleazar. The little party was about to set out for its long, slow, sad journey to London, but as they passed down towards the gates, a group of jeering men appeared, among them Aelward Ded. Stones were thrown, and shouts of "Stinking Jews. Filthy murderers. You got what you deserved. Rot in hell."

Unfortunately for them, Aelward had not thought to mention, or maybe had a short memory, the armed escort, which now appeared riding at speed down from the castle. Before they realised it, there were shouts, the thud of staves on shoulders, and they were driven up towards the castle.

"Don't wait for us, Masters," shouted one young soldier, "As soon as we've delivered this lot of shit to the Sheriff, we'll be with you every foot of the

364

way."

Anselm heard the whole story from the Bailiff the next day. The affair was soon over. All nine of them were thrown into the cells and brought up before the Sheriff the following morning. Those that had not been caught on the last occasion received the same sentences of fines, imprisonment, and community work. Aelward Ded received a year's hard labour. They were beginning to build some heavy stone fortifications down by the river. Said the Bailiff: "He couldn't say he wasn't warned. You heard it for yourself. Good riddance to bad rubbish, I say. Should keep him out of mischief for a while." And he went on his way whistling.

Perhaps that was why things had been quiet for so long, thought Anselm. Long might it keep so. The Sheriff was proving every bit as determined as his brother. There was, of course, the question of Bishop William's tenant, Simon de Novers. William was due home in October. All in all, it would be an interesting few weeks, especially as Margaret's child was expected in early November.

Michaelmas came, account books were made up for the quarter, and purple daisies blossomed in the gardens and hedgerows. And there would be a splendid crop of apples. And, thanks to the continual access to the gardens, as well as visits from the novices and, occasionally, Prior Elias,

Anselm's patients had kept well and cheerful.

At Chapter, on the Feast of Saint Denis, Prior Elias announced that Bishop William was expected to arrive within the next two days, depending on the roads. There would be a special mass to give thanks for his safe return.

Whether this news had triggered something, who could tell, but Anselm noticed more little gatherings in the streets than usual. More pleasing, though, he occasionally noticed Frideswide, walking calmly and serenely through the streets, dressed neatly and cleanly, and carrying a rush basket for her shopping, as if she had never been cursed by nightmares. His sleeping potions had helped, said Audrey, but after a week or so, there was no need. Was that a miracle? Did it matter? Well, only if it were misused. And did we really need a young boy for them? The power of the body and spirit to heal was a wonderful thing. That, in itself, was the real miracle.

Bishop William arrived with his retinue, looking tired, but cheerful. His visits had obviously been successful. After the celebratory Mass, there was meat at supper and wine, although Thomas made his usual renunciation which, truth to tell, nobody took any notice of anymore.

The Bishop retired to his palace to rest. But not for long. The next morning, Sir William's clerk

366

arrived with some documents and a letter. "Your Grace, Sir William says please to read these, and he would then appreciate an audience." He bowed, and left, so did not see William's face as he broke the seal and started to read.

He read, he re-read, and then, his face dark with anger, he sat down and dictated a reply. Sir William, receiving the letter an hour or so later, was not totally surprised. From what his brother had been able to tell him, and from what he had learned from others, Bishop William was behaving true to type, and closing ranks. Yet he was surprised not even to receive the courtesy of an interview.

He, too, thought, and then summoned the Bailiff.

"I have just received a reply from the Bishop, in answer to my report about Sir Simon de Novers. I should like to read it to you. It is not totally unexpected, but even so...

'Sir William,

I was surprised to receive your letter and its accompanying documents, regarding some little trouble in respect of the Jew, Eleazar Deulesalt. My tenant, Sir Simon de Novers, may indeed owe some trifling sum to the Jews, but that does not in any way implicate him in the man's death, whatever the scurrilous rumours. If you can furnish me with any proof, I shall of course speak to Sir Simon, but until then, as far as I am concerned, the matter is closed. And as for the citizens who took part in the affrays, they are not my responsibility. I repudiate absolutely any suggestion that they were incited by a member of my community. Pure gossip and an attempt to evade punishment.

And perhaps I should remind you that there is still the matter outstanding of a true and proper trial of the Jews in connection with their murder of the boy, William. I have it on good authority that they are involved, and can produce various firm evidence against them and their crucifying of the boy.

Thus, until a case is brought against them, and settled, I intend taking this matter no further. Take it to the King, if you wish. I suggest your petition will prove fruitless...'

"He's right, of course. Without more information, we cannot arrest Sir Simon, and we cannot insist on the Bishop's assistance. But as to his own firm evidence, we know it is a pack of lies. Just diversionary tactics. My brother oversaw the inquest on young William, at which the Bishop, as Prior, was present. Reading the reports, none of this nonsense was mentioned. Surely his memory is not that short?"

The Bailiff looked grave. "The laws being what they are, we can hardly accuse the Bishop of lying, or arrest him for spreading false information. Our only hope is to find proof that Sir Simon was involved, as well as find the true murderer of the lad. And even then, folks being what they are, I doubt it will stop the rumours."

"You mean, we shall be accused of covering up evidence? That's ridiculous, man."

"Sir William, you have seen the sort of men who were involved. Credulous. If you were someone like them, whom would you believe? A man of the cloth or the man who threw them in gaol because of their behaviour? My advice would be to write to the king just as a matter of information." He turned to Rolande, who was sitting at a desk in the corner, examining some tithing returns.

"Now, here's a young man of sense. What does he have to say about it?"

Rolande smiled. "I think you are both right. On the matter of informing the King, as someone who benefits from the Jewish bankers, and who has them under his protection, he would want to know the full story. Just as a matter of courtesy."

Sir William smiled back. "It seems we have all come to the same conclusion. Three heads are better than one. I do hope you do not follow up on that idea of yours of joining the Crusade,

369

Rolande. We should miss you here. Common sense has been sadly missing in this town since the boy's murder."

"I shall send a brief note. I think the Bishop needs to be reminded that he was at that inquest, which he seems conveniently to have forgotten. And we can leave it at that for the time being. But we really cannot have these disputes between town and Church."

A letter was drawn up to be carried to King Stephen, along with copies of the documents sent to the Bishop. There were other items to go to London, so it would not be a waste of a week. The note to the Bishop needed careful thought. He had read his brother's accounts of earlier meetings when William was Prior. Thank heavens for meticulous record-keeping. It was of help having the full facts. He would sleep on it, and a note could go tomorrow at the same time as his messenger rode to London. He could drop it off on his way.

When he read the note, the Bishop looked sour at being reminded of the original evidence at William's inquest. The Sheriff had quoted extensively from the minutes taken by the Clerk. He had also taken great pains to include the conclusion:

'That he had been killed by a heavy blow to the head by a sharp item – possibly a mace, but spiked. There were no other marks or injuries,' with the rider, "as you yourself will remember, your Grace, being there in person."

Also included were the remarks of Aelward, disproven as idle and malicious, a man currently in prison for the second time for affray. It was stressed that there was no evidence at all pointing towards the Jews, in spite of anything said by one Theobald, from a non-existent community in Cambridge, about a non-existent Council in Narbonne.

An impudent letter. There would be no reply.

Of course, there was talk. Everywhere. Sir Simon de Novers was not much known, except to his peers. Some people had not even got his name right. The news that he had borrowed money from a Jewish usurer caused some chatter. If you were poor, you assumed that the nobility were rich. One old man knew a bit more, as he told his listeners, gathered round him in the late October sunshine.

"Yes, my father worked for Sir Simon's grandfather years ago, as a shepherd. He was a landowner with vast estates. Came over with the Conqueror, so no wonder. No worries about money there."

"So, what's Sir Simon done with it, then?"

"Blessed if I know. I only knew the grandfather, William. Thirty-three Norfolk manors, he had.

371

Off the Conqueror. Thirty-three. They say it's all in the Domesday Book. So, your guess is as good as mine, young Cedric. But I'll tell you one thing for free. If he did arrange for that murder, he won't be found guilty."

"Yer, the rich can always buy their way out of trouble." A shout from the back of the little crowd.

"I think that's enough of this gossip, don't you? And you had better keep a hold on that tongue of yours, Limp Hamon, or you might just find yourself joining Aelward Ded in a nice damp cell. Me, I'm away to my supper." And that was that for the time being.

XLIV

There was a late burst of Summer at the end of the month, then with All Hallows Eve, the skies clouded over, and a chill descended. Churches were full for the services and vigils, and there was little time or inclination for idle chatter. If there were anything to chatter about. Master Eleazar's murderers were never discovered, Ded was kept busy heaving and chipping at stone down by the river banks, and Thomas was seldom seen in the Priory, let alone in the town.

On the whole, Anselm had few visitors to the infirmary, apart from Brother Edmund, complaining of a toothache. Anselm did what he could but was taken aback when the Brother announced that he would take himself to the tomb of the Blessed William.

"And you think that will have an effect?"

"Brother, did not the Sheriff's clerk, Gaufridus, find a cure?"

"Edmund, Master Gaufridus had a gum boil which burst. Nothing to do with the stone of William's tomb. The pain later came back, and the sheriff's farrier had to pull the tooth out with pliers. There was no miracle."

"But Brother Thomas..."

"Brother Thomas nothing, young man. I know what I saw, and the farrier will vouch for it. Try it if you wish, and then come back to me."

Edmund did not return, so either there was a miracle, or he did not like the idea of the pliers. The mind was a powerful medicine. However, that did not stop the rumours going round, accompanied by celebratory alleluias from Thomas.

Martinmas passed, and then news came from Sprowston. Lady Margaret had been delivered of her child, a girl. She would be named Cecily, because she was born on Saint Cecilia's Day. The baptism would be in their local, beautiful, round-towered, church, the 'church in the fields of gold,' as the parishioners called it, and administered by the rector. Luke did not have Revil's ideas of grandeur. They hoped that Anselm could attend, and then return with them to celebrate, his Prior permitting. Father Elias did permit. Following the dreadful event of Eleazar's murder, his personal feeling was that the more contact there was between town and Church, the better.

374

Rumours got round, and he was not unaware of the bad feeling generated by Bishop de Turbeville.

It was the same traditional ceremony but without the grandeur of the cathedral. The rector, an elderly, kindly man, welcomed them, and the deacon held open the north door to let the demons escape. Alys, as godmother, passed the child to him and, just like the baby Elizabeth, Cecily remained placid as she was dipped in the font, and then wrapped in the chrysom. Then it was back to the house for a simple celebration.

'Why was it this house always seemed so calm and welcoming?' thought Anselm. That was what the Priory and cathedral should be. Instead, there was sometimes a distinct feeling of excess, of worry. Conscious that with his thoughts about the pseudo-miracles he might be in some way contributing to this, he determined he would take up again his old decision to think kindly of Thomas.

The meal was full of talk of the crusades. So far, a year almost to the day since the call of Pope Eugene, with Papal Bull, *Quantum praedecessores*, there had been no definite call to England, but it might not be long now. The weather was not good for crossing the Channel, so probably April would be the expected time. It seemed that Conrad of Germany and King Louis of France were leading it, the first time kings had led a crusade. What the exact aim of this campaign was, nobody seemed to know. Certainly, it was to recapture Edessa on the edge of the Syrian desert, which had fallen two years before. Edessa had called for help but from what had filtered through to England, there seemed to be no other specific aim, apart from protecting holy Christian shrines and relics. As an encouragement, apart from remission of sins and time in purgatory, interest on loans could be suspended or cancelled.

Hugh summed it up for them when he said that it was all so terribly far away, in countries that no-one knew, and with no definite object. He had no doubt that people would join, though. Had not Sir William's Steward declared his intention? Or so Revil had said.

They changed the subject and talked about Christmas instead. They were planning the usual feasts, culminating in Twelfth Night. Revil said he was all in favour, provided he did not have to offer piggy-back to all the manor's youngsters. Last year his back had suffered for a month. The others accused him, laughing, of being a wet blanket. "Never mind," added Luke, "We'll let you take charge in the kitchens."

"Brother, what's happened to that strange monk of yours. Thomas, was it?"

"To tell the truth, we don't see him much these

days, except in the scriptorium, where I believe he is writing a history of our order in Norwich."

"I don't know about that," said Revil, "But he certainly makes visits to the castle."

They all turned to him. "The castle?"

"Yes, indeed. Or at least, according to Rolande. He comes to bring his spiritual succour to those in gaol, particularly the ones that were involved in the affray against the Jews. You did not know? But why would you? I wouldn't put it past him to be encouraging more support for his cuckoo ideas. Oh, yes, you did not think I was interested, did you? But it is so."

Anselm wondered whether the Prior knew. But, after all, that was one of the injunctions of our Lord – to visit those in prison.

Revil went on. "That man needs keeping an eye on. Dangerous, under all that sanctimonious bowing and scraping. Mark my words. There will be more trouble. I gather there's been another of his miracles. Toothache, was it?"

Anselm spoke gently. "No miracle, whatever Thomas says. I saw the Brother myself. A gumboil. And still giving him pain, although he refuses to admit it." Edmund had come to him only the day before, asking for some poppy seed infusion.

Revil went on spikily. "If I may say so, there seem to be rather too many tooth miracles. Better erect a shrine to Saint Apollonia, rather than a little apprentice. The world's gone mad."

"Don't you believe in miracles, Revil?" teased Luke.

"Not those that have been passing as miracles this past year. And if you are referring to that posy ring, which turned up on the hand of Our Lady's statue, that was no miracle, whatever that crazy monk was shouting. Now, if it had turned up on Alys's finger after she dropped it, I might just admit that it was extraordinary. No, Hugh, someone found it and kept it, and then realised they could not wear such an expensive piece without being noticed and slipped it onto the Virgin's finger when no-one was looking. Quite a beautiful gesture if I come to think about it. But now, if you will all excuse me, I will make my way back to Catton. Alys can stay on in my place and keep an eye on my sister." And he kissed her gently on the cheek and was off.

Anselm thought that if there was a miracle it was in Revil's behaviour. He seemed much easier and less taciturn these days, and there was none of that haunted look on Alys's face. Godyf came in to shoo the children off to bed, as it was getting dark. Anselm, too, took himself off, promising to come over after Christmas. Tomorrow was the start of Advent and the fasts. As he walked home, he reminded himself of his promise to be kinder to Thomas, so as soon as he got in, he walked over to the scriptorium. Empty. Maybe another time.

He put his nose round the door of Brother Nathaniel's office, but hardly had time to utter a greeting, when Nathaniel rose and seized him by the arm. "My word, you missed something this afternoon. Uproars on the streets of Norwich? No need to go outside for that. We had one of our own this afternoon."

"I am not sure I can believe it; maybe the one to ask is Brother Terence. He bore the brunt of it. Disgraceful. Since that man came here, we have had nothing but fantasy and furore. Go and see Terence now. I think he'd be glad of a visit. He was quite shaken, and you know how easy-going he is."

So, Anselm looked in on the infirmary, and then went off to find Terence, who was locking up his geese for the night. He was only too ready to talk.

"I had a message from the Prior to bring over some more quills for the scriptorium. As simple as that."

"But when I got there, I was grabbed by Brother Thomas, who flew into a great rage and accused me of stealing his manuscripts. I tell you, Brother, he was ranting so much, I thought he had gone mad. I couldn't even loosen his grip on my arm, which still feels it, even through these woollen sleeves. I told him I did not know what he was talking about; there were no papers. Nathaniel came in to see what was going on, and I was just about to ask him to fetch you, when Father Elias came in. Of course, I cannot recall what he said, word for word, but he was quite angry. He told Thomas that he had called in to see Nathaniel, seen the empty scriptorium and found one of the young cats had got in and had knocked over a pot of quills, and was batting them about. He had removed the papers for safety and put them in the cupboard. And ordered some more quills."

"So, what did Thomas say?"

"Nothing, absolutely nothing, not one word of apology. He didn't quite abase himself, or grovel at Father Elias' feet, but he looked as if he were going to. Elias said if he did not trust the honesty of a Brother monk, then maybe he should finish with the book. He would have a word with the Bishop. Perhaps someone else could take over the work. And he sent Thomas packing to 'reflect on his behaviour and ask God's forgiveness.' I remember that bit. Anyway, Thomas bowed and went off, and that was that. Father Elias asked if I was all right and went back to talk to Nathaniel. Just what is in those writings that is so secret? It cannot just be a history of the past fifty years. Mark my words, that won't be the end of it."

Anselm thought he was probably right. Then

took himself into Vespers.

XLV

However, over the next few days it did appear that things had calmed down. Until the day that Bishop William appeared at Chapter.

As the meeting drew to its end, and they bowed their heads for the blessing, there was a sudden shuffling, and looking up, Anselm saw Thomas rising to his feet, his arms upraised in prayer. "Father Losinga, Father Losinga."

Anselm bowed his head to shut out the sight. Surely nobody was going to believe this.

"Father, I bless thee for having commissioned me to carry out this holy work for the Blessed William. I do truly repent my shortcomings. I vow to keep my promise to you. I vow this great work will continue, as you have asked."

Anselm took a quick look. Elias was looking distinctly annoyed. Bishop William was unperturbed. Thomas was gazing up to the ceiling, his arms in the wide sleeves flapping like some enormous black bird.

What next? A faint? A fit? Yes, a faint. Should he go and see to him? He would wait for instructions. There was a silence.

Then Elias spoke. "Brother Anselm, would you see to our sick Brother. Thank you."

He turned to the community.

"Alas, our poor Brother has succumbed again. Sympathetic as we are to our Brother's failings, may I remind you all once more that a season of fasting does not mean making yourself ill. Those that fast to excess do a great disservice to the community, since they have to pick up the pieces, as it were, and it lays more work on Brother Anselm. In addition, it could possibly be construed as the sin of pride."

Bishop William's expression was an interesting one, thought Anselm, as he dragged Thomas to his feet. He could have sworn that he was about to say something when Elias had intervened.

As he led Thomas through the door, Bishop William spoke. "Alas, my poor son. Brother Thomas, when you are fully recovered, perhaps you would come to see me. And Father Prior, perhaps we could talk now, in my Parlour? And maybe Brother Anselm would join you? No hurry. Look after Thomas first."

Was that a note of threat, thought Anselm. But why? He wondered what it was that William had been about to say before he was interrupted.

Thomas, of course, did not want any help. He refused any offer of soothing potions, so Thomas left him. He didn't believe one jot of the so-called visitation of Bishop Losinga. Dunstan caught his arm as he passed through the garden. "I've just got all my youngsters settled, with study, games, sports and visits to the older monks, and he starts it all up again. Terence told me about the stolen documents. Now locked up, I gather. Well, that puts a stop to that idea."

"What idea? No, you surely weren't going to read the book?"

"Now, don't tell me the idea did not occur to you, Anselm. I saw that look on your face. The next time Thomas has one of his faints would be the time." And he winked.

Anselm pondered the idea as he made his way across to the Palace. The Bishop and the Prior were seated at a long table. The Bishop nodded to Anselm and bade him sit down. "We were just discussing Brother Thomas's state of health. Might we have your opinion, Brother Anselm. Was it a case of too much fasting? Or would you say there was something else? Brother Anselm, you can be quite honest with us."

Anselm saw Elias looking at him intently and tried to read the expression in his eyes. Honest it was, then. How to phrase it. He could hardly say that Thomas was a charlatan. He thought for a moment.

"Your Grace, it is not for one Brother to speak out against another. However, I can confirm that I believe many, maybe even all, of Thomas's faints and visions to be caused by over-zealous fasting. It even had a very bad effect on the younger Brothers. I believe Brother Dunstan had to speak to them on the subject. It may also be that hunger had led him to speak out sharply or behave unreasonably on several occasions. Or even to incite the townspeople to inexcusable behaviour or imaginary miracles. Your Grace may remember several of these events. If it was not hunger, then maybe it is something else that's troubling him. But I am not an expert in sickness of the mind, so I cannot say more."

He then stopped, aghast. He had just given the Bishop the excuse he wanted.

"Yes, that is it entirely, Brother Anselm. Something else. I will speak frankly. As I have said before, I truly believe that our Brother is blessed by God and has come among us to endow us with a great gift, that of the young Martyr William."

"So, I shall not be disciplining him. His is a frail and gentle spirit, which has been blessed with great visions. I shall continue to keep him under my wing and encourage him in his great work.

What happened the other day was regrettable, but understandable. When he is better, I will counsel him. And I am sure Father Prior will support me in this." And there was a brief nod of dismissal.

Anselm took himself back to the infirmary. He would calm his mind by giving Brother Felix a game of chequers.

However, Felix had other ideas.

"Brother, we were all there when Brother Thomas had his last fainting fit. How is he now?"

Anselm looked at him shrewdly. Then Felix said what he really meant: "Can you tell us anything more?"

"Not really, Brother. He will be in the care of the Bishop, supported by Prior Elias."

"Why?" Felix was blunt.

"Brother, you know the rules on gossip. Shall we just leave it there?"

"Well, I could, but I don't see it will stop there," and he pulled the chequers board towards him. "Humour an old man. Let me show you what I mean."

"Someone is playing a game. Let us start by looking at the empty board. Now, here is a little black counter. It starts with rumours or suggestions of sweet odours. Here is a white counter, which blocks it. Black counter moves to the side with stories of lights. White counter

386

disproves them. Another block. Black counter moves the other way, cheered on by rumours against the Jews. It visits Jewry. White counter arrives to block it. Black counter is sent away. Here ends the first part of the story."

"Ah, but look. Black counter returns, bringing rumours with it. It moves up to the next space to announce lights in the cemetery. It is joined by another black counter. No, two. First the spiritual visitation, then the faint."

"Game is looking bad for white, as black counter progresses to attacking a young maidservant, and terrifying the lady in labour. But white counter sends black counter to prison and writes to black counter's master."

"Black counter announces a demonic pig. When that is blocked by white, more blacks appear in the form of rumours and faked lights. Black counter sent away, then returns to spread more martyrdom rumours, lights, visions. Incitements to violence. Accusations of theft. Blocked by reprimand. Then comes another vision. Frankly, an awful lot of cheating." He covered the board in black counters. "Like a plague."

"I could go on. Especially with all those fake miracles. Do you see what I mean, Brother? Block one event and another pops up. Black does not want to lose. It does not play by any recognised rules as regards moves. So, I ask, what's the prize?"

Anselm was amazed. "How do you know everything that's been going on, Felix, stuck in here all day?"

Felix smiled. "We get visitors, Anselm, and you know what effect this is having on our community. It would be strange if none of it came down this end. All I am saying is, this is a battle that will be very hard for us to win. Let's hope our black counter is kept busy with his writing."

"And now, I am about to beat you in a very honest game of chequers."

XLVI

The Advent Fast continued, Margaret went for her churching to her local church, the Adam and Eve Day apple trees scented the churches once more, and the world welcomed in the Christ Child. Celebrations in the Priory were modest, but Anselm took the opportunity of visiting Godwin's family, and over the Twelve Days, went to Sprowston, where both families had gathered.

There was a delightful scent of green herbs and branches of leaves. The Hall was overflowing, not just with servants and their families, but also host to Sir William and his wife, as well as Rolande, looking distinctly dishevelled, with an ivy crown on his head. Yet, he still managed to look elegant, thought Anselm. And in spite of what he had said, Revil was again taking turns carrying small children on his shoulders, and throwing his son, Stephen, up into the air and catching him, to the child's great delight.

Margaret was being waited on – no role of servant this year, not so soon after the birth. She looked well, he thought.

Edward and Henry, swamped in large aprons, came over to offer hazel nuts, and Twelfth Night cake – or what was left of it. It looked as if Rolande had found the bean – hence the ivy crown.

Talk was about the Crusades. Sir William confirmed that nothing had arrived from the Pope, though doubtless it would, as soon as the warmer weather began. "And it looks as if I may very well lose Rolande. He will be very difficult to replace." Anselm caught sight of Revil's face, as he sat down recovering from his role as horse. What was that look? Anger? Sadness? A mixture of both. Now, just what was bothering him now? New Year, just passed, was a time for reflection and change. He had honestly thought that things were happier now at Catton. It was the talk of Crusade that seemed to have brought it on. But why?

The talk then turned to the miracles, and the need for truth. Anselm suddenly noticed two very small faces huddled up to their father and listening in. Was this really a talk for seven-year-olds, or younger, he asked himself. He was soon to find out.

A very serious Henry looked up at him.

"Brother Anselm, what is truth?"

"Come now, Henry," said Luke, "don't bother the Brother. You know what truth is. I think you should not be listening in to grown-up conversation."

"No, Luke, maybe he's right," said Anselm. "Maybe it's something we should all be asking ourselves, surrounded as we are by all these rumours. Let me talk to him."

"Henry, and Edward, too, sometimes we find it difficult to know what is true and what is not true. Let's have a little story. Suppose I came into the hall, and kicked Edward, and I then said I was sorry, as it was an accident."

"Now, suppose you had not seen the kick, but someone had told you I had done it on purpose. Who would you believe? Edward, who had not told you the story, or the person who told you that I had been a very bad man."

The child nodded. "I suppose I would think that the story was true. Only, Brother Anselm, you don't kick people. You are really kind. So, I might not believe it."

"Good, good. So, what would be the truth? My kicking Edward, which was an accident, but was true; or my kicking Edward to hurt him? And suppose it had not even been a kick, but I had bumped into him?"

Edward eagerly interrupted. "You mean, people

391

tell lies? They change the truth?"

"Well done, Edward. But one more thing. Suppose nothing had happened at all, but someone had told the first man that it had?"

"Then I suppose we sometimes cannot tell whether it is true or not." He looked worried.

"Don't look so worried, Edward. You have just said a very sensible thing. If we always tell the truth, and our friends and family do the same, then we can always trust each other. Otherwise, it might be sensible to ask ourselves a question whenever we hear something unusual or strange. Is this really true? Does the other person really know the true story? Or is someone telling lies?"

Sir William intervened. "Well, done, Brother. An excellent homily that it would be as well for everyone to accept."

"I am sorry, Sir William, I did not mean to preach. It was just intended for the little ones."

"Not at all, Brother. Sometimes we all need to have these things spelled out to us in very simple terms. If lies are not corrected at the beginning, they have a habit of turning into something very nasty indeed. Because eventually, there will be nobody left who remembers the true story."

What a wise man, thought Anselm. Maybe someone should be writing the true version of the past three years, and not what he suspected might very well be in Thomas's magnum opus. Of course, the one thing he had not mentioned in his little parable was what happened if people had some kind of dream which they genuinely believed to be true. But that was not an argument for tiny children.

At that moment Rolande intervened. "Come, all this talk is becoming far too serious for an evening such as this. As King for the day, I command all the gentlemen to dance. The branle, I think. Come, Revil, Hugh, Luke, and you, too, Sir William, up on your feet. Show the company what you can do."

He signed to the musicians taking a rest in the corner, and they struck up – bagpipe, vielle, flute. The men got to their feet reluctantly, until the hilarity of the situation took hold. "Master Rolande, please remember that I am your overlord. I shall not forget this," said Sir William, smiling. "Ah, but Sir William, should I go on that Crusade, I shall gain remission of all my sins, even a very little one such as this. And look, I am joining you, just to show you how to do it. Your hand, please."

Within minutes the small chain had become a longer one, and then became a circle. There was laughter, and clapping, and cheers from the servants as Revil and Sir William cut some neat footwork. Margaret, coming down from the solar, where she had been seeing to Cecily, was amazed when she saw Revil. Where did he learn to dance like that? He was always the first to disappear when dancing was suggested.

In the end, the company were too tired to continue, and collapsed onto benches, taking advantage of the jugs of cider and ale. Some of the chain had broken apart and gone outside to continue the dance elsewhere, with more people joining them as they made for the big barn.

Sir William approached his host. "It is time we returned to the castle. Revil, Luke, Margaret, Hugh, Alys – thank you for including us all in our first Twelfth Night celebrations since we arrived. Just what was needed after these past few months. I shall certainly sleep well."

Anselm called in to the infirmary, where he was glad to see a happy group of youngsters playing chess and chequers with Felix and the others, as well as noticing that one of the young cats had made itself at home on Brother Udo's lap. Udo looked up and smiled, his craggy face beaming with pleasure.

When Anselm glanced into the scriptorium, he found it empty, although Brother Nathaniel was hard at work nearby. All in all, a very pleasant end to the Christmas celebrations, with tomorrow the Feast of the Epiphany. Then a nasty thought struck him. Remembering what Felix had surmised about every block being followed by an event, he wondered if another happening was about to take place. But nothing had happened last year, nor the year before, so why now?

The Special Sermon, preached by the Bishop, dealt with the meaning of truth, although on a level more suited to monks. It set Anselm thinking again, and he vowed to stop the dreadful suspicion that something was about to happen.

XLVII

He visited this vow several times as the weeks passed, leading up to Candlemas, and the Feast of the Purification. He remembered a reading on one of the Feasts, probably several years back now. An account of the Feast 700 years ago by a woman pilgrim in Rome. He thought her name was Egeria. He could not remember the exact words, but thought that it was a description of how everyone went to the Church of the Resurrection, in procession, and joyfully, rather like Easter. All the priests preached, as did the Bishop, reminding his congregation what Simon said when Jesus was presented by Joseph and Mary, and then ending with a mass.

He found the idea comforting that it was such a very old rite, and he remembered that the Crusades were set up to protect churches such as that one. The ceremony of blessing the candles must have come later.

That morning the cathedral was full of people bringing their candles to be blessed. He was glad to see that the sky was clear, denoting a good year for beekeepers. They would all be pleased, especially Brother Paulinus. He remembered that he needed to re-stock his shelves with honey. With a sudden jerk, he remembered that this would also have been William's 15th birthday.

There were candles on the grave, and fresh flowers, including some rowan. Was this from Elviva? Although Elias had passed by earlier, and must surely have seen them, he had said nothing. He decided he must go and visit the family. It had been far too long.

When he passed by again, he saw Elviva praying by the grave. Nearby, Leviva was waiting for her, and when she saw Anselm, she slipped quietly over to him. "Come and see us, Brother. It has been very difficult since Wlward left us and now, today being William's birthday, well.... We shall be leaving shortly. Will you walk back with us? I know Godwin would also be glad of your company."

Anselm nodded. "When I saw the rowan, I thought of you all. Yes, I shall certainly come back with you. I will wait by the main gate."

The walk was slow and silent. Elviva seemed wrapped up in herself. And even Leviva did not say much. However, just as they were approaching the house, a figure in black came hurtling towards them, chased by Godwin. Leviva pushed Elviva behind her, and to the side, as if to protect her.

A furious Godwin was shouting at Brother Thomas to get out, get away, leave them alone. Thomas stopped when he saw the little group. He gesticulated at Godwin.

"This man denies you your rightful place as the blessed mother of our sacred William. He will burn in hell." He knelt at Elviva's feet. "Come, gentle mother, let me do you due homage."

Godwin seized him by the cowl and dragged him to his feet. "Haven't you caused enough damage already with your gossip and lies? Get back to your priory before I call the watch. Are you not ashamed to let one of your community see how you behave?"

Anselm took Thomas by the arm to lead him away, but Thomas shook him off. "Why do you consort with this heathen, Brother? I am just doing my duty as the Blessed William's Sacristan."

Godwin looked surprised. "Sacristan?"

Anselm shook his head. "There is no Sacristan. There is no shrine, just a resting place for a young child. You delude yourself, Brother. Should this good man decide to call the watch it will bring great shame on our community. If you do not confess your fault in Chapter tomorrow, then I will do it for you."

At that moment Baldwin the smith passed by. "Anything I can do to help, Brother? Father?"

"Yes," said Godwin, "He needs some assistance in returning to the Priory."

Baldwin moved to take Thomas by the arm but by then he was on his way home, muttering under his breath. "Seems to me that bell would have been better round his neck." And he moved on, whistling.

Godwin seized Anselm in an embrace, and once inside, sat him down for all the latest news, in particular any further information on Thomas. He had heard – who had not – of the so-called visitation of Bishop Losinga. It had got back to Elviva, which had only made her condition worse.

"You have just seen how Thomas is. Knocks on our door, demanding to see her."

Leviva added: "She has now suddenly remembered a dream of when she was pregnant. Something to do with a fish. Brother, there was no dream. Was I not with her at the time? Would not Wenstan or even my father have mentioned it, especially as my father was well known as an interpreter of dreams. This man puts ideas into her head, I am sure of it. He should not be allowed out. Truly."

"I am not sure what the full situation is about

Thomas, but I heard it from a reliable source in authority that he often goes to the castle to speak to the prisoners. Godwin, it is so difficult to know what do. Elias is on our side - if one can put it like that – but then, there is the business of Bishop William, who refuses to hear anything against him. Have you heard anything?"

"Not really. But who knows whom he visits and when? I do sometimes see him in the streets, though. Usually talking to small groups of men. And what did happen in the end about Master Eleazar?"

"Absolutely nothing. The Bishop says he will do nothing about his tenant, Sir Simon, until the Jews have been tried for murdering William. The Sheriff was going to write to King Stephen, since Bishop William's arguments were based on lies. I am not sure whether he did, as at the moment he is concerned with losing his steward, Rolande, to the Crusade."

Leviva brought out some little cakes and a jug of ale and sat with them by the fire. "Could you send us some more of those calming potions, Brother? They do seem to help Elviva when she has had one of her crying fits."

"I will bring some tomorrow, as I have some other patients to visit. When the weather is bad, some of the older folk find it difficult to get out."

A thought struck him. "I seem to remember one

or other of us – or maybe it was Wlward – thinking that believing William was a saint might have helped Elviva in some way?"

Leviva looked sad. "There is no joy there. How could there be when our William was murdered? I am not sure it even eases her soul. There is some bitterness from believing the Jews were responsible. Which she never thought before, but which I am sure is due to that dreadful monk. Sorry, Brother, I know he is part of your community, but I say what I mean."

A thought struck Godwin. "The next time there is a Synod, I shall be attending. I shall raise it there. Even if they turn me out, at least I shall have said something. And they should have to record my words. Mind you, they did not do a very good job last time. All I did was speak out to inform them about the Jewish feasts and customs to say they could not have been involved, and then mention the inquest. And we all know how that was reported."

Anselm looked concerned. "Of course, you must say something, but remember the last time, when a rumour spread that you and Wlward had accused the Jews. Then the rumour went round that Elviva believed it, too. We know this was untrue but do take care. Make it clear to as many people as possible what you have said."

"At present, it is quiet, although I make no

doubt that Brother Thomas is hard at work somewhere. There are probably just a handful of gossipmongers, especially after Sheriff William put most of them out of our way. I do not think they will try anything just yet."

He rose to go. "I will call in again tomorrow, or else send Brother Martin with the potions. I have been neglecting you, dear friends. I shall call more often."

As he walked home, he debated about mentioning Thomas in Chapter. It was his duty, although most Brothers confessed for themselves. But with Thomas it was different. He wondered if there would now be another event, to counteract this afternoon's fracas.

The next morning, on his way to Chapter, he thought he saw Godwin coming out of Prior Elias's parlour. No, he must have been wrong. Had something happened?

The normal business was announced. Then there were the usual self-accusations – on the whole, small and passed over with an admonition to spend a little more time in prayer. There was then a silence. Should he say something?

Then Elias rose. "Brother Thomas, we have just heard the admissions of some of our brethren. Do you have anything to add?"

"No, Father Prior. I think you have dealt with them well and justly."

There was a gasp, and Prior Elias tightened his lips.

"I was not referring to the others, but to you, Brother Thomas. Do you have anything to say in your own regard?"

Thomas looked smug. "No, Father Prior. Of course, I have occasionally been overzealous in my pursuit of the truth, such is my delight in the Lord."

Elias continued. "If you consider yourself entirely without fault, then might I suggest you come to my office after Chapter. Perhaps Brother Anselm might join us."

Anselm was glad he hadn't said anything. It looked as if Godwin just might have got there first. He saw Dunstan staring at him. Surely he didn't think he was in trouble, did he? He shook his head imperceptibly, and touched his lips, to indicate: 'Talk later.'

Elias was writing in a daybook when Anselm arrived. He asked Anselm to sit down, and while they waited for Thomas, he asked Anselm if he knew anything about an incident in town yesterday. Anselm nodded.

"Thank you, Brother Anselm. Once I have heard Brother Thomas's side of the story, I will ask you for confirmation of the events, and anything you have to add. Had you been thinking of reporting it yourself?"

"I had been rather hoping that Brother Thomas would do it for himself, Father. It is not pleasant to point the finger at another Brother."

Elias smiled. "Fortunately – if that is the word – Father Godwin Sturt did it for you. I gather you went there to offer comfort. That was very kindly done. I recollect that it would have been his nephew's fifteenth birthday yesterday – a very sad day for them all."

There was a knock on the door, and Thomas swept in. No sign of repentance there. As Peter was fond of saying, one could use him like a broom. He looked at Anselm. Was he wondering whether Anselm had said anything?

"Brother Thomas, this morning I received a visit from a local priest, with some very disturbing news about your behaviour. Not just yesterday, but in the past months. May I know why you have been paying visits to his house?"

"If you are referring to Godwin Sturt, the married priest – and he stressed the word married with some disdain – I go to bring comfort to his sister-in-law, the mother of the Blessed William."

"Would you say you were welcome there? Did they ask you to call?"

"There should be no need. I call wherever I feel I am needed."

"Answer, please. Did they ask you to call?"

"As I said, my vocation takes me where I am needed."

"And what do these visits entail?"

"I pray with them."

"And 'them' is – who?"

"The mother of the Blessed Saint William."

"For once and for all, young William is not a saint. Neither does he have a shrine. And neither are you his Sacristan, which various sources have told me you claim to be. Nor are you a missionary. Furthermore, your visits have greatly disturbed the mind of William's mother, so much so that on several times you have been asked to leave. Yesterday was the latest example. I count it a disgrace that you should bring our order into such disrepute. I understand that even a passing townsman offered to see you safely back here. You are fortunate indeed that Brother Anselm, whom I understand saw the whole thing, did not choose to raise the matter in Chapter."

"Brother Anselm is on their side. He believes the Jews. He believes the Sturts."

"Brother Anselm is an esteemed member of our order who brings help and joy to the community both inside and outside the Priory. Anselm, is what I have said about Thomas's visits correct?"

"Yes, Father. We did try to calm the situation but were unsuccessful. The local smith tried to help, too, but fortunately, by that time, Brother

Thomas left. Dame Elviva was very upset and frightened, and had to be calmed by her sister."

"Then it seems to me the answer is straightforward. Thomas, you will spend the night in prayer, and for the next two months you are forbidden to leave the Priory. In addition, for the next month, you will help the Priory swineherd with his animals, and work on the farm spreading manure. And in future you will under no circumstances visit the Sturt family. Have you anything to say?"

"This is most unfair. May I remind you I receive visions from heaven and from Bishop Losinga. I am the chosen one. The Bishop is my protector. He shall hear of this."

"I daresay he will – only from me. I am writing the report now. He is away for the next month, but after that, we shall see. May I remind you, one of the tenets of our order is obedience. Think on that. You are dismissed. Anselm, you may stay."

Thomas gave a perfunctory bow and flounced out of the room. Elias sighed.

"I am sorry to have to drag you into this, Anselm. Thomas is the Bishop's protégé, and I just cannot intervene. I hope that by confining Thomas to the Priory and its grounds, we may avoid the worst of his excesses. Do not be over-careful on holding back. I have the care of the community, both here and outside, always in my thoughts."

They spent the next ten minutes discussing Godwin and his family, and then Anselm returned to the infirmary where, as he had thought, Dunstan was waiting. When Anselm had finished, all he said was "Good for Father Elias. Two months peace and quiet."

But Felix, who had been sitting nearby, added, "Mark my words, there will be another event soon."

XLVIII

Everyone spent a quiet night, although it was possible that Thomas did not, sentenced as he had been to spend the night in prayer. Not a scream, not a chant, not even a light.

When Anselm set off to Colegate the next day, he felt curiously light-hearted. His rush basket contained the calming potions for Elviva, as well as some embrocation for Rolf. Martin had been sent to see Mistress Webbe, with instructions to stay as long as he wished. Jerome was left in charge until they got back.

Godwin looked very cheerful when he came to the door. He raised his eyebrows in query.

"You saved me having to make an eternal enemy of Brother Thomas," said Anselm.

"You mean, Prior Elias did something about it?"

"He certainly did: two months confined within the Priory, including a month working with the pigs and muck spreading. He has been ordered never to come near you again. What made you change your mind and come to see the Prior?"

"It was Elviva. She had a dreadful night. Half of her wants to believe that William is a saint; the other believes that it is sheer hubris, and she will be punished. That wretched man has bullied her into believing these things. I couldn't let it go, so straight after early service, I asked to see the Prior. He has been to see us on the odd occasion, so I knew he would not turn me away. I only wish I had mentioned it before."

"Let's hope that is it for the time being, Godwin. Although Brother Felix thinks that having been blocked in one of his enterprises, Thomas will sooner or later have another experience. But at least it will be within the walls and will not be bruited about the town."

His next stop was Rolf and Eda. "My feet are so much better, Brother, I am not sure I need any of that oil. It is really good stuff, although that Brother Thomas has been spreading round that it was really a miracle from the Blessed William, and that he had prayed for the saint's intervention." He saw Anselm's face and looked shamefaced. "Not that I believed it, Brother, but that's what he's been saying. He's such a difficult chap to get rid of, always pushing his way in."

"Then if it will make you feel safer, he has been told he is not allowed out of the Priory for the

409

next two months. He's now helping with the muck-spreading. If he ever does turn up again, send me word. You and your neighbours need to stick together on this. I'll leave the oil anyway – just in case."

He reached home at the same time as Martin. "Mistress Webbe's son came in as I was leaving – you know, Matthew from Sprowston. He says that the Sheriff's Steward is definitely joining the Crusade, not just a rumour. It's caused a bit of an upset, because he is so good at his job, and will be sorely missed. But I think you maybe already knew most of that. And Matthew says he is thinking of joining the campaign himself. His mother was very upset. He is all she has, her other children having moved up north."

Anselm dropped his basket in to the infirmary, then set off to see Brother Terence – ostensibly for some more quills for his labels, but really to see what Thomas was up to. He didn't want him wandering anywhere near the infirmary garden, even if the gate was locked shut.

Terence was pleased to see him. He knew about Thomas, of course.

"I'm not sure what help he can be around here. The pigs aren't my responsibility, but personally, I wouldn't let him anywhere near my geese. And as for muck-spreading. Dear God. Still, I suppose you've all had more than your fair ration of him, so it's only fair we share the load for a bit. But just let him come anywhere near here and I'll set the geese on him. Rome's Capitol will have nothing on them."

At supper Thomas was absent. Afterwards, in the warming room, Brother Jerome let it slip that Thomas was refusing supper, because he had said he would humbly share the food of his charges.

"What, you don't mean the pigs?"

"Yes, I do mean that. Apparently, he had a vision of Saint Anthony and his pig. Mind you, it all comes out of our kitchens, anyway, plus a few acorns, so at least it's not wasted."

"Anything else?"

"No, not that I've heard. But it's early days."

Dunstan added: "Let's hope the news doesn't reach my lads. Everything's going well at the moment, We don't want any more of his nitwittery. Saint Anthony, indeed. I've never heard such nonsense. Well, not since the last of Thomas's performances."

Whatever the farming Brothers had to put up with, it certainly took the pressure off the others. Apart from the morning when Thomas came into Chapter smelling distinctly porcine and was reprimanded by Elias for not having washed or changed his habit. Anselm began to feel sorry for him again.

Easter was late that year, so when Bishop

William returned, it was shortly after Lady Day, in the middle of Lent. At Chapter he made an announcement.

"My children, here in the Priory I am conscious you are protected from the outside world. Nevertheless, such is our care for the shrines and sacred places of the Holy Land, I can confirm that the call to Crusade for England has been received, following the Papal Bull of December First, 1145. Thousands in Europe have already replied to the call. Now it is our turn, and although we are forbidden to take up arms, our prayers will be with the sacred warriors. As Pope Eugenius writes:

"Quantum praedecessores nostri Romani p7ontifices pro liberatione Orientalis Ecclesiae laboraverunt, antiquorum relatione didicimus, et in gestis eorum scriptum reperimus."
"How much our predecessors the Roman pontiffs did labour for the deliverance of the Oriental Church, we have learned from the accounts of the ancients and have found it written in their acts."

"It has been decided that a contingent of Englishmen will prepare to leave to sail directly for the Holy Land in May, from the port of Dartmouth. Those of you who have relatives within easy reach who are considering joining the Holy War will be permitted a modicum of leave in order to say your goodbyes. And lest you feel cut off from the town, you are privileged to have been given the news before Sheriff William has it announced in the Marketplace."

Anselm knew Dartmouth. Not that well, it being some 30 miles from Exeter, but well enough to recall the deep-water harbour, and the beautiful countryside roundabout. His uncle farmed up the hill, in Townstal. A good place from which to say farewell to England for what could probably be years, he thought.

The next morning there was the loud banging of a drum and the ringing of a handbell from the town. Anselm picked up the basket of items for his various visits and set off. The Crier was already calling out Oyez, Oyez – Hear ye, hear ye - and people were rushing from all corners to hear the announcement. When it seemed that as many people as could cram into the marketplace had arrived, then the Bailiff took over and read out the Pope's letter – or rather, the substance of it, including the remission of sins and time in Purgatory.

"Sir William wishes to make it clear that not everyone can go, since we have harvests to gather and seed to sow, and law and order must be maintained. And furthermore, only people trained in weaponry will be welcome. However, His Holiness accords the same grace of remission to those who, whilst unable to join the Crusade, give generously in support. This notice will be affixed to the Council House."

The uproar of many voices was almost deafening. Many people asked where Dartmouth was? Others asked where they could obtain a weapon? A hauberk? Not everyone was enthusiastic, probably for reasons of work, amongst other concerns. And as Sir William had said, they were hardly trained in weaponry. What about sea sickness? The Bailiff had mentioned a fleet of over 150 ships sailing on 19th day of May. That was a lot of men, said one old man, who had been a sailor. Thinking about it, and doing some rough calculations in his head, he thought maybe ten thousand men.

Anselm tried to imagine ten thousand men billeted at Dartmouth. He wondered just who would enlist. He supposed they would follow their lords. Where would they find their weapons? Did Matthew even possess a sword? No peasant possessed any kind of armour. They were completely untrained. And then he remembered the stories he had heard about Peter the Hermit and the peasant crusaders - rampaging everywhere, and certainly unwanted by the Emperor Alexios. As he seemed to recall, Peter had been able to enthral people with his sermons, so that people believed they were impregnable. And thousands were slaughtered. As they themselves had killed Jews and Muslims. And here we were again, he thought, back to charismatic persuasion and the meaning of truth.

No, people such as that would be unwelcome, as Sir William had politely put it. Maybe Mistress Webbe would keep her son after all.

As he passed from house to house, he was able to give reassurances to his patients, who were now becoming worried about losing their sons, their brothers, their fathers.

The atmosphere calmed down somewhat over the coming weeks, although prayers were said daily. Maundy Thursday passed, as did Good Friday and Easter Sunday.

On Monday the marketplace was thronged again, as people came out to watch the crusaders start their long journey to Dartmouth. He counted the number of men, each wearing a white tabard with a red cross. He counted around fifty, gathered round their individual Lords. And, as he would have expected, they were all armed. There were no obvious peasants. And certainly, no Matthew. He saw Revil in the crowd, so he was not going. He was talking to Rolande, on his black horse, wearing the Cross, and a jaunty feather in his cap. They were deep in conversation.

Then Bishop William appeared, flanked by his Priors and monks, to give the blessing. The cross was held high as all knelt or bowed their heads. There was a silence, then the answer was given to lead off. Anselm noticed that Revil rode by Rolande's side, obviously accompanying him part of the way.

The air was sombre and people seemed deep in thought and were already beginning to return to their homes or places of work.

Suddenly, there were voices raised. Anselm could not see who it was. Just a few men and, surely that wasn't Thomas standing nearby? Of course, his two months of seclusion were over, and he had probably just come out with his brethren for the blessing.

But the words were ugly. "How about the Jews? Why haven't they given money? They want our men to die. Christ killers. Murderers. Kill the Jews."

But it suddenly stopped there as the Sheriff and the Bailiff rode over.

"Bailiff, arrest these men. Now."

What happened next was unexpected but, as Anselm thought afterwards, truly heart-warming. Sir William dismounted and handed the reins to his servant. He leapt onto a market stall, first checking that it would bear his weight, and reassuring the startled stallholder.

There was a sudden silence, and he took full advantage. He raised his arms.

"Citizens, gentlefolk, everyone – man, woman, child – listen to me."

When he had their attention, he continued.

"Today you have seen some brave men go off to fight in far distant lands. They go on your behalf, to protect the sacred places. They may not return. Most of you will not remember the last crusade, but I assure you, it is so. Many will not return."

"Others who are unable to go because of their duties here – bringing in the harvests that you may all eat; defending the laws so that you are safe; making things that we need for our daily lives; protecting our young children, our older folk – many of these have given money to support the King in this cause. And I should remind you that our Jewish community – our community, I say, lends money to King Stephen without interest."

"Citizens, this is not the time for hate. Or lies. Or violence. When is it ever? This should be a time when we all join hands in common cause – to look after each other, to protect each other. To give extra assistance in times of harvest, sowing, famine. Some time ago, I heard a little child ask one of our Brothers from the Priory what Truth was. And this was explained to him in very simple terms. As someone said then, if lies are not corrected at the beginning, they have a habit of turning into something very nasty indeed. Because eventually, there will be nobody left who remembers the true story. And I think I will leave it there. You have many wise men to deliver sermons; you do not need me. And now, I had better get down before I destroy this good man's stall."

There was a silence, and then, suddenly, everyone started clapping, even cheering. A thickset man made his way over to the stall, followed by a monk, who tried to catch him by the sleeve. The man turned to the monk, shook him off, and deliberately turned his back on him.

"Sir, Sir, Sir William Sir."

Sir William looked down. "Ah, Master Ded, I trust you are recovered from your holiday." And he smiled.

"Yes, Sir, thank you, Sir. I just wanted to say, Sir, that you were right. You are right. I'm with you all the way. And I am truly sorry for what I did." The man was almost crying.

Sir William took him by the hand. "You are a good man at heart, Master Ded. Thank you for your honesty and courage."

In the distance, a gangling, black-robed figure hurried away into the late afternoon.

So that was that, thought Anselm. There would

418

be no news for at least three months. Speaking for himself, he was glad that Matthew had not left with them.

XLIX

The ditching and ploughing passed, followed by the haymaking, the shearing. The weather kept fine, although there were storms at the end of May. He thought about the 150 boats sailing to the Holy Land. He thought about Rolande, whom he hardly knew, but who had seemed a merry young man. He wondered who was fulfilling his duties up at the castle.

Midsummer passed into July. Whether Sir William's speech had had any effect, he did not know. But there were no more disturbances, not even any miracles. Brother Thomas was seldom to be seen, unless he had taken to wandering round the town again in search of disciples. Anselm's elderly gentlemen were safe in the garden. There was almost no need for the lock on the gate.

He was invited to the harvest supper at Sprowston. This year it was held in the middle of

September, as there were other crops still being harvested, including the soft fruits. Again, Prior Elias gladly gave him permission to go. He had stayed behind that day in April and heard what Sir William had said. Anselm had the distinct impression that he was glad. All in all, the atmosphere everywhere was light and unburdened. Mind you, that might just be the effect of the sun, thought Anselm, as he took the path between the yellow fields and green hedgerows towards Sprowston.

The celebrations had already started. Long tables had been laid out in the barns and in the large courtyard. Ornate harvest loaves lay on each, with jugs of beer and cider. There were also some splendid cheeses. Plates of cold meats and small pies were brought out. Here and there were plates of plums and cherries. In the corner of the yard a small group of minstrels set people's feet tapping. Later there would be dancing. He noticed that the family sat among their servants and labourers, while all the children had a table to themselves, under the eye of Godyf and Brangwen, who were themselves being admired by the younger, unmarried servants.

The talk was of the Crusades. There had been very little news, except to say that, due to bad weather conditions, the ships had had to dock at Porto in the middle of June. It seemed they had

421

then agreed to assist King Alfonso in his attempt to dislodge the Moors from Lisbon. Apart from this, they knew nothing. It was assumed the siege had already begun. This information had also been confirmed in brief letters which Revil and Sir William had received from Rolande a week or so ago.

Anselm saw that Sir William, his wife and young daughters were there, oblivious of the compliments about his speech. News had obviously spread even this far. That speech of his might not have been that unexpected. Anselm now knew that Sir William had just founded Sibton Abbey and was a donor to other religious institutions.

Margaret and Luke came over to him, wanting the latest news. Cecily was now ten months old, and idolised by her brothers, who insisted on carrying her everywhere. Hugh and Revil were deep in conversation with Luke's reeve, but Anselm thought how sad Revil looked. He mentioned it to Margaret.

"Yes, he's been like that since they all left for the crusade."

"Would he have liked to have gone himself?"

"To be honest, I don't really know, and Alys does not say anything. We are not a family that has ever had anything much to do with wars, although, when called, we have a duty to King

422

Stephen. But Revil's work here is exacting, and I think he is also assisting Sir William, now that Rolande has gone away. Were you there when Sir William gave that speech? Hugh says he referred to young Edward."

"Yes, although not by name. It obviously referred to him. But it made a great impression, partly I think because who would have expected such an important officer to make such a speech? It even had an effect on one of the worst of the troublemakers."

"He is a good man, Brother. We are fortunate to have him."

"Actually, I was wondering. Brangwen knows Ardith – you know, the maid of Master Jacob, now that Eleazar has gone. Has there been any news as to how they are dealing with the situation of the murder? It's now over a year."

"I think you might have to ask Sir William. All I know is that when all this started, he did write to King Stephen. I am not sure that I would be told anything, anyway. And Brangwen hasn't mentioned any more trouble."

"What's that, sister?" It was Revil.

"Brother Anselm was just asking what was happening over the murder of Master Eleazar."

"And why is that, Brother?"

"Just because in an ideal world, we do not like mysteries, and it would be good to know that

Master Jacob and his community are safe."

Revil smiled cynically.

"But we do not live in an ideal world, Brother, as you have seen these past three years. Obviously, I cannot share Sir William's business with the world but since you have always taken a care for us all, and law and order must be maintained, I can tell you that all the details of the event were sent to His Majesty at the time."

"And it would not be gossip, since you may have heard that Bishop William refuses to deal with his tenant, unless the Jews are brought to trial over their supposed involvement in the murder of young William. You did not know? Ah, well, I am sure you are discreet."

"There was a reply, eventually. You know how long these things take. But only to say that business kept him away. And now, of course, there is the Crusade. The King said something to the effect that the Jews were under his protection, so would be safe, and he would deal with Sir Simon – if necessary - when he next came this way. Which Sir William assumed would be around the New Year. Not ideal, I know, but we must admit, the town has been peaceful these past five months."

He turned away and went over to talk to Luke.

"Well, that is unusual for Revil. He is usually unforthcoming and discreet. We shall just have to wait."

Anselm got back to the Priory as the light was changing. He had really spent too long away, but he needed to be reassured about events. He noticed that someone had put some sealed pots on his workbench. Honey. Of course, he had forgotten they would be harvesting the honey. He must take a walk over to the skeps to thank Brother Paulinus.

"There is more to come, Brother," said Paulinus. "But I thought these would do to start your stocking up for winter. You look very cheerful. Do I take it that you have been over to Sprowston?"

"Yes, indeed. They are all well, and still busy with harvesting. I'm afraid I was away rather longer than I intended. But it's always an opportunity to catch up on the news."

"And was there any?"

"Not really. Just to say that it is likely His Majesty will come to Norwich in the New Year to deal with the case of the murder of Master Eleazar. But apart from that, it seems that things have been calm in the town. For which may God be praised."

"And the Crusade?"

"Only that bad weather caused an unexpected stop in Porto, and the Crusaders are now in Lisbon, fighting the Moors. And from this lack of full information, we may learn patience."

He looked in on Brother Nathaniel, who was bringing the quarterly accounts up to date. There was no one in the scriptorium. He thought again about Brother Felix's theory. Was it the calm before the storm?

L

At the end of September, the sheep were brought down from the higher pastures, and over the next month work was given over to ploughing, and the sowing of the winter crops. Beechnuts and acorns were gathered, and cows and pigs turned over to pannage.

In the Priory, as elsewhere, wild Autumn fruits and berries were gathered, with some of them given to the lay Brothers to supplement their diet. The daily life in the Priory continued peacefully, and Anselm busied himself in stocking up his dispensary. Feast Days passed, among them that for Saint Luke, Patron Saint of Physicians, thought Anselm, with daily prayers for those on Crusade. Occasionally, flowers were left on the grave of young William.

Outside, the trees had turned, and bushes were laden with berries. Everything smelled of damp earth and bark. The last of the swallows and

427

swifts had left before the bad weather, and it soon became rather too cold to sit outside in the garden, much to the chagrin of the older patients, but the novices were given permission to occasionally wheel them round the town, with strict instructions not to go too fast.

And then it started again. He was not quite sure how. Indeed, he could not even ascribe it to Thomas, as he had not been seen near the infirmary. What it boiled down to, he thought, was that an older monk, also named Thomas, had come to him complaining that he had not been able to sleep for three nights.

"Brother, this is quite normal at your age, although I have to say that with the many late-night offices which we have to attend, it is rather odd that you do not drop off as soon as you return to bed. Have you returned to your old habits of pottering round at night, as you did the last time you were in here?"

Brother Martin put him to bed, and Anselm gave him a calming draught, telling him he was to stay in bed, and not get up and upset the other Brothers. To his irritation, the man then began to pray, out loud, and not the usual prayers before sleeping.

"Oh, blessed Saint William, if you are of so great in estimation as people say, grant your servant some rest." He then went out like a light, but when he woke up later after a good night's sleep, he claimed a miracle, and seemed conveniently to have forgotten the sleeping draught.

Anselm sighed. Well, at least the man had slept well, whatever he ascribed it to. But if Brother Thomas had a finger in this somewhere, it would not be long before the hysteria started again. And, of course, just as he had thought, the rumours went round; whether anyone believed them depended on whether they knew about the sleeping draught. And if Thomas were involved, he wouldn't be content with anything as mundane as loss of sleep. Luckily, now that William was no longer housed in the graveyard, there would be no-one sleeping out there in the cold, damp weather, especially with All Saints on the way.

The rumour may have been creeping round, but nothing was mentioned in Chapter. The insomniac hadn't actually said he had seen anything, so maybe Brother Thomas thought it unworthy of mention.

But gold rings were another thing entirely. Strangely, it reminded him of the lost ring of Alys, and the mysterious ring that appeared on the hand of the statue of the Virgin, claimed as a miracle by Brother Thomas. And it was all announced in Chapter, probably having gone round the monastery first, and probably also out into the town.

Before Elias or anyone could stop him, Brother Thomas rose to his feet, his face glowing.

"Father Prior, Brothers, I wish to share with you another most glorious miracle of which I have received notice. A noble lady was visited in a dream by our Blessed William, who asked of her the ring on her finger, as a sign of her great love for him. When she awoke, she found the ring almost falling off her finger, as if the saint had indeed tried to remove it, and so she asked her husband what she should do. And he immediately said she should come to Norwich to declare the miracle, which she did last afternoon, to me, as the Sacrist of the tomb."

There was a shocked silence. Did he not understand what he was saying? Did he not realise the discourtesy in this lady coming first to him, rather than to the Prior? And then waiting until now to say anything?

Prior Elias rose.

"Brother Thomas, I have no doubt that the lady had a dream in which she believed young William appeared to her. But may I remind you, yet again, of several things. Firstly, William is not a saint, neither is he Blessed. Secondly, you are not a Sacrist. Thirdly, you have caused this lady, and your Community, a great discourtesy by not

430

immediately directing her to me. Is there nothing that we can say that will persuade you? Do I have to send you into seclusion once again?"

"But she herself has proved that William is a saint, since he appeared in her dream."

"Brother Thomas, a dream is not proof. You will come to me later and furnish full details of this meeting. It may be that an apology is necessary to save us from embarrassment. Did she give you anything?"

"A ring."

"Then you will bring that with you. Obviously, we cannot return it, but this is most unsatisfactory. I trust you will not repeat this story to anyone. And that goes for the whole community."

Anselm thought, from Thomas's face, that it was probably already running round all the taverns and market stalls of the town. He hoped it would not reach Alys and Revil – it would bring back too many difficult memories.

But it certainly reached residents of the town, how he did not know, but maybe Thomas had already been at work before he made the announcement in Chapter. Anselm spent some time correcting the story which seemed to have grown somewhat in the telling, and in some way had become entangled with the story of the ring on the statue of the Virgin.

431

With late October and early November, the Priory was again much involved in fasting and the vigils for All Hallows and All Souls. Folks came to pray at William's grave, which sometimes made life awkward, as they had to be kept away during the hours of Chapter. And Peter still had to clean up after them. And if it wasn't the Chapter House, it was the cathedral. And the many candles had to be moved out of harm's way, in case they set fire to someone or something. Anselm had a theory that people were being told that William liked candles.

"For two pins I'd suggest to Father Prior that Brother Thomas take over as cleaner. Just look at this bucket – nutshells, apple cores, plum stones. Where is he, by the way? I haven't seen him since his last outburst. I sincerely hope he is being kept out of mischief."

"I can set your mind at rest. Brother Thomas is confined to his bed for a day or so. He reported to me with a very large bump on his head, and a sore wrist, which will stop him writing for a week or so. Apparently, he slipped on some plum skins outside the Chapter House. I cannot for the life of me think how they got there, can you?"

There were no more miracles or rumours, and life pottered gently towards Advent, then Christmas. On Christmas Eve it was announced in the Marketplace that the siege of Lisbon, which had begun on the first of July, had concluded after seventeen weeks, with the rulers agreeing to surrender to King Alphonso. Some of the crusaders were staying on, but the rest were continuing to the Holy Land. There was no news of any local casualties. It looked as if people could rest easy over the Christmas period and New Year.

LI

Anselm caught up with the news at the Twelfth Night celebrations, being held at Sprowston. Truth to tell, he was not sure he should be involved in all the conversations, but they seemed to treat him like one of the family. Revil seemed more cheerful and was to be seen bouncing Stephen in the air and joining in the round dance. Sir William was there with his family, although Anselm thought he looked rather serious.

"The King is coming to Norwich, Brother," said Hugh. "Partly to deal with the case of the murder of Master Eleazar. The Sheriff has to find accommodation for the King and his officials in the castle, although Revil has offered hospitality to two of them at Catton. I gather that Sir William is concerned that the Jews should receive a fair hearing, since the response from Bishop William was exceptionally unhelpful. And Sir Simon is denying the charges. Says he sent his

Squire to accompany Master Eleazar to Sir Simon's house to collect the debt, but that they were attacked by armed men. This defence came out much later, so that Sir William was unable to check that this squire was actually attacked. But all the documents concerning young William and Master Eleazar, including notes on William's death and inquest, have already been sent to the King, so he will be well informed."

Anselm thought for a while. "Does it not seem that these stories are similar? Young William is supposedly murdered in a wood by Jews, and now Master Eleazar is murdered in a wood, supposedly by Christians? Oh, yes, there are still rumours about William, none of them proved, and most of them lies, since I was there at the receiving of his body."

Hugh looked grave. "I think you may be right, but perhaps you should keep this to yourself for the moment. It is possible that Master Eleazar's murder was an attempt to avoid repayment of the debt, but as we cannot know that, we shall just have to wait for the trial. But, with all due respect to you and your order, Brother, I can see how Bishop William might use this as some sort of delaying tactic. First try the Jews for murdering William, then we shall see. He said as much in his letter to Sir William."

He saw Anselm's face. "You did not know? Of

course, why would you. You are hardly the Bishop's secretary. Then I am sorry to have burdened you with this extra knowledge. But as Revil says, we know you are discreet."

Anselm thought he now knew what this move was. Not just to defend Sir Simon, but also to try and prove that William had been martyred by the Jews, and could then become a saint, with all the glory and prestige that came with it. Over the past months he had seen support for the supposed martyrdom dwindle, and rumours had more or less ceased. So, someone was trying another tack. Another black counter in the Devil's game.

He tried hard to take his mind off the affair over the rest of the afternoon. There was nothing he could do. As Hugh said, they would just have to wait. He wondered if he would be called as a witness, should the Jews be brought to trial. And they could hardly try a dead man, could they. Unless they were going for conspiracy.

Epiphany passed, then Candlemas, with more candles appearing on William's grave in the Chapter House. Anselm was helping Brother Peter clear away the stubs and wicks, and scrape off the grease, when Brother Thomas passed by. He looked at them pityingly.

"Never mind. In a short while you will no longer have to do this."

"May we ask why, Brother?" asked Peter, politely.

"Because the Blessed Saint and Martyr will be translated to the cathedral. Bishop William is already drawing up plans." And he swept smugly on.

"Hmmph, and what makes him think that a new resting place in the cathedral will put a stop to all this mess? Is the young lad to have his own private household?"

But Anselm was more concerned with the idea of William being moved into the cathedral itself. It did rather seem to tie up with his earlier suspicions.

When the news of the King's visit was finally announced in Chapter and in the Marketplace, for Anselm, at least, it was rather an ante-climax, so long had he been waiting to hear. For the townsfolk it was another thing entirely. He had thought there might be more talk of Jews getting their just deserts but strangely, this was not the case. Most people seemed more interested in how many soldiers would come; how many servants; would he bring the Queen; how would His Majesty be dressed. Several wondered if he would be wearing a crown.

As for himself, he busied himself with his work, and spent rather more time than usual praying, this time for a just outcome to both cases. He assumed the case of Master Eleazar would be heard first, since the Sheriff had raised it. He would dearly love to be present, but humble monks would certainly not be invited. He wondered whether the Bishop would be called into court.

When the day arrived, the streets were packed. Men-at-arms lined the roads, and the Constable and Bailiff kept watch for troublemakers. A cheer went up when King Stephen appeared on his black mare, accompanied by soldiers and officers. There was no sign of the Queen, nor did he wear a crown, just a simple circlet. And his clothing was plain, fit for long hours in the saddle, with a fur-lined cloak against the winter weather. This was not a king who wasted money on fripperies, whatever his handsome, easy-going face might suggest.

He had been greeted by the Sheriff at the entrance to the town and accompanied to the castle. And that was the last any of the townsfolk saw of him for the next few days. It seemed that Stephen wanted it all over and done with. He did not even spend any time hunting. All the people had left to stare at were the baggage wagons which arrived later.

The proceedings of the Jews' petition to the King came out piece by piece. In Anselm's case it was shared with him by Hugh, who had been present, and, strangely, by Matthew, through Brangwen, who was related to Ardith, who was able to share some of the reactions she had observed in the Jewish household. The Bailiff was also forthcoming.

"I know what a care you have for our community in general, Brother Anselm, so no harm in telling you. It is not a secret. Many of our leading citizens were present at the hearing. The fact is, Master Jacob petitioned His Majesty for justice, laying forth his case clearly, but Sir Simon denied it all. Then Bishop William declared his tenant innocent, and accused the Jews of murdering young William, saying that this must be discussed first, before he defended Sir Simon."

"His Majesty then said that this was all dragging on somewhat, and he had other business to attend to, so the case has been deferred to take place in London at a later date, in front of more churchmen and nobility, I daresay. And the Lord knows when that will be. It does, of course, make it more difficult to deal with the murder of young William, since I doubt any of those who found him will be invited down to London. His grandfather is dead, to start with."

"Indeed," thought Anselm, wearily. The last person Bishop William would need was anyone who was able to attest to the absence of nail or thorn wounds. He supposed this would drag on for another year, another year in which a nobleman would probably remain unpunished for killing a Jew, and in which the true murderer of William would never be found. He had another, even more unwelcome, thought. It would shortly be the Anniversary of William's murder, followed by Easter. He hoped this recent trial, if it could be called that, did not lead to any violence.

In memory of William's murder, Thomas had another vision. On the way to Mass, in view of the congregation sitting that side of the screen, and, after his outburst, falling on the slabs by the entrance to the choir. It was the usual vision confirming the Blessedness and Martyrdom of William, making sure that the business of the dual murders and the trial was not allowed to slip away. The Jews had a mention this time, as did the vengeance upon them through the murder of Eleazar. Brief but excessive, said Anselm to himself, as he and Dunstan dragged Thomas, still shouting ecstatically, to the infirmary.

As Anselm enthusiastically splashed water on Thomas's face, he consoled himself with the thought that maybe this would keep Thomas inside for a while. And maybe the congregation would not gossip. He wondered what King Stephen would have thought, had he been present. Had this been intended for him? Did

Thomas not realise that Stephen had already left that morning for his next destination?

Easter passed, and the world turned again toward the summer. There were some short notices about the progress of the Crusade, but nothing of any detail.

In Chapter it was announced that Bishop William would shortly be leaving for London in defence of Sir Simon de Novers, in a hearing taking place at the end of May, and so would be absent from the diocese for the next few weeks. And, as Anselm suspected, neither he nor anyone else were summoned to London as witnesses in the case of the boy William.

As expected, the community turned out with prayers for Bishop William's safe journey. He set off somewhat earlier than Sir William, who was not encumbered by so many trappings. Both departures were watched with interest by quite a few of the townsfolk. Apart from Lord Revil, who was being seen off by Alys and Hugh, Sir William was also accompanied by four guards, and a small baggage mule. Anselm supposed the leather saddle bags contained copies of the documents relating to Master Eleazar and the inquest on William. He wondered what people knew of the recent hearing; not a lot, he suspected.

Leaving just before Sir William was a small party consisting of Master Jacob, his younger brother, Isaac, two senior members of his community, and three armed guards, supplied by Sir William. Thankfully the weather was dry and pleasant. It would be a few weeks before any news arrived, but Anselm thought he might call in on Sprowston anyway. He knew he was always welcome. He waited a few days first, to let the changes in daily routine settle.

Margaret was pleased to see him. "These past months have been very busy for Revil but now, thank the Lord, Sir William has a replacement Steward, which means that Revil could accompany Sir William to London. His presence is essential, since both he and Hugh were present at that inquest. The Bailiff is in charge during their absence, and with the leading actors, as he calls them, out of town, it is hoped the rumours will not start up again. We heard the story of the ring, and friends tell us that Brother Thomas had another fit last month."

He was interested that she called it a fit. But what else could one call it? A vision? A side-show?

"Lady Margaret, I am sure I am not talking out of turn, and I know you will be discreet, but there is nothing wrong with Brother Thomas." He thought he had better be charitable. "Except, perhaps, for an overactive imagination."

"So, it is not another move towards getting William declared a martyr?"

Now where had she got that idea from? She saw his quizzical look. "No, Brother, it was not my idea to start with, but mainly what comes back to this house through Revil and Hugh. And even Sir William, although, like you, he is discreet. Which is why, I suppose, these latest hearings in London are so important."

She has a superior intelligence, he thought. She seemed different to other high-born ladies he had encountered. He could not quite see her spending all her time embroidering or making tapestries, although he had seen her mending the boys' socks, and also knitting them. What a pity women were never allowed into government and study.

They walked into the garden, where the white roses were already in full bloom. Alys and the children were staying with them during Revil's absence, so Catton must feel rather empty.

"We moved out here when the King came, Brother, as Revil wished to host two of the King's officers. Catton is large but not that large." She laughed. "Elizabeth was rather worried they might steal her poppets. I saw the gentlemen – middle-aged and rather portly. I cannot imagine it, somehow. Anyway, we brought them all here. I am glad to be here. Catton is very lonely at the moment, with Revil away, and Hugh with extra work in assisting the Reeve. We never see him."

Godyf appeared with a tray of ale and small

cakes, and they sat and watched the children playing. Anselm thought how perfect a world would be in which all children had a childhood just like this.

"What are you thinking, Brother?" asked Margaret.

"Just that not all children have a gentle and easy childhood. I was remembering young William apprenticed at eight years old. I admit it was to prepare him for a useful life, but he was the same age as young Edward here. Tell me, are you going to be sending him away?"

"To another manor, you mean? To learn manners, and how to wait at table and bow to the ladies? To learn how to read? But he already knows all that. Anything he needs to know, he can learn here. Or go and stay with Alys. It's the same thing. And as for learning how to fight, their uncles can teach them. I always say, we could run a small school here. Our boys even know how to collect eggs, nuts and windfalls – not a necessary skill for a noble boy, I grant you, but a very useful one, nevertheless. And if they were to go away, I would really miss them."

He asked after Ardith. "She must be feeling strange with her Master away."

"Brangwen is here if you want to talk to her," said Alys. Brangwen was all too ready to talk.

"Ardith is fine, Brother. Well, you know her,

just gets on with life. And the family are fond of her. But she does worry a bit, sometimes, especially with this business of Master Eleazar's murder. If she left, they would be very sorry to lose her."

"Is it that bad?"

"Well, Brother, she says that strange monk has come calling yet again. The last time was the day after they left for London. I supposed he thought there would be no-one to forbid him entrance."

"And what happened?"

"Well, Brother, from what I can understand, it was all very strange. He wanted to look at a wall."

"A wall?"

"Yes, Brother, I know. Anyway, she wasn't having any of that nonsense, so she shouted for help, and Reuben – that's the head servant, Brother – soon sent him packing. I think if you don't mind, she might welcome a visit. She didn't rightly know who to go to, Masters Jacob and Reuben being away. I said I would tell someone here, when I had a chance."

"Then I shall pay a visit tomorrow. Thank you for this, Brangwen. It is all very strange, but I am sure we can get to the bottom of it."

They changed the subject to lighter matters, and then Anselm said his goodbyes, and took what was becoming one of his favourite walks, between the green hedgerows, busy with small

445

birds, and with the yellow and green fields beyond.

When he got back to the Priory, he wondered whether he should tell Prior Elias about Thomas's odd behaviour. Then he decided to wait and see what Ardith had to say. It might be nothing. Just some eccentricity. But he did not think so, somehow.

He put his head into the scriptorium. Thomas was busy writing, but was so engrossed, he did not see him.

LII

Anselm had rather a lot to do the next morning, but as soon as he could, he left for the Jewry.

He passed the Constable on his way, and thought he might just briefly mention Thomas's visit. "I was wondering whether there were any guards on duty outside the house?"

"Well, Brother, they were offered, but Master Jacob refused. He said it might give the impression they were afraid. But I can look in, if you think it's a good idea. Are you going there now? Why don't you drop into the guardroom on your way back, and let me know if there are any problems."

When Anselm arrived, Reuben recognised him, and let him in, and took him round the back. Ardith was filling a pail with fresh water from the well.

"Oh, Brother, did Brangwen tell you what happened?"

"She did indeed, but I must confess I am rather puzzled. He came to look at a wall, you say?"

"Just that, Brother. I'm not sure who let him in – it was probably the new servant, who didn't know who he was. He wanted to look at the walls - said he was looking for nails and nail marks. Plenty of those - the house is made of wood and stone. Then he tried to come into the kitchen. He fair scared the life out of me, and I had to shout for Reuben to get rid of him. Even then, Reuben had a time of it, as he didn't want to leave. But he went in the end, causing no end of a fuss."

"Ardith, do you think it would help if I asked the Constable to station one of his guards nearby? I wouldn't want to go against your Master, but maybe if the man were to stand outside at the end of the lane. There is no other way in, is there?"

"No, Brother. The houses are just in this one great block."

"Then I will do that and mention it to Reuben on the way out. I am sure the household is in no danger, but Brother Thomas being such a nuisance, we need to keep him well away."

The Constable was only too ready to put someone on guard. "If you ask me, that Brother Thomas needs putting away somewhere safe. Begging your pardon, you being a physician and that, but people like him are a lot more dangerous than you'd think."

Anselm pondered on the situation. This was a new black counter to add to what was now becoming quite a collection. Walls? Nail marks? Just what was he up to this time?

There were no more incidents. At least, none that he knew of, although who knew what Thomas was telling people on his peregrinations round the town. He obviously hadn't been put into seclusion. Perhaps Prior Elias was trying a different approach.

Towards the end of June, Sir William and his party returned to Norwich. They rode past Anselm as he was crossing Elm Lane. Both the Sheriff and Revil looked stern, grim even. It looked as if things had not gone too well. At Chapter, it was announced that Bishop William was taking the opportunity of visiting other parts of the diocese. Master Isaac and his party returned a day or so later. Well, Anselm supposed he would learn what had happened, some way or another.

When he called in on Sprowston, a couple of days later, he found that Revil had already called by to accompany Alys and the children back to Catton. But Hugh was staying on and was only too willing to share what he had learned.

"It was just a repeat of what happened here. Master Isaac presented his petition, and then Bishop William was called into court. He did exactly the same thing, said he would defend his tenant only after the Jews had been tried for the murder of William. I wish I'd been there to see it, but Revil said his speech was an elegant tangle of arguments and quotations proving that it was all a big conspiracy cooked up in Narbonne four years ago, that the Jews had crucified William, and so until they were punished, he was doing nothing about Sir Simon."

At this point Revil joined them. "I wasn't going to say anything, but my brother is quite right. A carefully crafted tangle, quoting various Jewish traditions, and using little-known scholars, all designed to lead people astray and make them believe things that weren't true. I was called as a witness and made it quite clear that the boy had not been crucified, neither were there any marks of that nature on the boy's body, and this was backed up by Sir William, who had all the records from the inquest, and who supported Master Eleazar and his community. But the Bishop kept on insisting that Master Eleazar had kidnapped the child and tortured him and killed him."

"And was your testimony accepted, brother? asked Margaret.

"By the Bishop? Not a bit of it. He even had the gall (sorry, Brother) to talk about Thomas's crony, Theobald of Cambridge, whom everyone knows is an impostor, and who appears to have

450

disappeared off the face of the earth."

"So, what was the verdict?"

"There wasn't one. The King said he had had enough, it proved nothing, and the Jews were under his protection anyway. Of course, that meant that the case against Sir Simon could not go forward, as the Bishop would have nothing to do with it. In any case, it could not exactly be proved. The Bishop had already said in his preamble that Master Eleazar had been murdered by passing thieves. But the long and short of it is, that's the end of it all. A complete waste of time. The Bishop has a satisfied tenant who has not, as far as we can make out, repaid his debt, and the Jews have not had justice. As has been said before, if you were a rich baron, and there were plenty of them at the hearing, who would you believe? A man of the Church or a Jewish banker? I am not a supporter of the Jews, but I do support justice. And this was not justice."

Margaret stared. "Revil, I have never seen you so fired up before. I am glad you are on my side. I should not like you as an enemy."

He calmed down, and smiled, sheepishly. "I've learned a lot over the past three years, Margaret. From you, from your family, and from our Sheriffs. And even from you, Brother Anselm. But now I must get the family back to Catton before it gets dark," and he hugged Margaret, shook

451

Anselm's hand, and slapped Luke on the back. "I'll see you at Catton later, Hugh."

And they were off.

Margaret asked Anselm what had happened over Ardith. When he mentioned the nails and nail marks, and Thomas's threatening behaviour, she was speechless. Her immediate reaction was that Thomas must be ill. And that maybe the Sheriff should be told. Or at least Revil. Then, with her quick brain, she changed her mind.

"No, Brother, there is something else. There has to be. I am not sure what Sir William could do. It has to be up to the Bishop, and from what you have said, that would go nowhere. I am glad her Master has returned to protect the household. And thank you for acting so promptly and arranging for a guard. Brangwen was quite worried."

"You can thank the Constable for that. He was more than willing."

He stayed a little longer, then walked back to the Priory, thinking that he really must tidy up his still room and cupboards. On the way, he had noticed that there were great numbers of green holly berries, yet to turn orange then red in the late autumn. Bright against the dark green, unlike the inconspicuous, short-lived, and easily missed flowers. White, but often delicately tinted pinkish or yellow. Were they in for a hard winter?

Maybe, or so the tales went. He made a mental note to look at his herb beds, particularly at the mint, sage, henbane and coriander. A hard winter would mean coughs and colds. He had also been thinking, ever since Thomas busied himself with his history, that maybe now was the time to update his book of receipts. Knowledge never stayed still, and he had learned a few things over the past two years or so. Oddly, Jerome had also proved informative.

Later, as he browsed among the herb beds, he thought the henbane was running rather too riotously. Used in the wrong amounts, it could cause hallucinations and strange dreams. One wouldn't want it to get into the wrong hands. He put on some gloves, and started to prune vigorously, taking some of the cuttings away to dry for future use. Felix was sitting nearby, one of the cats on his lap.

"You're being rather hard on those poor plants, Brother."

"For a good reason. One cannot be too careful. This innocuous-looking plant, used wrongly, can cause hallucinations."

"I should have thought we already have enough of those in this Priory. As you say, better to take care. Not that I think our dear Brother Thomas could get in here, not with the gate being locked. Surely he wouldn't be that irresponsible."

"No, I don't think so. But I am just being careful. And, what with one thing and another, I have rather neglected the weeding and pruning."

"Yes, I heard about Brother Thomas and the Jews' maid."

"Did you now? My word, how news gets around. May I ask?"

"It's become common knowledge. Brother Jerome said that Thomas came back in what he could only describe as a mood, and with the case against the Jews gone nowhere, I imagine he'll be working a little bit harder at his latest schemes."

Anselm thought, he's worse than me. Did he feel guilty? Not a bit of it. This nonsense had to be stopped. Knowledge was power.

Before he knew it, the harvesting had begun, and once more, folks held their harvest suppers; later, churches were filled with greenery and lammas loaves to celebrate the fruits of the land, and a safe harvest. They all helped with the Priory apple crop, and the shelves in the barns were soon filled with apples and pears, ready for the winter, while Brother Terence and his team prepared for the cider making. He was always surprised at how quickly the years came round again, but it seemed to have happened faster in these past two or three years.

He wondered whether it was because his life was no longer a matter of routine but invaded by extraordinary events.

LIII

It was somewhere round about mid-October that it happened. Anselm was going into the scriptorium to look for discards of the papery sheets used for unofficial notes. He was not surprised to find nothing in the baskets apart from one or two scraps, which he thought would do for labels. So he tucked them in his sleeve and was about to leave, when he saw a couple of torn sheets lying under a bench. As he stooped to pick them up, in case they had been thrown away in error, he started to read. He re-read. He read again and stood staring at them.

In his workroom at the end of the infirmary, he sat down calmly, and began to read again. More slowly this time.

They were obviously not complete pages but rather notes, or draughts. Some of it had been scratched through with a penknife but was still legible.

'...a certain poor Christian woman who was a maidservant among them was getting ready some boiling water in the kitchen as she had been bidden... Through the chink of the door, she saw the boy fastened to a post... she could not see it with both eyes but she saw it with one... if the Jews knew she was mistress of their secret they would conspire and put her to death...

...she pointed out to us on the timbers of the house the marks of the boy's martyrdom...

I cannot further pass over the death of the Sheriff John which I must believe to have been wrought by the vengeance of God... heavily bribed... began to labour under an incurable disorder... The blood began to flow for two years... The great deserts of his wickedness provoked the anger of God...

...that most crafty and avaricious race, the Jews... so foul a crime has remained unpunished...;

His knees shook, even though he was sitting down. What was he to make of this? Was this what Thomas had been writing for the past three years? Why was he writing such lies? Was it Thomas? Or was it someone else? But if so, who? As far as he knew, Thomas was the only regular user of the scriptorium. Was this why he had gone to seek out Ardith? To gather some colour – a description of the kitchen, maybe - to support his claim of the martyrdom?

More to the point, what was he to do? He could hardly go to the Sheriff, as he had a vow of loyalty to the Bishop. And writing lies was not against the law, although disseminating them was. Of course, unless Bishop William knew about this and approved, then he would be right to go and see him. But if not?

He tucked the sheets away and decided he would talk to Brother Dunstan. It was possible he had misunderstood something, but he did not think so. His own Latin was good, but Dunstan's would be better, because he taught it to his boys. Then he remembered the other scraps he had taken from the basket. But there was nothing on them of note – they appeared to be a list of herbs and flowers. And he was sure that the sheets he had picked up had not been thrown away. They must have dropped out of whatever manuscripts Thomas, if it were he, took away with him.

What else was he writing? Was Dunstan right? Should he try and gain access to the book itself? And if he did, and found it not to his liking, what could he do about it?

When Dunstan saw the sheets, he took them over to the desk and looked at them closely. Then the former lawyer gave his judgement.

"No, Brother, you haven't misunderstood. Whoever he is – and we probably know who it is – he writes good Latin. What were you proposing to do about it? The Sheriff should be told, as he has had to deal with the rumours and riots, but the Church is not under his jurisdiction. Until these are read or shared in some way, it cannot be construed as incitement to a crime. I doubt Bishop William will care – I suspect he is more than in favour of a saint for the cathedral – and showing them to Father Elias would put him in a very difficult situation. And if these sheets left your hands, then the evidence would be lost."

"So should we tuck them away somewhere?"

"I would say yes. Either you or I. And maybe share the contents with a few others. It's not ideal but as I believe I once heard you say, knowledge is power." He was silent for a while. "I suppose you are not thinking of playing housebreaker? Don't look so shocked. I know we have joked about it, but if these are a sample of the poison in that book, maybe it might be considered."

"Yes, and what would we do then? Showing them would be admitting our guilt, and we would be punished, secluded and probably thrown out of the order. Perhaps just showing these to the Sheriff, and then letting it go for a while?"

"He won't like that paragraph about his brother. But I think, if you have an opportunity, why not?

How well do you get on with Lord Revil? Or his brother Hugh? Could you use them as intermediaries?"

They decided that was a good idea, and Anselm said he would wait for an opportunity.

He returned to his work, feeling strangely exhausted. Even Vespers could not calm him and lift his spirits. And this was the case over the next few weeks as the October days became shorter, and passed into the time of All Hallows and All Souls, with their fasting and vigils.

Life was so busy, he had no time to go to Catton to speak to Sir Revil. The Chapter House received many visitors in those weeks, all declaring they had been cured by the Blessed William and donating gifts of money to the cathedral. In the end, to prevent more of Thomas's performances in Church and Chapter, Prior Elias asked him to make a list of the cures, and then read it out in Chapter. When he heard it, Anselm thought he understood why Elias had done this. Whilst not wishing to insult the needs of the populace, the list was banal in the extreme, and since there had been no examination of the people in question prior to their visits, it was difficult to know if these could actually be described as miracles. Some certainly were not, although the bad language of the blasphemer was famous.

A boy's falcon being healed.

460

A boy vomiting up a live viper and its young. *Note to self by Anselm: This man and his father were regularly seen in fair grounds doing the same trick.*

The servant of the Dean cured of blaspheming through seeing William in a dream.

People cured of toothache, the fever and headaches.

But however banal these events were, it did not stop people queuing up at the grave, and handing over candles, and money, to Thomas.

The weather was indeed inclement, with early snows and bitter winds. Anselm had never known anything like it. He was hard put to it to get round to all his patients with cough mixtures and embrocations. On one or two occasions he met Matthew who was delivering warm blankets, baby clothes and thick socks donated by Margaret. The Almoner opened the gates of the Priory every day to give bread and soup to those in need.

However, two weeks or so before Christmas, the weather softened slightly, and he was able to walk to Catton where, by good chance, he found Lord Revil at home. It was a sobering visit. Revil looked pale and ill, as if he had not slept for a week, and was not in a good mood. However, he did grant Anselm a short interview.

"Good to see you, Brother. You are always

461

welcome. But I cannot spare you much time, as I have just received some bad news. What have you brought me?"

When he had read the pieces of paper, he almost exploded with anger.

"Brother, my Latin is not of the best, so you had better tell me if my translation is correct," and he carefully read out what he understood of the writings. "Am I right?"

"Indeed, you are, Sir Revil. I took the same precautions and checked with another myself."

"And who is the writer of these scurrilous lies, do you know?"

"We believe we know, Sir, but our only recourse was to come to you, such is the relationship between the Bishop and Sir William at the moment."

Revil's old cynical expression returned. "And you do not think you are being disloyal to your overlords? No, don't answer that. As one who has always had a care for our community, you could do no less than share this. So, what do you wish me to do? Lies on a piece of paper are not a hanging matter, as I am sure you realise."

"I thought, Sir Revil, if you were able to share this with Sir William? Just to forewarn him, as it were. More people are starting to visit the tomb, and the old rumour of the Jews is being whispered again, here and there."

"Well, I can certainly do that, although what he will say about the lies about his brother, John, I do not care to think. Will you leave these with me? They will be quite safe. Now, go down into the kitchen, and get something hot inside you before you leave. I hope we shall see you over Christmas, maybe at Sprowston. I know I am not speaking out of turn when I say that my sister and her family would welcome you. I shall mention it to them, when next I go over in a day or so."

Anselm bowed and did not forget to go to the kitchens for some spiced ale. He marvelled at how much Revil had softened in the past four years. Still harsh on occasion, still with that touch of cynicism, but nevertheless, softer and kinder. But he did look ill, haunted even.

When he reached home, he went straight to the warming room, leaving his damp cloak on the rack, and stuffing his boots with rags to help them dry out. They were of good leather – the Priory did not stint – and so his thick socks were still dry.

Dunstan was anxious to know what had happened over the writings.

"The sooner those things get passed to the Sheriff, the better. Thomas has been scratching away in the scriptorium like a man possessed for the past two hours. I am wondering what he will come up with next. Did you hear that there had been some news about the crusades? I heard it from Jerome, who had been up to visit Mistress Webbe with some cough mixture; he said that he thought it best not to wait until you got back. The usual, he said. The one with mullein, coltsfoot and horehound, plus elderberries. I think I've got that right."

"You have indeed, as has he. But what was this news?"

"You'd maybe better ask him. He's over there."

Jerome looked worried. Anselm was reassuring. "Don't look so worried, Jerome, you did the right thing. That was exactly the right mixture."

"No, it wasn't that exactly. There has been some news about the Crusade. It seems that Master Rolande, the Sheriff's Steward, was injured in the Siege of Damascus. He was carried back to Jerusalem after they abandoned the city but died on the way. He has been buried out there, and a letter sent to the Sheriff. It took more than three months to reach him. The only other thing that was returned was a box and a letter addressed to Lord Revil. Which I assume he has by now."

Anselm remembered the young man. He wondered if that was the bad news which Revil had mentioned. It must be hard to lose a colleague. He wondered whether Rolande had family here. He had rather got the impression he might be French.

He decided he would go into the cathedral and say a few prayers. It would soon be Advent, then Christmas; it was not the time for families to lose loved ones.

As November passed into December the weather became even more bitter. The infirmary began to fill up with patients from outside, the majority of them with chesty coughs and fevers. Some came to have ankles and wrists seen to and strapped up, after they had slipped on icy cobbles. The cold struck up through the stone paving, and the Almoner was kept busy feeding the queues of people at the gate. Matthew called by with knitted socks, mittens and caps sent by Margaret. As Anselm had guessed, she was not the sort of person to sit and embroider; she was far too busy knitting.

Mistress Webbe recovered and was under strict instructions to stay indoors. A message came from Sprowston to say that Anselm would be welcome over the Christmas period, weather permitting. But it never got that far. Ten days later another message came asking him to call in, as Revil had had a fall.

LIV

Revil was lying, pale and twisted, his head wrapped in bandages.

"How long has he been like this?"

Margaret looked embarrassed.

"Over a week, but he would not let us call anyone, not even his own physician. He was on his way here when he was thrown from his horse. It may have been the ice, but someone saw him riding like a mad thing. They saw it happen and were able to fetch help. He always did take risks, but recently he seems not to care. And now he sleeps most of the time. When he comes to, he won't even see Alys."

Anselm took Revil's hand. It was cold, with *pulsus serratus*. Obviously, phlegm on the lung.

"Does he take anything? Is he in pain?"

"A little wine. Some gruel. And as for pain, he sometimes groans and has bad dreams. And he coughs a lot."

466

Anselm drew back the covers. Revil opened his eyes and coughed.

"Oh, it's you, Brother. Come to read the last rites? I'm not dead yet."

His voice was breathless and frail. His body was pale and bruised. Anselm suspected several broken ribs. Revil winced when he probed.

Anselm tried to smile, while not making light of the situation, which was not good. "You have some broken ribs, my lord. I shall apply some balm, then strap them up. I shall try not to hurt you too much. Perhaps then you will be more comfortable."

As he worked, he thought that if only Revil had had attention earlier, he might not now be at risk of Winter Fever. He could hear the wheezing from the chest. The short, rapid breaths. It might be too late, as he knew that there was no cure that really worked.

"May I sit and watch with him for a while? It might help me consider further treatment."

"Yes, Brother. I will send up something to eat. You must be cold after that long walk, and I was so concerned about Revil, I am afraid I was inconsiderate."

Anselm sat watching Revil fall asleep. He took out his breviary and read. Then Godyf came in with a tray of bread and cheese and hot soup. Meanwhile Revil tossed in pain, muttering, as if

467

he had something on his mind. At one point he said, "Papers... papers... sorry... Sir William... sorry." Then he dropped off again.

Anselm wondered if he were referring to the pieces of manuscript. If he had not given them to the Sheriff, well, it was too late now. There were more important things.

Anselm nodded off, and was awakened by Margaret, who had come in to take over. "Best go home and get some rest, Brother. Matthew will take you."

"No, I will stay here, if I may. Maybe if you can find me a quiet spot for a few hours. If there is any change, call me."

"It's not good, is it, Brother?"

"No, but there is always hope. He is still young and strong. He may recover."

"Then you can rest in the still room. It is warm, as Godyf has been working there. I'll make sure you have some warm blankets."

Anselm slept fitfully, but was not awakened early. There was no change, although he saw that Alys was now sitting with Revil, holding his hand, and trying to warm it. He put his ear to Revil's chest. No better. But no worse, either. He opened his shirt, and gently rubbed some warming embrocation on his chest and throat to ease the breathing. Revil said, "Thank you, Alys," then dropped off again.

Alys's eyes were filled with tears. "He thought it was me. Is he going to be alright, Brother?"

"It would be unfair to say that he will definitely recover. There is a chance, but a very slim one. Stay here with him, if you can. Your presence may help."

"Oh, Brother. He had been so kind these past two years. Quite changed. When I remember how..."

"Perhaps he has learned the meaning of love. It is a very powerful gift. Now, tell me about the family. Oh, do not worry about your husband. Gentle conversations will not hurt him; indeed, the sound of voices may serve to keep him with us."

So, they spent the next hour or so discussing the children, the bad weather, the work she and Margaret were doing to make warm clothing and medicines, the news brought by Brangwen from her cousin working in the Jewry.

"Alys, you haven't heard anything about Ardith wishing to leave their employ?"

"No, Brother. Apart from her work in the kitchen, she loves the children. Brangwen says that apparently someone in the town offered her work, but she turned it down. Said she was very happy where she was."

A sad look came into her face.

"I wish we could find out who really killed that

little boy. Just think. He would have been sixteen in a few months. Old enough to go on crusade, although, from what Hugh said, many who went this time did not come back. The Sheriff's steward among them. It upset Revil a lot, as he had worked closely with him over the past few years. I also heard from Brangwen that a cousin of hers was wounded, although not too badly. He is now on his way home."

Hugh put his head round the door. "How is my brother? What a relief to have you with us, Brother Anselm. It was the Devil's (sorry, Brother) own job to get him to agree to let us send for you. He then became too weak to object. How is he doing?"

Anselm drew him away from the bed. "Not that well, but there is still hope. Keep visiting. Take his hand now and then. Talk to him, even if you think he does not hear. Lend him some of your strength. Can you stay?"

"I can indeed. I have asked Matthew to take you back to the Priory. We will send for you if there is any change. Margaret can take over from me, and we shall both of us look after Alys. And we have Luke as back up. What should we be doing?"

"A little water. Some poppy-seed cordial if he is in pain. The dose is on the label. If he can eat, some bread soaked in wine. A little thin broth."

Walking back towards his infirmary, Anselm

felt exhausted. Not from anything he had done, but from the emotions, the sadness, which he had felt all around him. Was it all to come to this? A young man who had started to find something positive in his life to fade away like the dew? And leaving a young widow, and two little children. He tried to tell himself that there was always hope. But the signs were not good.

He was almost knocked over by Thomas, leaving the infirmary obviously in a hurry. What on earth?

It all seemed calm. Martin was stirring some broth, Jerome vigorously pounding some herbs. The usual cat had found its way to the warmth of the stove, and was busily cleaning itself in a hurried, rather affronted manner, and all the inmates seemed rested. Felix looked up. "You just missed something, Brother." "Oh?"

"Yes, Brother Thomas dropped in to give us one of his little talks."

"No. What about?"

"Something to do with the Jews and their – now, how did he put it? – their 'ritual murders.'"

"And did he? Talk to you, I mean?"

"He didn't get a chance, Brother. Martin and Jerome told him to leave. Then he said he had the Bishop's permission to be here. Then Jerome said he believed that was only if you were here, and in any case, we all needed our rest. I then added my groat's worth."

"Which was?"

Martin intervened. "Do let me tell it. You should have heard him, Brother. He told him that he had been a Hebrew and Greek scholar and teacher before he took the cowl, and if anyone knew about Jewish ritual killings, it would be him. Only there was no such thing, and if he wanted a debate on the subject, he would give him one. Perhaps he could call the Bishop in as well. And maybe Dunstan could bring his pupils. Why not the Archbishop of Canterbury? Let all come. Where would he like it to take place? In the marketplace? That seemed to be his chosen place for spreading his pernicious lies."

Felix smiled. "Yes, I think I did rather well. I offered him a dissertation on Purim or Passover, assuring him that neither of them involved the slightest drop of blood." He winked. "You do realise there will now be another miracle?"

Jerome added, "I particularly liked the phrase, 'I warn you, young man, I shall make mincemeat of you.' And everyone cheered, too. Anyway, he slammed out in a hurry, and almost fell over the cat. It bit him."

Anselm suddenly felt cheered. Even the cat was on his side.

LV

A day or so later, Matthew brought the message that Lord Revil was worsening. Anselm wasted no time. He gave orders to Martin and Jerome, obtained permission from the Prior, and left with Matthew.

The family were waiting for him, but there was little he could do. Revil was now semi-delirious and seemed troubled about something. Among his mutterings, Anselm caught the words... box... no... love... sorry... Alys. He looked at Hugh and Margaret.

"I think you need to send for a priest. Maybe your own. This sometimes helps, but if not, then it is time to say goodbye." There was a sob from Alys, who had laid her head against Revil's chest, and was holding his hand. Margaret stroked his hair, damp with sweat, and put a cloth soaked in lavender water on his forehead. Hugh held his other hand, telling him to pull through, talking about the good times they had had together as boys. The two children were brought in to kiss their father goodbye although, as Margaret said afterwards, they were completely mystified.

It passed very quickly. The local priest came to receive Revil's repentance of his sins, anointing him with holy oil, and whispering words of comfort into his ear. He slipped away quietly after the sacrament, to the sound of his family at prayer. Anselm thought that after the words of forgiveness, whatever it was that had been troubling him seemed to have gone. There was just a great peace. And candles.

When he finally left, it was to promise that he would attend the funeral, and that prayers would be said in the community. Hugh said that the Bishop had agreed months back that Revil and his family would be buried in the cathedral. Nothing ostentatious. Just a modest slab in the north aisle. It just remained to talk to Prior Elias to arrange a day for the Requiem Mass and the burial.

Dame Maud and Margaret washed and prepared the body, and it was laid out in the same room, which was shrouded in black, but lit by many candles. Alys found some late flowering Michaelmas daisies, and some hellebore, plus holly, and placed them round the room. She remembered the story they had all been told by their mother when they were young. A holly bush had sprouted leaves and thorns to hide the child Jesus from Herod's soldiers, and it was for this grace that Jesus had made the holly an evergreen.

Many people came to pay their respects, among them the Sheriff. Revil had not been an easy man, reflected Margaret, but he was respected as honest and good to his tenants. She supposed Hugh would now take over until Stephen reached his majority. It would be a sad Christmas this year. Just as Revil was getting to know his children.

There was also a mass in the local church at Catton, attended by so many people, they were having to stand in the doorways. The funeral and burial would be held in the cathedral, on the Feast of the Holy Family.

The streets were lined with townspeople, many of whom had benefited from the charity of the dead man's family. Hugh and Luke walked behind the coffin, and Margaret supported Alys. Even Master Jacob and his brother followed discreetly at the end of the procession. He had paid a call on the family to pay his respects since, as he had said to Hugh:

"In the most difficult times, he supported us against the rumours. He gave up his time to ride to London to witness for us. He believed in justice. As it is said, the Lord loves the just and will not forsake his faithful ones. So may it be with the Lord Revil."

As Margaret said to Anselm some time later, "Brother, so many people respected my brother. I had no idea. It has been a great comfort to us all. In fact, Hugh and I decided that the slab should be engraved with that exact verse."

But Anselm thought: You did not hear what Thomas said after your brother's coffin was lowered beneath the cathedral, and the slab moved into place. I am glad you did not hear that. No-one should have had to hear it. It was a wicked thing.

Thomas, seated in the stalls for the celebration of the mass, had muttered to his neighbour, "That man supported those murderous Jews in London, and is buried here, in the cathedral. Blasphemy. Yet the Blessed William is confined to a humble place in the Chapter House."

It was heard by several of the monks but, as far as Anselm could ascertain, no-one reported it to the Prior, much less to the Bishop who was officiating. And the next day, Thomas continued his games with another vision. Just as Felix had warned.

Two days before Christmas. The notices had been given out, and all were preparing to leave, when Thomas threw himself down before Elias.

"A dream! Last night I had another dream, a

vision, a glorious vision. Bishop de Losinga appeared to me, his thoughts, as ever, for the Blessed William. He charged me to bring this message to you and to the Bishop. His very words, his very own words."

"This day you have blasphemed in my holy place, the place which I have founded. A supporter of the murderous Jews, who martyred the Blessed William, was buried in my cathedral. Shame upon you. A curse upon you."

There was a gasp in the Chapter.

"You will translate the body of the Blessed William to a place near my tomb. This I command. Or his punishment on you will be great."

And Thomas started writhing on the floor, in what Anselm knew was a complete playact. He glanced at Elias, who stood there, coolly regarding the performance, before saying, as he had so often said before: "Take him away. I will deal with this uncalled-for show later. In the meantime, Brother, you are confined to your cell. I am not unaware of what you said yesterday during the mass for Lord Revil."

Terence and Peter pulled Thomas to his feet – not without some difficulty – and hurried him out, still shouting, to his cell.

Anselm caught Dunstan's eye. Was this the time? He mimed 'Talk later.'

Later that morning, shortly after Terce, Dunstan appeared at the infirmary asking for some ointment for one of his novices, "Nothing serious, Brother. Something for chilblains. It's the sudden cold spell."

Anselm took him into the side room. "So, Anselm, are we on?"

"Dunstan, I wasn't aware we had actually arranged anything. Didn't we think it was rather risky?"

"Yes, but with Brother Thomas confined to barracks, as it were, and after those scurrilous writings – did you take them to Lord Revil, by the way – this is perhaps our only chance. You heard him this morning, screaming and roaring, as Brother Terence would have delicately put it."

"And if we find anything, what would we do?"

"Brother, let's deal with that when we come to it. Now. The scriptorium is empty – I just checked. And there are a few bits and pieces lying around. For someone who is always so anxious to hide what he is up to, he is extraordinarily slipshod."

So, they walked as unobtrusively as possible into the room, and immediately saw some manuscripts lying on the desk. "You keep watch," said Dunstan. "I'll just have a quick skim." And he leaned over the sheets.

"Not a lot. Seems to have it in for Sheriff William. And something about a grave. Oh, and

478

Father Elias, too. No, we need more. Wait now, what's in here? Not even locked," and leaning down he pulled out a thick pile of script.

"My word, he's been a busy little soul. But there's far too much to read here. Let's take it back with us and read it more slowly. We can always say we took it away for safety. And don't look like that, Brother. It's not weasel words, although I grant you, I did look in the cupboard. But I've had enough of this. One of my lads actually believed what Thomas said this morning. And two of the others heard what he said during the mass yesterday. So much for trying to teach them critical thinking. If I am punished for this, I am willing to take whatever Father Prior dishes out. Come on. Perhaps my room would be best."

Dunstan's little room was neat and organised. He cleared the desk, and they sat down facing each other, so that Dunstan could keep an eye on the door. The first few pages were in the form of a Prologue. "Hmm, makes interesting reading, Brother. No false modesty, our Thomas. Just listen to this:

"I have preferred at any rate to sacrifice my own modesty rather than that the many and great Virtues of the holy martyr William should pass away in oblivion or through the rust of ignorance: and because the good wishes

of the brethren has demanded that this passion
and miracles should be put into shape upon
my anvil, I set myself to comply with this pious
wish of the believers...

        ... and so on and so forth."

"He does go on. There are pages of it. Which brethren is he referring to, do you think? Us? Let's move on."

"Ah, So that's why he was poking round Master Jacob's kitchen. Listen to this:

And we, after enquiring into the matter very
diligently, did both find the house and discover
some certain marks in it of what had been
done there...

...there, instead of a cross, a post set up
between two other posts, and a beam stretched
across the midmost post and attached to the
other on either side. And as we afterwards
discovered, from the marks of the wounds and
of the bands...

"Here, you take half of the sheets and see what you can make out."

So, they both read for the next hour, sometimes sharing in disgust what they were reading. Anselm gave a start. "So that's why he was always trying to get me to say that there was an odour of sanctity...

'And when they drew near they were greatly astonished because, though so many days had passed by since the time when they suspected he had been put to death, yet there was absolutely no bad smell perceptible. But what seemed more deserving their wonder was - that though there was never a flower there nor any sweet - smelling herb growing thereabout, yet there the perfume of spring flowers and fragrant herbs was wafted to the nostrils of all present.'

And again:

"But to those who chanced to be standing near, as I was informed afterwards by some of them, it was granted to have a perception there of the sweet-smelling fragrance that I mentioned before."

"Nothing for it," said Dunstan. "He's an arrant liar. And arrogant. Listen to this:

"...and I stirred by zeal for the truth will never cease to oppose; whose rash insolence on the arena of this present page I intend to assault, and to stand up for innocence. I, a second David, hasten to confound the abusive

481

Philistines, running forth from the opposite ranks, drawing forth from the scrip of my mind certain spiritual weapons of reasoning as it were stones. Let one Goliath then on behalf of the rest, with his scoffs join battle with me for the Philistines. Lo! by the sling of my lips and its whirl and force I will crash through the shameless forehead with the smooth stone of the word, and with the sword of his own tongue I will pierce through the heart of the gainsayer. Wherefore whosoever he be who attributes to me the sin of presumption, and charges me with rashness, let him come forward, say I, let him come forward and speak out that which his wont was to babble and jabber! He has been saying, look you, it is very presumptuous..."

"I don't think I can bear to read any more."

"Dunstan, do you remember the Sheriff's clerk saying he had been healed of the toothache, whereas I just diagnosed a burst gumboil?"

"I do indeed. Toothache turned out to be the miracle of the month, if I remember correctly."

"...a certain clerk of William the Sheriff, Gaufridus by name, tortured by a very dreadful toothache, came to the sepulchre of the blessed martyr, a feeling of devotion drawing and leading him there. Prompted by his faith which taught him, he took a morsel of the cement of the sepulchre and touched his teeth, rubbing them with it, and immediately the pain was stilled as if he had had nothing the matter with him, and he went away from the sepulchre whole."

"In fact, the Sheriff told me that his farrier had pulled out the offending tooth. I even told our own Brother Edmund this."

There was more. In the end, they stopped reading.

They put the sheets by, checking that they were in the order in which they had found them.

Anselm looked worried. "What should we do? We can hardly go to the Prior, as we interfered with another Brother's work. If we had those pieces of paper I gave to Lord Revil, maybe he would listen. I did genuinely find them."

Dunstan agreed. "I would give the Bishop up as a bad job, if I were you. Judging from some of the stuff Thomas wrote at the beginning, he is probably encouraging him. But sadly, I suspect anything Father Elias has to say will be swept away. As I have said, I believe the Bishop wants the cathedral to have its own saint. And what better than a young, innocent martyr. Doesn't the cathedral have its own glorious dedication? The

Holy and Undivided Trinity? Why look for anything else?"

"Then we are agreed? I will go to the Sheriff and ask if he received anything from Lord Revil. I can mention that we have seen sight of the book. If he didn't, then I need to go to the family, and ask for the return of the papers. It is Christmas, and they are grieving, but they know I can be trusted. In fact, I'll go to the castle as soon as there is a break in the weather."

Dunstan looked grim. "For two pins I'd burn the lot, but it would not solve much, as you can't burn word of mouth and play acting. I wish you God's grace, Brother. Would you like me to come with you?"

"I'm not sure it would help. And I am not sure the Sheriff has any power, either. But at least he would be aware."

Dunstan moved over to the brazier. There was the smell of burning.

"Brother, what have you done?"

"Just given our friend a little extra homework. Burning twelve of the sheets. Style rather bathetic and exaggerated, you understand. Definitely needs to be done again. Now, shall we put this devil's work back in its den? Do you fancy a walk round the orchards? I think we both need some fresh air."

Christmas Eve and Christmas Day took

Anselm's mind off the matter for a short while. On Christmas Day, Thomas appeared at Mass. There was no work that day, so the scriptorium remained empty. As it did on Saint Stephen's Day. But on the Feast of the Holy Innocents, he finally acted.

LVI

The Christmas season had passed comfortably, the food more interesting than normal. But for Anselm there wasn't the usual light atmosphere. Whether that was because he had not called in on Sprowston, wishing to leave them to their grief, or because he still had an odd feeling of foreboding. That morning began badly. Thomas had barged into the infirmary very early – without permission, as usual, and with the frailer of the inpatients still sleeping, and started what Anselm could only describe as a rant.

"Where are they? What have you done with them?"

"Done with what, Brother?" asked Brother Jerome.

"I'm not addressing you. Where is Anselm?"

"Brother Anselm to you, Brother," added Felix, who was already up preparing to be wheeled into Prime. "Have a little respect, please."

"I know what you're all up to. What have you done to my book?"

Anselm came through from the dispensary. So, it had started. "And what book might that be, Brother?"

"You know quite well what I am talking about. My book. The book. You've seen me writing it. You and your cronies. You are all against me. Plotting to destroy my great work. Have no fear. I shall take this to the highest authority. I shall have you thrown out of the order."

Anselm remained calm. "Brother, unless you explain exactly what you are talking about, none of us can help you. We cannot cope with all this babble and jabber." He then realised that he had quoted from the book. Would Thomas realise? "Now, why not sit down calmly, and tell us what the problem is."

"No, I will not sit down. I will not spend another minute in this den of iniquity. I shall raise it in Chapter. Then we shall see." And he slammed out of the door.

Felix whistled in a most irreligious way. "Well, I shall look forward to that. Another of Brother Thomas's little outbursts, no doubt. I thought the last week had been rather too peaceful. Shall we go? I can't wait."

Prime was longer than usual, with extra prayers for those slain in the Crusades and for Lord Revil.

487

In Chapter, Prior Elias had barely got into the business of the day, when there was an interruption.

"Father Prior, there has been a crime. A great crime."

"Brother Thomas, this must wait until after we have concluded our business. Pray sit."

"I will not sit. My work. My great work has been interfered with, damaged."

Anselm glanced at Dunstan. Were they going to have to own up?

"Brother Thomas, you will please wait until we have finished. Do I have to yet again put you in seclusion for this discourtesy? You have only just come out, and that was only an indulgence because it was the Christmas season. If you cannot control yourself, then please leave."

Thomas sat down, twitching and fuming. Every time he made as if to rise, Sub-Prior Richard stretched out a restraining hand. Eventually all the business was concluded, and Thomas was made to wait until last.

Nobody escaped. They were all in it together. Someone had burned his book. The Prior was intrigued. "And which book might that be, Brother? A breviary, maybe? When I last looked in the scriptorium, it was rather disorganised. Papers lying about everywhere. And a brazier left uncovered."

"No, it was not my fault. And it was not my breviary, but my book about the Blessed William. The story of his murder by the Jews. All his many miracles. The visions. The dreams."

Elias continued to look interested. "Ah, I did not know about that. I was under the impression that you were writing a history of our order here in Norwich. You have not mentioned it to me."

"It does not concern you." There was a gasp. "Bishop William supports what I am doing. And jealous people have burned it. If you won't punish them, I shall go to the Bishop. You will lose your post."

Elias maintained his calm, but his eyes narrowed. "Brother Thomas, unless you can be more specific in your accusations, I can do nothing. How big was this book? There have not been very many of these so-called miracles. Or dreams. Where was it burned? When was it burned? Why did you not keep it safely locked up?"

"In the past two or three days while I have been away from my work. They must have gone into my cupboard. Some of the pages are missing."

"How many?"

"Twelve."

"Then you can rewrite them. And anyone who knows anything about this may come and see me. Now, please stand for the Blessing."

As they filed out, Anselm nodded at Dunstan, who later came into the garden. "On your way, then? I think we got off lightly. I shall make confession to the Lord in my prayers tonight. Although He will already know what I have done."

Anselm slipped into the cathedral to send up a quick prayer for guidance, and a positive end to this terrible affair. Then he passed through the gates and set off for the castle. Fortunately, it was not raining or sleeting. The ground was damp, but not icy, and he was there sooner than he had expected. He hoped the Sheriff was at home, and not away visiting.

Sir William was seated at the table talking to the new Steward. He rose when he saw Anselm and bade him take a seat. His clerk took Anselm's cloak and placed it near the fire.

Anselm did not know where to begin. Had it not been for him having now seen the book, it might have been easier. He began by just asking whether Sir William had received what Anselm had given to Lord Revil.

"No, Brother, although..." and he stopped. "A day or so before Lord Revil had his fall, I had to deliver some letters and a box to Catton, and at the time he was searching for something which he said you had asked him to pass on. He said it was most important, but then could not find what

490

he was looking for. He said he would bring it over as soon as he had found it. Something to do with those anti-Jewish rumours, if I remember rightly."

Anselm nodded. "Yes, it was some writings that I had occasion to pick up and read. They were only extracts from some kind of draft, but they were fabrications about Master Eleazar's maid and her supposed witnessing of the crime against William. They also mentioned your brother."

"By fabrications, you mean lies?"

"Yes, Sir William. I just wanted you and Sir Revil to be aware."

Sir Wiliam looked at him shrewdly. "But, if I read your face aright, Brother, there is something more, isn't there?"

"The fact is – and I feel somewhat ashamed – I and another Brother gained access to a book, whose contents were of the same character, but much more numerous, inaccurate and harmful. Pages and pages. There will be more."

"Go on."

"Our order demands complete obedience, so you will understand my unease. I cannot show you the book, but at least the pieces which I passed to Lord Revil might reassure you that I am speaking the truth."

"Brother Anselm, I have not the slightest doubt that what you are saying is completely true.

491

Remember, my brother took care to apprise me of the history of this case. You realise, of course, that even if I were in possession of these drafts, there would be nothing I could do, as the Church is subject to other jurisdiction. Am I right in assuming that you have not taken the matter to your Prior? The Bishop will be out of the question. No, have no fear, I have already experienced Bishop de Turbeville's attitude, and I knew about the book. I had assumed it was the history of your order at Norwich, but I am now beginning to think differently. But however little influence I may have, two things are sure. First, I shall be forewarned and secondly, I can pass this on to the King. His task is a difficult one. He must keep the barons and the Church on his side, but he must also protect the Jews."

Anselm nodded in agreement.

"Then, let us do this. My Steward is about to go to Catton. Why doesn't he take you with him, and you can ask about the drafts. Sir Hugh and his sister and sister-in-law are there dealing with the estate. If they have come across what we are looking for, my Steward can bring it back with him. I cannot believe it will be lost. Sir Revil was most insistent that I should have it, and he has always been organised and meticulous in his dealings. If it is at Catton, then it will have been found."

"Now, some spiced ale before you leave. We shall have snow soon."

Unlike his predecessor, the new Steward was fair, stolid and taciturn, which gave Anselm time to think. How he wished he had not become involved in this story, for story it was, with its influence felt on several families, three communities and the town, and even the King. He still could not rid himself of that sense of foreboding, and this stayed with him as he dismounted and followed the Steward into the Hall, where Hugh was bundling up some documents.

"Ah, Brother Anselm. I am so glad you are come. It means I can set your mind at rest over those scraps of manuscript which you gave to my brother. I am afraid he mislaid them and when he was first ill, he impressed on me that I should find them and send them on. Which I am doing now. See, he had already wrapped and sealed them. I came across them later, but by then he was too ill to understand. And he had other things on his mind, too."

He handed them over to the Steward, together with a satchel of other documents. "Now, Brother, why don't you go and say hello to the ladies? There is a box to investigate, and then we are done. I can give you a ride back to the Priory later. Margaret wants me to deliver more socks and

493

caps. And I am sure Master Yves here would like to get back to his work."

Anselm followed Hugh to the office, where Margaret and Alys had just opened a long, narrow box, and were putting its contents on the table.

"Look, Hugh, Revil must have already opened it. Such a curious assortment of things. That looks rather like Revil's lost brooch. In fact, that is it exactly."

It now lay on the table, together with a large gold ring, two pennies and a small penknife.

Alys put her hands in and brought out a long object wrapped in stained yellow silk. As she made to unwrap it, something fell to the floor. Anselm picked it up. It was a note, its seal broken. He handed it to Hugh.

"And look, Hugh. What do you think this strange thing is?"

He would never forget the frozen expression on Hugh's face as he looked at what Alys was holding in her small white hands.

It was long and thin and metallic, with a rounded head, spiked like a horse chestnut fruit, and the faded blond hair caught among the cruel spikes was stained a rusty brown. Hugh read the lightly crumpled note:

"'Dearest. What I did, I did to protect our love.

494

Remember me. R'"

Postscript &
historical note

On Easter Saturday, 1144 a twelve-year-old boy called William, a tanner's apprentice, was found murdered in a wood outside Norwich.

Very little about him was recorded at the time. Even some of that information may have been added at a later date.

In 1172, a seven volume book was published about the Life and Passion of Saint William. It was written over the space of around 20 years or so, probably at the instigation of Bishop William de Turbeville who, at the time of the murder, was Prior of the Benedictine order and the cathedral. The book was written by Brother Thomas of Monmouth. The assumption is that he was originally from Monmouth, and then joined the Benedictine community in Norwich.

He wrote in good Latin and seemed well educated. Apart from that nothing is known about him. But what he wrote was poison.

Over the years a handful of scholars, among them M.R. James, attempted to disentangle what was more or less, a farrago of lies and fantasy, which increased the income of the Church by reporting miracles and other snippets of William's life, the cathedral becoming a shrine and a place of influence. As Umberto Eco wrote, in another context:

'Baudolino knew that a good relic could change the fate of a city, cause it to become the destination of uninterrupted pilgrimage, transform a simple church into a shrine.'

Some of the characters mentioned by Thomas did exist, but whether events attributed by Thomas to Sir William de Chesney, for example, are true is another thing, for it seems that Thomas 'had it in for him.' He also had it in for his older brother, John. Certainly, had all the so-called witnesses in the book spoken up at the time, it would all have been done and dusted. Why wait years and years before coming out with your little story? And who was Theobald of Cambridge, for example?

According to Thomas, he was a Jewish convert, yet there was no sign of any Jews in Cambridge at that time; those came later. Other records of the time are sparse, so we do not even know when Thomas was born. What we do know is that his book added greatly to the blood libel against the Jews. In fact, it probably started it in England.

Even today, the ballad of Little Sir William can be found in books and in a song setting by Benjamin Britten, although here the murderer is the school wife with a little penknife. But you get the drift.

I had always wondered who had murdered William. This is my idea, It is 95 per cent complete fiction, and written for my own enjoyment. For my part, some of my characters did exist - Sir John de Chesney, Sir William's elder brother, and Sheriff before him; the Jews; the Bishops, the Priors, the Sub-Prior, the various Popes, Simon de Novers, not forgetting King Stephen and even Aelwyn Ded.

One or two of the events have been brought forward by a year or so, in order to make a more fluent story. Given Thomas's own propensity for fiction, I do not feel any guilt whatsoever. Like Thomas's book, mine, too, is mainly fiction.

Susan Ekins
October 8, 2023

The Real Press

If you enjoyed this book, check out our website at www.theRealPress.co.uk, where you will find - among other historical titles - this one, also set in the twelfth century.

And while you are there, why not sign up for your free ebook - a copy of *Scandal,* a non-fiction book set in Victorian England...

Printed in Great Britain
by Amazon

53582307R00290